At the end of World War II, roughly 300,000 American GIs were deployed as occupation forces in Germany. Many of them quickly developed intimate relations with their former enemies. Those informal interactions played a significant role in the transformation of Germany from enemy to ally of the United States, argues Petra Goedde in her engrossing book.

Goedde finds that as American soldiers fraternized with German civilians, particularly as they formed sexual relationships with women, they developed a feminized image of Germany that contrasted sharply with their wartime image of the aggressive Nazi storm trooper. A perception of German "victimhood" emerged that was fostered by the German population and adopted by Americans. According to Goedde, this new view of Germany provided a foundation

GIs

and

Germans

GIs and Germans: Culture, Gender, and Foreign Relations, 1945–1949

Petra Goedde

Yale University Press   New Haven & London

Set in Minion type by Keystone Typesetting, Inc.
Printed in the United States of America by Sheridan Books.

ISBN: 0-300-09022-6

A catalogue record for this book is available from the Library of Congress
and the British Library.

The paper in this book meets the guidelines for permanence and durability
of the Committee on Production Guidelines for Book Longevity of the
Council on Library Resources.

10 9 8 7 6 5 4 3 2 1

For Drew

Contents

Acknowledgments

When I began graduate work in history in the United States, I never envisioned that it would lead to the publication of this book. It would not have happened if not for the enormous encouragement and support I received along the way from many institutions, advisers, colleagues, friends, and family members.

Foremost among those who guided this project from its earliest stages was my adviser at Northwestern University, Michael S. Sherry. His probing questions, extensive comments and suggestions on countless drafts, and his unfailing support throughout have been formative for this project. I also benefited greatly from the expertise and advice of other Northwestern colleagues, among them Karen Halttunen, Peter Hayes, Walter Hixson, Nancy McLean, and Arthur F. McEvoy. I was fortunate to receive a fellowship from the Deutsche Akademische Austauschdienst (DAAD) during my first year of graduate work at Northwestern, and subsequent financial support from the Northwestern history department.

During a year of teaching at the University of Puget Sound, I derived much inspiration from the cross-disciplinary atmosphere particularly from interactions with members of the women's studies and political science departments. The friendship of Suzanne Barnett, Bill Barry, Bill Breitenbach, Nancy Bristow, Mott Greene, Liz

Norville, John Lear, and David Smith made it a truly pleasurable experience.

I had the good fortune to be able to begin the process of revising the manuscript as a fellow at the Charles Warren Center for Studies in American History at Harvard University. My greatest debt since then goes to Akira Iriye who has been consistently supportive beyond any measure and whose advice and expertise have been instrumental in the shaping of the final project. The biweekly seminars of the center, run by Ernest May, were always thought-provoking and influenced my work in countless ways. What made this a truly memorable year was the friendship and support of the fellows at the Warren Center, Tom Knock, Tim Naftali, Phil Nash, Lu Soo Chun, Daniela Rossini, Rafia Zafar, and Susan Hunt.

Princeton University provided a stimulating intellectual environment. Along the way several colleagues gave advice, showed support, and changed my way of thinking about my project. Among them were Karen Merrill, Arno Mayer, Anson Rabinbach, Dan Rodgers, and Eileen Scully. I want to thank Richard Challener in particular who took some time one afternoon to share his experience as a member of the occupying forces in Germany at the end of the war.

No research project can succeed without the help of librarians and archivists who are willing to track down obscure books, go the extra mile to retrieve a lost document and the like. I received generous help from several archives and research libraries, most notably the National Archives, Harvard's Widener Library, Northwestern Library, Princeton's Firestone Library and the Seeley G. Mudd Manuscript Library, the Bundesarchiv Koblenz, Landesarchiv Berlin and the Landesbildstelle Berlin, Bayrisches Hauptstaatsarchiv in München, Baden-Württembergisches Hauptstaatsarchiv in Stuttgart, Hessisches Hauptstaatsarchiv in Wiesbaden, Institut für Publizistik at the Westfälische Wilhelms-Universität Münster, and the Archiv des Instituts für Zeitungsforschung, Dortmund.

I would also like to thank the editors at Yale University Press, above all Lara Heimert and Margaret Otzel who have guided this project through to its publication. Lara's enthusiasm for the project was encouraging and her managing of the review process has impressed me greatly. Thanks also to the anonymous reviewers, who have been most generous in their comments and support for this project.

Over the years I have incurred huge debts to friends and family who have shown unfailing interest in this project, have given generously of their time when I needed to "talk things through," when I needed them to re-read a draft "yet again," when I needed to be distracted from my work and be told that there is a life, and a good life at that, beyond this book and beyond history. They are Katey Anderson, Andy Lohmeier, Naoko Shibusawa, Georg Schmundt-Thomas, Bettina Westerhoff, Chiqui Rulan Levy, Kyle Smith, Birgit Lindmeyer, Detlef Mebus, John and Lynn Hillman, Susan Friedman, Dan Cohen, Kurk Dorsey, Rosanne Currarino, Paul Miles, Anne and Bernd Lorenzen, Lisa and Rüdiger Thurm, and my parents, Franz-Josef and Elisabeth Gödde, for teaching me what really matters in life and for keeping their impatience with the duration of this project mostly to themselves.

Finally I want to thank my children, Kai, Elena, and Noah, for being, and for being who they are. And I want to thank Drew for being friend, family, colleague, and adviser all rolled into one. Without Drew this book would not be, without him this book would not be what it is.

Introduction

Three years after the end of World War II the sound of American military aircraft approaching Berlin was still familiar to its citizens. The American C-47s and C-54s did not carry bombs but delivered food, fuel, and other vital goods to the population in the city's western sectors around the clock. The Anglo-American airlift, one of the opening scenes of the cold war, was the western Allies' response to the Soviet blockade of West Berlin, itself a response to the introduction of a new currency in the western zones of Germany and the western sectors of Berlin. Unlike in 1944 and early 1945, when terrified Berliners rushed into underground air raid shelters at the sound of the approaching aircraft, in 1948 countless children rushed into the street. They were hoping to catch one of the little parachutes with candy attached to them that some flight crews playfully dropped out of their transport planes. The candy drops began as an initiative of a single Lieutenant, Gail S. Halvorsen, in July 1948. They became so popular that the U.S. Air Force soon formally adopted and expanded the practice to include a few drops over Soviet-occupied territory. A Soviet protest note calling the measure an "outrageous capitalist trick" soon put an end to those excursions, however.[1] Like Halvorsen, the citizens of West Berlin ironically contrasted the mission of the airlift with the late war affectionately calling all transport planes *Rosinenbomber* (raisin bombers).

The metamorphosis of war planes into Rosinenbomber during the year-long airlift epitomized the dramatic turnabout in
American-German relations since the end of the war. Germany and
the United States had resumed amicable relations and economic
cooperation after fighting on opposite sides in World War I, but
World War II produced a much deeper rift between the two countries. Nonetheless, the western part of Germany and the United
States managed to transform their animosity into an alliance that
encompassed economic, cultural, political, and—after West Germany's entry into NATO—military cooperation.[2] As American-
Soviet relations deteriorated and the eastern and western zones
of Germany separated, the West German parliamentary council
adopted a democratic constitution—the Basic Law—which bor-
rowed important elements from the American system of federal
government.[3] West Germany's political leaders chose integration
into the Western alliance over unification with East Germany. America had created in West Germany what the historian Manfred Jonas
called a "client state."[4]

How could this dramatic transformation have occurred in such a
short span of time? This question lies at the core of this book. It is by
no means a new question, yet unlike previous treatments of this
subject, which have focused on political and economic factors, this
study explores the question from a socio-cultural perspective. In
other words, it broadens the definition of foreign relations to mean
not only the interactions among politicians and diplomats but the
relationships among ordinary Americans and Germans, more specifically the interactions between U.S. occupation soldiers and the
civilian population in Germany. It asserts that these relationships
made a significant contribution to the rapidity of U.S.–German
rapprochement.

The study of informal relationships between members of the
occupying forces and German civilians has been largely neglected by

scholars of the American occupation. Research instead has focused primarily on political, military, and economic elites. These elites supposedly held the key to the two central questions that have dominated the historiography of the occupation: Did Americans achieve their objectives in Germany? And why did American policy toward Germany change between 1945 and 1949? Answers to the first question have varied widely. Most early researchers who evaluated the period as a whole judged the occupation a success.[5] Beginning in the 1970s, however, scholars increasingly concentrated on specific policies such as denazification, reeducation, political reconstruction, and economic reform.[6] Those accounts often revealed shortcomings of the occupation, especially in its denazification and reeducation efforts. Yet this new generation of historians still shared the assumption of its predecessors that the answer to their questions lay in administrative and political rather than social and cultural records.

Scholars have addressed the second question—why did American policy toward Germany change—within the larger context of the cold war. Their main focus revolved around whether or not the reconstruction of Germany served American global interests. Caught between East and West, Germany became either a territorial/ideological battleground, as realist historians assumed, or an economic one, as revisionist historians assumed. Scholars on both sides did not investigate whether the experiences of occupation troops in Germany had any bearing on policy formulations in Washington. They saw the cold war as a political phenomenon that might have had cultural and social consequences but not cultural or social roots. The improvement of American-German relations was therefore considered a matter of political expediency.[7]

Few historians of the occupation ventured into the cultural realm. Those who did confined themselves to the exploration of the American military government's cultural policies.[8] In recent years an increasing number of German historians have explored the question of Germany's cultural and economic Americanization after World War II, yet the occupation and especially the presence of U.S. troops in Germany often played a marginal role in these studies.[9] Focused on the agency of Germans in the transformation of their own culture, these scholars seldom explored the reciprocity between German and American cultural and political changes.

Over the past two decades, however, German social and women's historians have begun to shift the emphasis from elites to the experiences of ordinary Germans during the occupation.[10] Women figured prominently in these histories, not surprisingly, since they far outnumbered men after the war. Many of these studies addressed the impact of occupation troops on the social and cultural life within Germany.[11] These works significantly enriched our understanding of how ordinary Germans experienced the aftermath of the war and the presence of foreign troops in their communities.

Yet they shed little light on the way these experiences related to the larger political framework in which they occurred. One notable exception is Norman Naimark's study on the Russian presence in Germany after 1945. Drawing on political, economic, social, and cultural sources, Naimark explored the interactions between Russians and Germans. He found that East Germany's political and social development was very much a product of these interactions between Russians and Germans during the occupation. Rather than fostering good relations between the two countries, Naimark found that they damaged the Soviet reputation in East Germany and diminished the popular support for East Germany's communists.[12]

To date, no comparable study exists for the American presence in West Germany. Instead most American historians focused on the politics of the occupation and American agency in restructuring and reconstructing Germany, while most German historians focused on the German reception of an imaginary American culture and on German agency in shaping its own postwar history. Neither of them explored the process of interaction between the two cultures in any depth. What thus emerges is the development of two parallel historiographies, one concerned with the political impact of American occupation policies on Germany, the other with the social and cultural reconstruction of Germany. These two spheres overlap only rarely, for instance, when the former includes a discussion of cultural policies toward Germany, or when the latter includes a discussion of Germany's Americanization.

This book seeks to reconnect these two spheres. It assumes that culture and politics do not change independently. Indeed, politics—domestic and international—cannot be separated from the cultural context in which it unfolds. It does not try to provide a comprehensive political analysis of the German-American postwar relationship. Nor should it be understood as a social history of early postwar Germany. Rather, it tries to link the history of the cultural and social interactions between American soldiers and German civilians to the political history of the occupation. It builds on the excellent research done in the growing field of local and regional studies on early postwar Germany and attempts to link those findings to the field of American foreign relations.[13]

This study also does not try to render irrelevant the findings in the field of American-German political and economic postwar relations, nor does it try to diminish the importance and relevance of the cold war for this relationship. Rather it focuses on those aspects of the relationship that evolved prior to the onset of the cold war and seeks to show their contribution primarily in the realm of social and cultural interactions, to the shift in the relationship between the two countries. The objective of this study is thus twofold: first to investigate the social interactions between occupation forces and civilians and second to explore the ways in which these interactions related to the larger political context of the occupation.

This approach accomplishes two broad objectives. First, it links together social, cultural, and political changes in American-German relations and, second, it links together German and American domestic social and cultural history. The circumstances in early postwar Germany provide a unique opportunity to study international relations from a socio-cultural as well as political perspective because of the massive presence of foreign soldiers on German soil. The only historical precedent for this situation in the United States occurred in the aftermath of the Civil War when Northern troops occupied the South. Both the influx of large numbers of Northern troops after the war and the speed with which the former enemies buried their differences resembled the German case. After an initial period of radical reform in the South in the wake of the war, northerners allowed the antebellum political elite to resume power. In Germany, too, American efforts at denazification were soon compromised. Most histories of the reconstruction period initially focused on the political and economic reasons for the failure of reconstruction.[14] Yet when the historian Nina Silber investigated the process of North-South reconciliation from a socio-cultural perspective, she found that gender served as a crucial metaphor for the postbellum reunion. Gilded age Americans, she argued, increasingly viewed reconstruction as a northern courtship of an initially unwilling but eventually consenting feminized South.[15] The following study will reveal a similar dynamic in the relationships between Germans and Americans after World War II, pointing to the centrality of gender in the reconciliation between the two societies.

A contemporaneous reference point to the German case was the American occupation of Japan after World War II. Like Germany, Japan was a defeated and powerless nation subject to foreign occupation and the influx of thousands of American soldiers. Yet apart from this obvious similarity, there was more to separate than to unite the German and Japanese occupation experiences. Unlike Germany, Japan faced only the United States as an occupation power, giving the Supreme Commander of the Allied Forces, General Douglas MacArthur, extensive power of decision. Furthermore, while Americans left the basic political structures in place in Japan, above all the retention of the Emperor Hirohito, they insisted on the complete dismantling of Germany's political institutions. Concerning the constitution, however, Americans reversed their approach in the two countries. In Japan, American constitutional experts wrote the constitution without much input from Japanese officials, while in Germany the western Allies allowed the Germans in their zones some leeway in the composition of their constitution.[16]

Within the social and cultural realm, differences also outweighed similarities. Race played a crucial role in the American experience in Japan, establishing a barrier between occupiers and occupied. In Germany, the opposite was the case. Racial and cultural similarities between Germans and white Americans facilitated exchange, leading to a sense of cultural affinity rather than alienation. Yet in one crucial aspect the soldier-civilian interactions were remarkably similar in both countries. In Japan, like in Germany and the American South after the Civil War, gender and sexuality played a vital role in changing American perceptions of the defeated enemy. As John Dower argued, after defeating Japan, Americans conceived of it as a feminized nation.[17]

Most historians who apply gender analysis to the study of intercultural relations focus on peoples of different racial background. When Andrew Rotter, for instance, used gender in his analysis of the relationship between the United States and India, he identified Latin America, China, and Vietnam as additional loci for a gendered interpretation of foreign relations. Europe, on the other hand, he saw as a partner of equal, possibly male, stature in foreign relations.[18] The following study will show that gender also played a major part in the reconciliation between Americans and Germans. The Germany that American soldiers encountered after the war was weak,

submissive, and disproportionately female. Death and the imprison-
ment of millions of German soldiers at the end of the war—some
prisoners of war were not released until the 1950s—had significantly
reduced the male population between the ages of twenty and sixty.[19]
Partly but not exclusively as a result of this gender imbalance and the
GIs' overwhelming preference for female companionship, gender
functioned as a crucial reference point in the discourse about Germany's reconciliation with the United States. Within the first year of
occupation, American soldiers developed a feminized and infan-
tilized image of Germany that contrasted sharply with the masculine, wartime image of Nazi storm troopers.

The inclusion of culture and gender as analytical categories in
the study of international relations requires the borrowing of tools
from other disciplines. Cultural historians have long advocated an
interdisciplinary approach to history, looking to anthropology, sociology, and literary criticism for help. For historians of American
foreign relations, this undertaking is new and somewhat unusual.[20]
Of foremost importance is a working definition of culture and its
relationship to politics. I use the term "culture" in its broadest possible sense, denoting a system of customs, values, and beliefs shared by
a group of similar ethnic, national, and class background. As the
anthropologist Clifford Geertz has explained, politics and culture
are closely intertwined. Politics should thus be understood as an
expression of culture as well as a forum for cultural contestation.[21]

Yet both culture and politics are in a state of constant flux. This
book intends to explain how changes in the cultural realm can affect
changes in the political realm and vice versa. In the context of
American-German postwar relations, gender analysis helps to document this change. This does not mean that gender analysis can
explain every aspect of the American occupation. Rather it focuses
attention on one crucial aspect of the relationship between Germans
and Americans, namely the vast difference in power between the two

countries. Historians of American foreign relations and women's historians have utilized gender analysis as a way to signify relations of power between individuals as well as countries.[22] Within the context of this book, then, gender analysis helps explain the ways in which both Germans and Americans legitimized, accepted, and ultimately overcame this power imbalance. It is important to note that gender is a historically constructed concept whose meaning is conditioned by time and place and subject to change.[23] Gender served as a metaphor for the German-American relationship primarily within the specific context of the early postwar period. This book investigates both the concrete and normative realm of women's and men's roles in postwar Germany and the United States as well as the figurative use of gender difference in the cross-cultural relationship between the two nations.

Power was central to this relationship. More importantly, American power over Germans became infused with gendered meaning, creating the perception both among those who held the power and those who submitted to it, that the asymmetry between them was a natural phenomenon. American power over Germans extended from the military government's ability to set policy and appoint political officials in the American zone to the relationships between individual soldiers and German civilians. Many GIs filled a void in German society left by the war-related shortage of German men. They became male providers and protectors to young German women and on occasion functioned as male role models for young German boys. Yet at the same time both Germans and Americans remained very much aware of the soldiers' status as outsiders. Germans both accommodated to and resisted the intrusion of these foreign troops into their communities. Women and children were often more willing to accept the presence of American soldiers, in part because they benefited most from the GIs' relative economic wealth, but also because the soldiers' presence did not challenge their role within German society. For that very reason, older Germans and men often saw these foreigners as a threat to the established power structures within their own communities. The presence of American soldiers directly and in very personal ways challenged the power and masculinity of German men.[24] Yet ultimately even German men accepted cultural and political feminization as the best path toward their own country's international rehabilitation. They appropriated German women's experiences as the national experience, turning the *Trümmerfrau* (rubble woman), who cleared away the debris from bomb sites, into a national icon of postwar western Germany.[25]

The emphasis on social and cultural factors in the German-American relationship places the cold war in a broader context, showing the cultural and social aspects of the transformation of the German-American relationship that undergirded the emergence of the cold war. The socio-cultural approach also moves beyond the focus on the American-Soviet relationship as the only important variable in the postwar geo-political configuration. It shows that the greatest dynamic in the first two years of the postwar period lay in the U.S.-German rather than the U.S.-Soviet relationship. By 1947, Americans saw the Soviet Union as a greater threat to their security than Germany, not so much because the Soviet Union had become more of a threat but because Western Germany had become less of a threat. What had changed then was the relationship of the United States to Western Germany relative to the Soviet Union. The cold war was therefore as much a consequence as a cause of the improved relationship between Germany and the United States.

The Rosinenbomber that came roaring into Berlin in 1948–49 symbolized the new relationship between Germans and Americans. The airlift marked the culmination of the previous four years of gradual change rather than a turning point in U.S.–German relations. The personal interactions between American soldiers and

German civilians bridged the divide that the war had created between the two countries. In fact, by casting postwar Germany in feminine terms, Americans and Germans avoided confronting the Nazi past. Postwar Germany shed its aggressive masculine identity and took on the new, if temporary, identity of a feminized, victimized, and most importantly pacific, client state.

CHAPTER 1

"Know Your Enemy?"
American and German
Wartime Images

"I have always thought the Krauts would fight like devils for every inch of German soil," Sergeant Henry Giles wrote in his diary as he fought his way into Germany in February 1945, "and in a way they are." Many of the first American troops to enter Germany in late 1944 and early 1945 shared Giles's apprehension. Hardened by months of deadly exchanges with the German Wehrmacht, they feared that the intensity of the fighting would increase as German civilians joined soldiers to battle for their homeland. A month later Giles revised his judgment after entering town upon town in which civilians surrendered without a fight. "At first we were pretty nervous of them," he recorded in his journal, "for we'd been told all civilians would be sniping at us. If they have, we haven't seen or heard of it."[1] Giles's entries give an indication of the confusion that existed among GIs during their earliest encounters with German civilians. German responses to the American invasion were equally confused ranging from fierce resistance in some areas to abject defeatism in others.

The unpredictability of these first days of direct contact with the enemy have to be seen in the context of the complex and volatile images Americans and Germans had retained of each other throughout the war. Both countries' governments created aggressive propaganda campaigns designed to portray the enemy as their own antithesis. Those campaigns, however, did not operate in a cultural vacuum. Unlike the U.S. wartime propaganda campaign against Japan, for instance, a non-white nation against whom many Americans harbored prejudices and misconceptions long before the outbreak of war, the campaign against Germany occurred within the context of deep cultural and ethnic ties dating back to the nineteenth century. This difference resulted in not only far more subdued anti-German than anti-Japanese propaganda but also weakened the effect of the propaganda as many Americans, despite the war, maintained a more positive image of Germany. In Germany, too, the persistence of a subculture that admired American popular culture and its technical achievements undercut the official propaganda.

In both Germany and the United States in the 1930s and early 1940s, popular attitudes proved to be more resistant to change than politics. Most Americans found the Nazi regime's policies revolting. Yet throughout the war they debated the "Germanness" of National Socialism. Did the Nazis simply carry out what the German population had advocated for generations or did a small group of fanatics hold a largely passive and powerless population hostage? During the Nazi regime German attitudes toward the United States were equally ambiguous extending a pattern dating back to the Weimar Republic. Charges of American superficiality and lack of cultural sophistication existed side by side with a growing demand for the products of American technological innovation and popular culture.[2] Although the regime tried to restrict outside influences on German culture—especially from the United States—many Germans nurtured cultural ties to the United States until well into the war years.

Official propaganda and cultural debates on the home front were important elements in the formulation of both GIs' and German civilians' expectations of each other. These wartime debates help explain why during the transition from war to peace so many GIs developed friendly relationships with individual Germans while maintaining a collective negative image of a monolithic Nazi Germany. The juxtaposition between the private personal and the public collective was already evident in those wartime debates.

* * *

Throughout the 1930s and World War II, Americans struggled to understand Nazism's relationship to German history and culture. Some traced German aggression to the nation's long history of militarism and authoritarianism, assuming that Germany had developed a distinct culture that not only separated it from the rest of western civilization but permitted such extreme ideologies as Nazism to prosper. A sizable group of American intellectuals, however, separated Nazism from German culture.[3] Instead of characterizing Nazism as the natural outcome of German national culture, they interpreted it as an aberration of western civilization and therefore a problem not only of the German people but the entire western world. Most Americans found themselves somewhere between the extremes of cultural alienation and cultural affinity: they saw Nazis as quintessential Germans, but not all Germans as quintessential Nazis.

Americans who believed that Nazism exposed the fundamental differences between Germany and the rest of western civilization found considerable support within the U.S. government. The wartime anti-German campaign, conducted first by the Office of Facts and Figures (OFF) and, after 1942, the Office of War Information (OWI), depicted Nazism as the logical outcome of German history. Originally, the purpose of the information agency was solely to "coordinate the dissemination of war information by all federal agencies and to formulate and carry out, by means of the press, radio and motion pictures, programs designed to facilitate an understanding in the United States and abroad of the progress of the war effort and of the policies, activities, and aims of the Government."[4] Yet within the first year of OWI's operation, efforts to depict the American involvement in the war dispassionately gave way to more blunt ways of propagating the government's war policies and vilifying its enemies.

The work of the Hollywood filmmaker Frank Capra, OWI's most famous employee, had much to do with this shift. OWI considered his documentary series *Why We Fight* so successful that it extended its distribution from the original target audience of American troops to the general public. These documentaries created the impression of objectivity through the use of extensive original footage from the enemy countries' own propaganda films. "Let our boys hear the Nazis and the Japs shout their own claims of master-race crud," Capra argued, "and our fighting men will know why they are in uniform."[5] In *Prelude to War*—the first of the seven-part series—Capra pitted the American "free world" against the Axis "slave world." He pointed to the similarities among German, Japanese, and Italian militarism, nationalist ideologies, imperialism, racism, and authoritarianism. A display of a world map marked not only the areas which had already fallen victim to the Axis powers but also their alleged future targets, including the United States. The shift from past to future conquests was hardly recognizable in the film, as the blackened surface of the enemy countries spilled like an overturned inkwell over the entire globe. The Pacific and European theaters of war seemed to be encroaching upon the American continent. The message to Americans was unmistakable: they were no longer safe. The closing words of the film—"it's us or them"—powerfully underscored this sense of immediate danger.[6]

In Capra's films the Germans, Japanese, and Italians were barely distinguished, and there was no distinction between the populations of those countries and their leaders either. The roots of Nazism, according to *Prelude to War*, lay in Germany's cultural and militarist history, because "the Germans have an inborn national love for regimentation and harsh discipline."[7] *The Nazis Strike,* the second documentary in the series, traced the German desire for world domination to the nineteenth century. "The symbols and the leaders change," the commentator warned, "but Germany's maniacal urge to impose its will on others continues from generation to generation."[8] To underscore the barbarous nature of the regime, Capra compared Adolf Hitler's Germany to the rule of terror of Ghengis Khan's Mongolian empire in the thirteenth century. The film's emphasis on continuity suggested that the rise of National Socialism in Germany was the consequence rather than the source of Germany's will to war.

If German aggression transcended the current regime, then its roots had to lie in Germany's culture and society—precisely where the former British Permanent Undersecretary for Foreign Affairs Lord Vansittart located them. Debating the future of Germany with Dorothy Thompson in *Newsweek,* the British Lord took the hard line. For him, the principle for dealing with Germans was "not to trust them." He found Germans to be "utterly untrustworthy and appallingly tenacious of evil." He held no hope of "re-educating the present generation of German savages." Inherent German hooliganism, he continued, demanded the harshest possible terms after the war, grounded in a "well-founded distrust of the Germans as a whole, until we are sure, not only of reformation, but transformation."[9] The removal of Nazism from the German political landscape thus would not suffice to prevent future German aggression. Unless the Allies significantly transformed Germany's culture and society, there could be no peace in Europe.[10]

Vansittart's position built on that of a powerful group of writers and political commentators in the United States. The German-born writer Emil Ludwig had asserted a year earlier in *Collier's* that "the qualities which are dominant in the Germans today were developed in the first centuries after their appearance in civilized Europe." The Germans' lack of self-assurance, according to Ludwig, drove them to conquer their happier neighbors and to idealize conquest and militarism. "As a soldier, the German for 2,000 years has found satisfaction in seeing the fear he evokes in other countries. . . . He is happy when he knows that others are less happy than he."[11] By consistently using the singular pronoun, Ludwig implied the universality of the militaristic German character and its consistency over the last two millennia.

Ludwig acknowledged that there existed another side of Germany that produced great musicians, philosophers, and scientists. Those achievements, he argued, served only to mask Germany's darker side. Scientists, Ludwig explained, learned to apply to their studies the same robotic precision that Prussian militarists drilled into their armies, and the "romantic and musical side of the German character was always weaker than the side which worshiped the state—and above all, uniforms."[12] By setting up this contrast between art and militarism, Ludwig defined the national debate about Germany. In Ludwig's formulation, the two sides of the German character were masculine and feminine, with the masculine tendencies dominant.

Many of Ludwig's contemporaries shared his ideas about the continuity of German militarism throughout history.[13] In January 1944 F. W. Foerster claimed in *Commonweal* that "one hundred years of ever-growing Pan-Germanism, racial pride, militarism, glorification of war, and finally fifteen years of secret re-armament and propaganda for revenge were bound to produce the ruthless Fuehrer who brought the final conclusion to the long-prepared general madness."[14] He warned that even after Hitler and the Nazis had vanished the German danger would persist, unless Allied nations imposed a system of rigid and long-term control on Germany. Foerster claimed to know what he was talking about since his family combined the two major traits of German culture, military and muse. His father had been Director of the Berlin Conservatory and his grandfather a distinguished German officer. Like Ludwig before him, Foerster found the militaristic side dominating the artistic. This dialectic—however flawed—provided a way for Americans to make sense of their contradictory sentiments about Germany's national culture.

The assumption of Germany's historical predisposition toward Nazism influenced proposals for its postwar treatment. Siegrid Schultz, drawing on her experience as a *Chicago Tribune* correspondent in Berlin between 1919 and 1941, warned in her 1944 book *Germany Will Try It Again* that Hitler's Nazi ideas would live on even after the end of the war and cited World War I and its aftermath as proof of the continuity of pan-German ideas.[15] In his review of her monograph, the *Chicago Sun* correspondent F. W. Fodor credited Schultz with "probably [knowing] Germany better than any other correspondent." Fodor repeated Schultz's warning that the Germans might again exploit "the sympathies of the sentimental Anglo-Saxons for their cause," as they had done after the previous war.[16] Both Fodor and Schultz called for much tighter control over Germany than had occurred after the last war.

Louis Nizer, in *What to Do With Germany,* went even further. Nizer claimed that German aggression and totalitarianism had persisted throughout two thousand years of history. "It is not the leader of the day," he asserted, "whether he be Charlemagne, Barbarossa, Frederick Wilhelm, the Great Elector, Frederick the Great, Bismarck, the Kaiser or Hitler, who wages war against mankind. It is the German people." He proposed to take the whole country into "protective custody" after the war and to punish not only Nazi officials but also ranking officers of the German armed forces, party and government members, and administrators, "no matter how subordinate."[17] The complete eradication of the nation's bureaucratic apparatus would be the only road toward a peaceful Germany. Nizer and like-minded contemporaries identified Germany's national culture as the main source of aggression. The elimination of the German threat to world peace thus involved a fundamental purge of Germany's militarist culture rather than the mere eradication of its political system.

The German problem produced an equally lively debate in scientific circles. In *Is Germany Incurable?*, Richard M. Brickner argued that the answer to Germany's behavior lay not in its inherent militarism but in a mental pathology that had struck the nation collectively. Brickner, a neuro-psychiatrist at Columbia University's College of Physicians and Surgeons, asserted that Germany's national traits conformed to those observable in a paranoid individual. He claimed that all nations from time to time revealed paranoid streaks. In Germany, however, the frequency of the disease and its intensity made it a dominant trait. Even though clinical psychiatrists considered paranoia an incurable disease, Brickner harbored some hope for the infected nation. To cure the German people, he argued, one needed to re-educate them through what he called the "clear area," that part of a patient's mind which still responded to reason. Nazism thus became medicalized as a disease, the German nation became a mental patient, Nazi territory a psychiatric ward.[18]

Reviews of Brickner's bold theory illustrated the broad spectrum of popular attitudes toward Germany. Sigrid Undset, the Norwegian novelist and Nobel Prize winner, wholeheartedly supported Brickner's ideas. Though not a scientist and speaking only from personal experience, she found the notion that Germans were stricken by collective paranoia quite convincing. The Germans she had met, she argued, could never bear to be contradicted "with any semblance of grace." She suggested that because of the pathological nature of Germany's problems the Allied occupation should include a large contingent of medical experts. Furthermore, Undset proposed to allocate scholarships to students to "learn about the importance of mental diseases or mental health in the affairs of society."[19] The relationship between Americans and Germans would thus be one of scientific researchers toward mentally ill patients.

Brickner's proposition of a German collective paranoia also convinced Horace M. Kallen. He found it to be a reasonable explanation for what he called the "German enigma." He remained skeptical, however, about the "programmatic value of the 'paranoid' interpretation of Germany's *Kultur* as a guide in effecting the fundamental social revolution which post-Nazi Germany requires." Instead, he argued, "the bulk of the German people are not less assuredly prisoners of the *Deutschtum's* force and fraud than the French, Russian, and Polish slaves of the Nazi aggression." He believed that a minority of Nazi fanatics dominated the majority of the German people and that the paranoia that Dr. Brickner had described did not extend beyond this minority. The cure for Germany would therefore lie primarily in isolating those paranoid individuals from the rest of German society.[20]

American scientists did not uniformly adopt the depiction of the Germans as pathological. Two reviewers, Gregory Zilboorg and Frank Kingdon, dismissed Brickner's theory outright. Zilboorg, also a psychiatrist, accused his colleague of misusing science for the purpose of propaganda. He attacked Brickner's argument by posing a host of rhetorical questions: "Why would he [Brickner] not admit that we psychiatrists do not yet know how to treat whole cultures? How could a culture suffer from paranoia, any more than a culture could have pneumonia?" Brickner's approach to the German problem, Zilboorg charged, came perilously close to the Nazi ideology by identifying inferior and superior cultures, sick and healthy races. Rather, Zilboorg argued, European culture was "one and indivisible, and . . . we are as responsible for the birth of Mussolini and Hitler as the Italians and Germans themselves." The developments in Germany thus represented a darker side of the western cultural tradition rather than a peculiarity of the German cultural tradition. Kingdon objected to Brickner's thesis on similar grounds. He argued that Germany, like any other nation, contained within itself conflicting cultural trends. The dominance of one trend over others at a particular time depended on dynamic forces active within the nation but also on influences coming from the outside. The United States, France, and Great Britain, therefore, had to share responsibility for what happened in Germany. Kingdon and Zilboorg tried to explain German behavior within the realm of human rationality. They did not see the developments in Germany as a peculiar path of a pathological people. Both pointed to the common roots of American and German culture as part of the western tradition. To them, the question was not what peculiarities in the German national tradition caused them to follow a fanatical leader, but what went wrong with western civilization to enable such fanatics as Hitler, Mussolini, and Franco to rise to power.[21] The public dispute over Brickner's thesis reflected the larger contours of the debate about the Allied war against Germany. Did Americans fight to liberate the world from the German menace or did they fight to liberate Germany, and by extension western civilization, from the Nazi menace?

The debate extended to the inner circles of the Roosevelt administration. One faction, headed by Secretary of the Treasury Henry Morgenthau Jr., believed that Germany's threat transcended the problem of Nazism. In his 1945 book *Germany Is Our Problem*, Morgenthau asserted that Germans had long harbored the conviction that they were destined to rule over inferior peoples. "The Nazis," he found, "pushed these theories further in practice than any of their predecessors, but they could not have done it without the generations of preparation. The German people had to be cultivated intensively for nearly two hundred years before they could produce those finest Nazi flowers—the gas chambers of Maidanek and the massacre of Lidice."[22] Nazism, according to Morgenthau, represented the natural culmination of Germany's militarist tradition. Weeding out this tradition, Morgenthau asserted, required more than punishing the leaders of the regime. The only way to turn Germany into a peaceful nation, Morgenthau believed, was with a heavy dose of Jeffersonian agrarianism: dismantle Germany's heavy industry and send the people into the country to farm the land.[23] Morgenthau had presented this proposal to Roosevelt in 1944 as a blueprint for Germany's postwar treatment. The Morgenthau Plan, as it became known, suggested that the necessary radical transformation of Germany's economy and society must begin with the return to an agricultural society. Whereas Brickner located the roots of Nazism in Germany's national psyche, Morgenthau seemed to suggest that it had emerged from Germany's path toward industrialization. If, as Morgenthau assumed, Germany's cultural heritage had produced Nazism, then a lasting peace depended not only on the crushing of Nazism's ideology and elite but also the overhaul of Germany's economy, society, and culture.

Morgenthau's influence within the administration peaked when he accompanied the President to the Quebec Conference with the British Prime Minister Winston Churchill in September 1944. He succeeded in convincing both leaders to adopt core elements of the plan, including the dismantling of Germany's warmaking industry.[24] However, shortly after his return to Washington, Roosevelt retreated from Morgenthau's propositions and began to formulate a less rigorous alternative for Germany's postwar treatment. The President's shift on the question of Germany's future reflected his own ambivalence about Germany as well as the growing influence within his cabinet of a group opposed to the Morgenthau plan, headed by Secretary of War Henry L. Stimson.

Stimson, who had not attended conference, favored Germany's

economic rehabilitation over its complete destruction. Before the President departed for Quebec, Stimson warned him against the Morgenthau Plan, remarking that it was "not within the realm of possibility that a whole nation of seventy million people, who have been outstanding for many years in the arts and the sciences and who through their efficiency and energy have attained one of the highest industrial levels in Europe, can by force be required to abandon all their previous methods of life, be reduced to a peasant level with virtually complete control of industry and science left to other peoples." Whereas Morgenthau saw Germany's industrialization as the source of the current problem, Stimson saw it as the country's path to salvation. He invoked most of the dominant stereotypes about Germany, its efficiency, modernism, and its leadership in arts and sciences—all hallmarks of advanced civilization in Stimson's eyes. For Morgenthau, Stimson had little admiration. In his diary he noted that Morgenthau was "so biased by his Semitic grievances that he is really a very dangerous adviser to the president at this time."[25]

Stimson's admonitions appeared to have been too weak to impress Roosevelt at the time, yet strong enough to make him write ten days after the conference that "no one wants to make Germany a wholly agricultural nation again."[26] This statement signified a decisive retreat from the Morgenthau Plan. By October, FDR's ideas about Germany's future appeared even farther removed from the Quebec agreements. "Much of this economic subhead [on economic objectives]," he wrote to Secretary of State Hull, "is dependent on what we and the Allies find when we get into Germany."[27] This flexibility on Roosevelt's part prevented the formulation of a detailed blueprint for the conduct of the occupation. When Harry S. Truman succeeded Roosevelt as president in April 1945, he inherited considerable leeway in shaping the U.S. postwar mission in Germany.

Roosevelt shared with Morgenthau and most members of his

administration the call for Germany's unconditional surrender and the complete destruction of the Nazi empire. Yet he did not necessarily regard Nazism as the natural expression of Germany's cultural and social values. When the President and Churchill agreed in Casablanca in 1943 to call for the Axis powers' unconditional surrender, Roosevelt assured critics that this would not mean "the destruction of the population of Germany, Italy, and Japan, but it does mean the destruction of the philosophies in those countries which are based on conquest and the subjugation of other people."[28] His careful distinction between populations and political philosophies opened an avenue for postwar reconciliation.

Roosevelt also publicly questioned the idea of Germany's historical record of militarism. His own views on Germany were based in part on his frequent childhood visits to that country. Speaking to journalists on his return from the Yalta conference in February 1945, FDR recalled that Germany "was not a military-minded nation" when he went to school there during the reign of Emperor Wilhelm I.[29] Germany's path toward militarism and expansionism, he asserted, did not begin until Wilhelm II took office in 1889. Its quest for expansion thus appeared to be the result of the political ambitions of the country's leaders over the previous decades rather than its cultural history.

Roosevelt's apparent unwillingness to commit himself to either a harsh or a soft peace encouraged Germanophiles within the United States. Throughout the war they searched for ways to reconcile their past admiration for German culture with their present alienation. A 1943 poll showed that most Americans, like FDR, differentiated between the German people and their government. When asked to choose among three statements describing the Germans, forty-six percent thought that Germans did not like war but had shown to be too easily led into war by powerful leaders. Thirty-two percent thought that Germans did not like war and that they would become

Fig. 1.1 The Japanese "monkey" mimics the German mastermind. © 1942, *Washington Post*. Reprinted with permission.

good citizens of the world if they had the same chance as people in other countries. Only twenty-two percent shared Morgenthau's view that Germans would "always want to go to war to make themselves as powerful as possible." Thus even during the height of the war Morgenthau could muster the support of only a minority for his views.[30]

The tendency to place blame for German aggression upon the government was discernible in visual images as well. Newspaper cartoons often depicted German atrocities as "Nazi" rather than "German" crimes. A July 1942 *Washington Post* cartoon, for instance, associated German war crimes directly with Hitler by depicting his image looming over the ruins of Lidice and Lezaky (fig. 1.1).[31] The focus of public outrage on the personality of Hitler and the Nazi party permitted Americans to continue appreciating the common cultural heritage of the two nations.

The importance of cultural affinity emerged even more clearly when comparing American attitudes toward Germany with those toward Japan. The same *Washington Post* cartoon addressed Japanese atrocities in Cebu by showing a gorilla labeled "Japs" in the foreground. Worse still, the title "Mimic" suggested that the Japanese had simply followed the example of Nazi masterminds, who were, it seemed, even in their barbarism more highly evolved. Wartime cartoons often depicted the Japanese as bestial animals, in contrast to the personalized human image of Hitler in many anti-German cartoons (fig. 1.2). Americans were much less willing to distinguish between the Japanese people and their leaders than they were with respect to Germany.[32]

Opinion polls taken over the course of 1943 and 1944 corroborated this tendency. Sixty-two percent of the American people believed the Japanese would "always want to go to war to make themselves as powerful as possible." Only twenty-seven percent believed that in Japan people "might not like war, but they had shown that they were too easily led into war by powerful leaders." Even fewer, a mere eleven percent, believed that the Japanese "did not like war and that they would become good citizens of the world if they had the same chance as people in other countries (table 1.1)." The sharp differences between American characterizations of Japanese and Germans and the representation of Japanese as rats, roaches, or apes, reflected the endemic current of racism in the United States toward a non-white people.[33]

A shared cultural heritage, the presence of a large number of Americans of German descent in the United States, and excesses in

Fig. 1.2 World War II poster of the German enemy, who was usually portrayed as human, often through an image of Hitler. Reprinted from *Behind the Lines: Gender and the Two World Wars,* edited by Margaret Randolph Higonnet, Jane Jenson, Sonya Michel, and Margaret Collins Weitz. New Haven: Yale University Press, 1987.

the anti-German campaign during World War I dissuaded American propagandists from ridiculing Germans as they had the Japanese.[34] During much of the 1930s, prominent Americans, among them Henry Ford and Charles A. Lindbergh, had even sympathized with Hitler's policies. Anti-Semitism was on the rise and public personalities such as Gerald K. Smith, a preacher from Louisiana, and Father Charles Coughlin spread their anti-Semitic messages before numerous sympathetic listeners.[35] Throughout the war, the

Table 1.1: American public opinion about Germany and
Japan during World War II (by percentage)

	Germany	Japan
Will always want war	22	62
Too easily led	46	27
Do not like war	32	11

Source: *Public Opinion Quarterly* (Winter 1943), 755.

administration downplayed evidence pointing toward Hitler's annihilation of the Jews.[36] Even though openly fascist organizations such
as Fritz Kuhn's Bund and William Dudley Pelley's Silver Shirts remained marginal in the United States, complacency about anti-
Semitism and racism shaped the American response to the war in
the Pacific and in Europe.

The racial undercurrents of the war divided American opinions
about the enemy. African-Americans in particular pointed to the
irony that while the United States engaged in a crusade against the
"slave world," Jim Crow laws excluded black Americans from full
participation in the "free world." More than seventy years after their
emancipation from slavery, African-Americans remained second-
class citizens in their own country, suffering the effects of the segregation of public facilities and institutions. Their views of the war
against Germany and Japan reflected their concerns over racial discrimination at home.

According to wartime public opinion polls, African-Americans
tended to be less fearful of the Japanese than of the Germans. Many
sympathized with the Japanese nation as fellow "people of color" and
assumed that they would be less likely than white Americans to dis-
criminate against African-Americans. National Socialist racism on
the other hand represented a greater threat than American racism. A
survey conducted in early 1942 by the OFF revealed that eighteen
percent of the black population believed African-Americans would

be better off under Japanese rule since they were "also colored." Thirty-one percent believed that the Japanese would treat them the same, whereas only twenty-eight percent believed they would be worse off under Japanese rule. By contrast, fifty-one percent of white Americans expected Japanese treatment of blacks to be worse.[37] Their own racism toward the Japanese and their blindness toward the discrimination to which they subjected their own non-white compatriots prevented them from understanding the black point of view.

African-American activists focused less on the racial overtones of the war than on the hypocrisy of the American official propaganda. The Caribbean-born radical activist C. L. R. James saw no reason for black Americans to support the war effort in Europe and the Pacific. "Such is the democracy of the South," he declared, "that in many towns the Negroes wouldn't be able to sit in the same room with the whites to hear why they should die for 'democracy.'" James's opposition to the war stemmed from his conviction that "the democracy I want to fight for, Hitler is not depriving me of." He found few differences between Hitler's policies in Germany and Eastern Europe, Roosevelt's policies in the United States, and the imperialist policies of Great Britain, France, and Belgium in Africa and Asia. Instead of aiding white Americans in re-establishing their position of supremacy, James urged all non-white people in America, Asia, and Africa to unite in a struggle to end white colonialism.[38] The American writer Zora Neale Hurston expressed similar sentiments in a 1945 piece called "Crazy for this Democracy." In it she mocked the paradox of America's fight for democracy abroad and its denial of democratic participation for blacks at home. For African-Americans, the American war effort was more ambiguous than propagandists wanted them to believe.

Still, most blacks supported the war, though somewhat less enthusiastically than their white compatriots. The NAACP called on black citizens to fight the war on two fronts, against totalitarianism abroad as well as racism at home. By vowing to continue the struggle for racial equality in the United States during the war, the NAACP departed from the position of black activists during World War I.[39] At that time W. E. B. Du Bois had called on African-Americans to postpone the struggle for equality until after the war.[40] During World War II, African-Americans had increased their leverage not only because of the advances made in the wake of the last war, but also, and maybe more importantly, because of the racial undercurrents of the current war. Gunnar Myrdal, a Swedish sociologist who studied race relations in the United States in the 1940s, observed that the nature of the war forced the American government to support racial equality more openly. "In fighting fascism and nazism," Myrdal explained, "America had to stand before the whole world in favor of racial tolerance and cooperation and of racial equality. It had to denounce German racialism as a reversion to barbarism."[41]

Confronted with this dilemma, government officials as well as leading Republicans at least rhetorically lent their support to the cause of racial equality. When Republican Party chairman Wendell Willkie addressed the NAACP at its annual conference in July 1942 he admitted that "our very proclamations of what we are fighting for have rendered our own inequities self-evident. When we talk of freedom and opportunity for all nations the mocking paradoxes in our own society become so clear they can no longer be ignored."[42] Those verbal proclamations of support, however, did not translate into any immediate action on the part of the government, such as the desegregation of the armed forces or the repeal of Jim Crow laws in the South. Government officials still hoped that the immediacy of the foreign threat could convince African-Americans to delay their demands for equality until the end of the war. By making this a " 'people's' war for freedom" they thought they could "help clear up the alien problem, the Negro problem, the anti-Semitic problem."[43]

Yet they failed to unify the country to the extent often portrayed in war films and political rhetoric. As the frequent and violent race riots on Army bases and in major cities like Detroit testify, the war could not bridge the deep rifts that divided Americans along racial lines. To the contrary the war often exposed and deepened the existing divide.[44]

The wartime debate in the United States about Germany has to be seen in the context of this struggle to create a unified national identity. By defining Germany as the "other," fundamentally different from everything America stood for, American propagandists and government officials created an image of their own culture as homogenous. Nations thus became monolithic blocs defined by their dominant political, ideological, and cultural philosophy. Those in the United States, however, who pointed to the existence of both democratic and reactionary groups within Germany, implicitly acknowledged the diversity of the American polity. This assumption of diversity held both promise for Germany and perils for the rest of western civilization. Diversity within Germany entailed the possibility of the country's return to democracy and peaceful coexistence once anti-Nazi forces regained power. That same diversity also implied that the United States was not as unified as government officials would have liked the population to believe and, more importantly, that Nazism and fascism could thrive outside of Germany. Americans, critics of the official propaganda line warned, had to guard against fascist trends within their own society in order to prevent them from gaining dominance as they had in Germany.

Acceptance of cultural diversity within the United States went hand in hand with skepticism about cultural and political unity abroad. Negative attitudes toward Germany, therefore, did not always extend to the German people but instead concentrated on the personality of Hitler and the fanaticism of the Nazi party. Thus, while propaganda agencies tried to convince the public that Germany's culture and society contrasted sharply with the rest of the western world, skeptics saw a diverse society in which a minority of fanatics held the majority hostage.

Those who rejected the German monolith argument often pointed to the personality of Hitler and the oppressive power of the Nazi regime as the most plausible explanation for the nation's current warfare. Konrad Heiden's widely read 1944 biography of Hitler, *Der Führer,* argued that Hitler's power emanated from his ability to conquer the generals and make both the citizenry and the military tools of his grand scheme.[45] Dorothy Thompson praised the work as an objective and even-handed account of Hitler. Thompson shared Heiden's view that Hitler and his closest advisers rather than the entire German population were responsible for the war.[46] Without offering to exculpate the German nation, they both attributed primary responsibility to the leaders rather than the people.

Heiden and Thompson found support for their views in an unlikely place: the movie industry. Hollywood war films such as *The Moon Is Down, Watch on the Rhine* and *The Hitler Gang* all had their share of evil Nazi officials, often in the garb of the SS or Gestapo. Yet they also included Germans who were either disaffected with Nazism, active in the resistance, or victimized by the regime.[47] *The Hitler Gang* in particular laid all the blame for the current war on a small group of leading industrialists and generals who supported Hitler and terrorized the German population.[48] Even though the film supported unconditional surrender, it left the impression that ordinary Germans were not responsible for the war. Because films like *The Hitler Gang* portrayed only the Nazis as villains, they faced criticism from the OWI. The government agency feared that such portrayals would elicit sympathy for the German population among viewers and therefore erode support for a hard peace.[49]

Despite pressure from the OWI, Hollywood movies continued to include sympathetic German characters that allowed Americans to hold on to a pre-Hitlerian view of the German people. Therefore, when Dorothy Thompson criticized the idea of universal German national guilt in a 1944 *Newsweek* article, she expressed what the movies were portraying and many Americans wanted to believe. An ardent opponent of Nazism, she argued that "there is as much individualism among Germans as among any other people." She assumed that resistance groups within Germany were fighting against the regime and feared that "the Nazi terror is killing every conceivably decent German, and in every rank of society."[50] Cultural and political diversity existed, according to Thompson, in Germany as well as in any other country, including the United States. The overthrow of the Nazi regime would therefore help those democratic forces within Germany to regain the power they had lost with the onset of the Nazi regime.

Adherents of the theory of Germany's cultural diversity sometimes accused their opponents of employing the same rhetoric that Nazis used to discredit so-called "inferior races." In a scathing review of Luis Nizer's *What To Do With Germany*, Captain C. Brooks Peters criticized the author for "dash[ing] through several thousand years of German history with the alacrity and thoroughness of a Nazi schoolmaster."[51] The superficial treatment of some thousand years of history, Peters charged, obscured the complex reasons for Germany's current aggressions. He reminded readers that the distortion of the historical record was exactly what National Socialists were doing concerning Jews and other non-Aryans. Articles in major newspapers and magazines of the nation echoed this view. *New York Times* war correspondent James P. Warburg, for instance, found no difference between books "written to prove that the Germans are paranoid, or bloodthirsty, or militaristic, or aggressive" and the Nazis' way of writing about the Jews. He argued that Germany consisted of "good" as well as "bad" Germans. The fact that over the past eighty years "bad" had dominated over "good" was a matter of behavior rather than inherent racial or national characteristics.[52]

For Hollywood screenwriter Emmet Lavery the differences between Americans and Germans were all but non-existent. Lavery argued in *The Commonweal* that "to understand the enemy we have only to understand ourselves a little better." In an effort to demystify the super- or sub-human characterizations of the Japanese and the Germans, he reminded his readers that "whether we like to admit it or not, the enemy is a human being, a human being with all of our weaknesses as many of our virtues." He concluded that "we are, in many ways, the very things we oppose in the enemy."[53] Instead of seeing in Germany and Japan the antithesis of American society, Lavery saw in them mirror images of his own country's identity.

Others searched for signs of internal opposition to underscore the theory that not all Germans were Nazis. *Christian Century* reported on a German underground group which helped Allied pilots who had been forced to bail out over German territory.[54] In early 1945 press reports also focused attention on the thousands of political opponents languishing in Nazi concentration camps.[55] Some writers suggested that those political prisoners deserved a chance to play an active role in the reconstruction of a democratic Germany.[56] Acknowledgment of political and social diversity within the German population opened an avenue toward a more lenient postwar treatment of Germany than hard-liners such as Henry Morgenthau and Lord Vansittart advocated.

Americans who stressed diversity within Germany searched for ways to reconcile the contradiction between their prewar image of Germany and the present reality of German aggression. Although most of them deplored the Nazi regime, they interpreted it as an aberration rather than a continuity of the German cultural and political tradition. Germany, according to these critics, remained firmly embedded in the cultural tradition of western civilization. German Nazism had carried to an extreme what lay dormant in many other national cultures. The task of the western world would thus be to strengthen the progressive democratic forces within Germany in order to safeguard against future autocrats and fascists. The passionate debate between historical determinists and advocates of cultural diversity revealed the struggle in the United States not only to understand its enemies but also to come to terms with its own cultural diversity. Unlike Japanese culture, which seemed alien to most Americans, German culture had been closely intertwined with that of America and with the traditions of western civilization. If Americans acknowledged that German aggression grew out of those traditions, they would have to re-evaluate their own cultural heritage.

* * *

German images of the United States were no less ambiguous than American perceptions of Germany. This ambiguity surfaced both in official and popular attitudes toward the United States. Nazi propaganda turned openly anti-American only after the outbreak of war between the two countries. Until then no consistent National Socialist position toward the United States was discernible. For much of the 1930s, German readers of the government-censored press could find both laudatory and derogatory articles about the culture, society, and politics in the United States.[57] Many of the features on the United States built on common stereotypes of the Weimar Republic.[58] Nazi officials exploited the common notion of Americans as a people lacking the rich traditions of European high culture. Propagandists fused those traditional ideas with their own racial ideology claiming that black and Jewish influences were corrupting American culture, society, and politics.

Yet throughout the Nazi period America's technological achievements and popular culture found admirers among Germans. Since the 1920s, particularly young Germans were drawn to American jazz and swing music, its modern dance styles, and above all American movies. Even National Socialists, who tried to discredit American culture as preoccupied with materialism, emulated aspects of American consumer culture. By the same token, many Germans spurned American high culture but loved its popular music, films, and movie stars. In the areas of mass production and advanced technology, German economists continued to look toward the United States as a model. Part of Hitler's economic program aimed at achieving the same efficiency in mass production of goods as American manufacturers, above all the Ford Motor Company.[59] The persistence of these positive images of the United States throughout the Nazi period shaped German expectations of their postwar relationship with the United States.

During the prewar years Nazi propaganda was not particularly anti-American but rather focused on anything un-German. The campaign for the cultural purification of Germany was in the hands of the Ministry of Public Enlightenment and Propaganda (Ministerium für Volksaufklärung und Propaganda) under the leadership of Joseph Goebbels. Soon after Hitler came to power, the ministry established its hold over newspapers, magazines, and other publications. The censorship of the media was only part of the regime's move toward *Gleichschaltung* (coordination) that included replacing the labor unions with the Deutsche Arbeitsfront (German Labor Front—DAF), independent women's organizations with Nazi organizations such as the Frauenschaft (National Socialist Women's Group) and the Deutsches Frauenwerk (German Women's Union), and forced youth out of traditional organizations into the Hitlerjugend (Hitler Youth) and the Bund Deutscher Mädel (Confederation of German Girls). The party's goal was not only to force the population to participate in the public display of Nazi power but also to establish total control over all social and cultural activities within the state.[60]

Nazi propagandists began their crusade to purify national culture by removing Jewish and other so-called un-German cultural products from bookshelves, museum walls, and theaters. Stripped of their freedom of expression, prominent German artists and writers, including the painters Max Beckmann and George Grosz, and the writers Thomas Mann and Bertolt Brecht, left the country. Many of them eventually moved to the United States. The assault on the cultural avant-garde in Germany began with book burnings in 1933 and culminated in the confiscation of over 16,000 works of art by the Ministry of Public Enlightenment and Propaganda in 1937. The government displayed some of these works in the Munich exhibition *Entartete Kunst* (Degenerate Art). The exhibition was enormously popular. Within four months more than two million visitors passed through the halls in Munich and another million people viewed the exhibition as it toured several German and Austrian cities over the next three years.[61] Its popularity was by no means an indicator of the level of support for the Nazi assault on avant-garde art, since it also attracted visitors who admired the works displayed in the exhibition. In all likelihood, however, most Germans supported the "process of national purification" since avant-garde art did not enjoy broad-based popular support.

The purging of disturbing pieces of art appealed to those longing for order, a traditional notion of aesthetics, and moral conservatism. The shift toward cultural conservatism had actually begun prior to the Nazis' rise to power. Cultural critics noticed as early as 1930 a move away from the avant-garde experimentation of the 1920s.[62] The gradual change in popular sentiment brought with it a growing antagonism toward the United States as the epitome of modernism. Critics increasingly derided modern art as "degenerate" and categorized it as part of "Jewish" or "Negro" culture.[63] The same critics also lamented the dehumanization of modern life and culture and saw both as the inevitable consequence of the modern emphasis on rationalization and technology—all attributes associated with the United States.[64] Nazi propagandists exploited this popular antagonism against both the Weimar Republic and the United States when they launched their campaign for cultural nationalism.

The National Socialists' ideal of their own national culture shaped their interpretation of the United States. Like the OWI's official portrayal of Germany, German government publications often described the United States as Germany's antithesis. This juxtaposition turned Germany into a model society of cultural and racial purity that contrasted with America's supposed hodgepodge of cultures and ethnicities. Stability and order in Germany stood opposite social chaos in the United States.[65]

Anti-Semitism soon became the focal point of Germany's anti-American propaganda. Jewish conspirators allegedly dominated American finance and politics and were dragging an innocent nation into war. The Austrian-born journalist and writer Colin Ross was one of the most prolific exponents of these theories in Germany. A descendant of the British explorer John Ross, the younger Ross was the author of a wide variety of travelogues and became an informal adviser to the foreign ministry during the war.[66] In several books on the United States he commented on its major geographical, social, and political characteristics.[67] His interpretations reflected the central tenets of Nazi propaganda against Americans.[68] Ross asserted that Roosevelt's plans for American domination of the world were the product of a Jewish conspiracy. Jewish domination of American politics, he found, was a "difficult, even inexplicable phenomenon," since, as he asserted, the majority of Americans were anti-Semites. He recalled several conversations in which Americans themselves expressed their aversion to the enormous political and financial power of Jews in their own country. According to these descriptions, a minority of powerful Jews held a largely anti-Semitic country hostage.[69]

Paradoxically, Ross blamed the new wave of anti-German propaganda in the United States on the rise of anti-Semitism in the United States in the 1930s. Influential Jews with close ties to the government and the President, he explained, realized that something had to be done to stop the rising tide of anti-Semitism. Therefore, Ross continued, "protective measures of the national socialist state" were translated into horror tales and grossly distorted for propaganda purposes. Jewish domination of the press, he argued, facilitated the depiction of developments in Germany as a regression to barbarism and medieval practices. Ross's portrayal of the contradiction between the majority's anti-Semitism and the government's pro-Jewish sentiments mirrored his own conflicted image of the United States. He admired American achievements in economy, science, and technology, and identified with the racist ideologies of some Americans. Yet the failure of the government to translate these popular notions into federal policies disappointed him. The only explanation for this contradiction was, according to Ross, the enormous power of Jewish financial tycoons in the government.[70]

Wartime German propaganda films further exploited the Jewish theme. They portrayed America as the epitome of racial impurity, a place where the superior Aryan races of Northern Europe mingled freely with the lesser breeds of blacks and Jews. According to these "documentaries" Americans had fallen victim not only to the dictatorship of the Jewish financial monopoly but also to subhuman jazz and swing that corrupted European-American culture. Jewish financiers and businessmen were singled out for particular vilification. One of the films, *Rund um die Freiheitsstatue: Ein Spaziergang durch die USA,* held Jews responsible for the Great Depression and accused them of showing no compassion toward the suffering of unemployed workers and impoverished families. As proof the film showed policemen, allegedly hired by Jewish business moguls, beating striking workers in the streets. The film also portrayed the New Deal as a hideous scheme by which Jews accumulated more capital and the population fell deeper into misery.[71] Just as they did in Germany, Nazis blamed Jews for the worldwide economic depression of the 1930s.

The racial connotations of Germany's anti-American propaganda began to dominate only with the American entry into the war in 1941. For much of the 1930s, Nazis allowed the German press considerable leeway in its reporting on the United States. In particular Roosevelt's New Deal program received much attention, some surprisingly positive. A 1934 article in *Die Neue Rundschau* lauded the New Deal as an abdication of the gospel of unfettered free capitalism. The author pointed out some crucial parallels between the Nazi Arbeitsfront (labor front) and the New Deal work projects such as the Civilian Conservation Corps and the Public Works Administration.[72] Another went even further by declaring that Roosevelt's program inevitably moved toward the establishment of National Socialism in the United States.[73] The search for similarities between the German and American approach to the Great Depression suggests that Germans tried to reassure themselves of the soundness of their own economic approach by looking toward the United States, the economic powerhouse of the twentieth century.

Criticism of the New Deal increased throughout the 1930s especially after its failures in the economic realm became apparent.[74] Yet with the declaration of war against the United States at the end of 1941, propagandists focused increasingly on racial arguments to discredit the New Deal. At a conference of the directors of the Reich propaganda departments in July 1942, for instance, Curt Ludwig Freiherr von Gienanth, an official in the Propaganda ministry, mocked the United States' "deranged" efforts to deal with the

Depression. "The people tried to master the crisis," he asserted, "in a typically Jewish way, influenced by Jewish financiers, by applying the most eccentric measures." He related that officials in Chicago destroyed six million pigs and nine million cattle and dumped them into Lake Michigan for the sole purpose of keeping the market price high. American hypocrisy had reached new heights, von Gienanth scoffed, when Roosevelt tolerated those miserable conditions in his own country yet vigorously complained "when a Jew is beheaded here." He ascribed these actions to the enormous influence of such Jews close to the President as Henry Morgenthau Jr. By blaming Jews within the government German propagandists were able to isolate Jews from those members of American society they still deemed admirable and worth emulating.[75]

In the cultural realm, the anti-American propaganda campaign played on common stereotypes that existed prior to the Nazi ascendancy. As Germans became increasingly interested in American popular music, films, and other forms of entertainment in the 1920s, cultural purists had warned against the growing influence of American popular culture in Germany. As they began to develop a consumer culture modeled on that of the United States, cultural nationalists warned that American influences would dilute German culture and lead to Germany's decline into materialism.[76] During the Third Reich, those skeptics compared Americans to a kulturlose Herde (cultureless herd) who had no interest in or understanding of the high culture of the European tradition.[77] In addition, what had been a cultural argument in the 1920s, now became heavily infused with racial connotations. The propaganda film *Herr Roosevelt Plaudert* (Mr. Roosevelt Chats), for instance, singled out black Americans singing gospel music and dancing swing in the streets as representative of American culture. Deriding it as *Hexenbeschwörung* (witch worshipping), the commentator scorned the *Kulturlosigkeit* (lack of culture) of Americans, "in a country which claims to save the culture of the world."[78] The notion that the United States lacked the cultural sophistication of the European continent had been widespread in Germany long before the Nazis took power. Propagandists skillfully meshed those long-standing stereotypes with racial overtones in order to stir anti-American sentiments among Germans.

While Nazis explored almost every avenue to discredit American culture and politics, they were careful not to condemn the American people collectively. This caution revealed the desire—at least until the outbreak of war—to keep the United States neutral as well as the recognition of the sizable German-American population within the United States. Both Freiherr von Gienanth and Colin Ross emphasized the existence of pro-German and anti-Semitic voices in America. Von Gienanth commended the faction around Charles Lindbergh as "people, who hopefully will replace Roosevelt in the future, people with a healthy human intellect, people who won't be bullied by England, people who deep down in their hearts are anti-Semites."[79] The problem, Nazis found, was that while American gentiles were socially anti-Semitic, politically they were not. Ross found hope for the American people in the person of Henry Ford, an ardent anti-Semite, who, according to Ross, was the first American to point out publicly the danger radiating from the presence of Jews in the United States. He admired Ford's crusade against the "International Jew" and alleged Jewish control of America's finance and policy.[80] Yet, Ross concluded, not even Ford was strong enough to avert the Jewish menace and thus had to watch on the sidelines as five million Jews drove 125 million Americans into a Jewish war.

Hitler himself maintained conflicting images of the American people and their President. In his earlier writings he expressed some admiration for American technical and scientific achievements, crediting the Aryan elements within America's population with this success.[81] Later on, however, especially after Germany had declared war on the United States, his attitude became more disdainful and hostile. In a conversation recorded in January 1942 by Heinrich Heim, a civil servant in the Reich Ministry, Hitler expressed nothing but contempt for the United States. "I don't see much future for the Americans," he lamented. "In my view it's a decayed country. And they have their racial problem, and the problem of social inequality." He further declared that his "feelings against Americanism are feelings of hatred and deep repugnance. . . . Everything about the behavior of American society reveals that it is half Judaized and the other half negrified."[82] As the political relationship between Germany and the United States deteriorated, Hitler increasingly couched his disdain for the United States in cultural and racial terms. America's racial inferiority, in his mind, was responsible for the outbreak of hostilities between the two countries.

Anti-American propaganda seemed to have had little effect on popular opinion. Germans were most receptive to Nazi propaganda whenever it confirmed their preconceived notions, for instance, that Americans were materialist, that they lacked cultural sophistication, and that they always placed their individual gain above the common good.[83] Those negative attitudes, however, competed with equally powerful positive images of the United States represented by Hollywood movies, jazz, swing, and technological expertise. Even when Nazi propagandists tried to curb the circulation of American movies, literature, and music, determined fans found ways to cultivate their interests. The apparent contradiction between German public images of Americans and the private interests of many consumers prompted literary historian Hans Dieter Schäfer to speak of a German "split consciousness" during the Third Reich.[84] In this environment both positive and negative images about the United States persisted side by side throughout the Nazi period largely unaffected by propaganda or even the war.

One source of German fascination with the United States lay in the age-old myth of the American frontier. The myth was fueled in the late nineteenth century by the writings of Karl May. Since then, generations of youth have grown up with May's adventure stories. Even though May did not visit the United States until after he had written his books about the fictional Apache chief Winnetou, his descriptions became the basis for countless youths' dreams of pioneering the American West.[85] Germans drew further inspiration from Buffalo Bill's Wild West show, which was quite popular in Germany and Western Europe before World War I. The German fascination with the American West and Native Americans continued unabated throughout the Nazi regime, bolstered by numerous articles in popular magazines.[86] Some aspects of the American frontier myth dovetailed with National Socialist ideology. According to Schäfer, Nazis saw parallels between the American expansion westward and their own quest for "Lebensraum" in the East.[87] In this context, Native Americans, just as the non-Aryan populations of Eastern Europe, had to make way for the superior Aryans of Northern Europe.

In Karl May's stories, however, and in the imagination of many German Wild West fans, American Indians were heroic figures. Nazis did not seem to take offense at the free intermingling of the races in his books. To the contrary, Hitler himself was an ardent fan of May's books. In 1939, the government honored Fritz Steuben, another Wild West fiction author, with the Fritz Schemm Prize, the Nazi party's most prestigious award for youth literature. Steuben, also known as Erhard Witteke, had written a series of novels based on the Shawnee chief Tecumseh, who led Indian resistance to U.S. expansion in the Ohio Valley in the early nineteenth century. The stories appealed to young readers primarily for the heroism of the Indian leader. Despite the obvious racial inversion—non-Aryans portrayed as heroes in the fight against whites—the books appealed to Nazi leaders for their emphasis on military action and the glorification of war.[88] The success of the Tecumseh stories during the Third Reich illustrates not only the contradictions inherent in the German attitude toward the United States but also the Nazis' own adaptation and modification of traditional myths toward their own ends. Native Americans served both as models of a heroic warrior culture and proof of the ultimate submission of non-white races to the superior Aryan races of Northern Europe.

Another example of the Nazis' partial adaptation and modification of popular German stereotypes about the United States was the fate of jazz during the Third Reich. Propagandists regularly derided jazz and swing as inferior products of black and Jewish culture. Jazz became the main target of the Nazi campaign for the revival of *völkische Kultur* (folk culture). The government realized that jazz's emphasis on improvisation and free musical expression could become a powerful symbol for democracy and freedom of expression in Germany and therefore began to curtail its dissemination as early as 1933.[89] Traditional enemies of jazz—that is, those who criticized the genre for its alleged failure to prove its artistic merits—helped Nazi ideologues in their campaign. They drew support mainly from groups that despised all aspects of American popular culture. Nazi propagandists added a racial component to the fight against jazz, by first dismissing it as "nigger music," and later identifying it with Jewish culture. In 1936, a Hitler Youth leader explained that "the nigger has a very pronounced feeling for rhythm, and his 'art' was perhaps indigenous but nevertheless offensive to our sentiments. Surely, such stuff belongs among the Hottentots and not in a German dance hall. The Jew, on the other hand, has cooked up those aberrations on purpose."[90] By meshing traditional stereotypes with racial ideology, Nazi ideologues reshaped the debate about jazz toward their own ends.

Nazi administrators, however, could not prevent the playing of jazz music on the radio, in live performances, or even the sale of jazz records in stores. Chief propagandist Joseph Goebbels proceeded cautiously in his assault on jazz because of its widespread popularity among young Germans. He initially refrained from imposing a categorical ban on jazz and swing on German radio programs because it would have prompted most listeners to turn to foreign broadcasts such as the BBC and Radio Luxemburg.[91] When in October 1935, the propaganda ministry reversed that decision, the difficulties in enforcing the ban became immediately apparent. No strict definitions existed about what constituted jazz. A number of German-speaking musicians had developed a domestic form of jazz that could be passed off as another genre of popular music. Furthermore, in order to ensure the sale of German records in foreign countries, Germans had to allow the influx of some foreign records, including jazz, onto the domestic market. In an effort to keep the demand for foreign jazz down, Nazi administrators encouraged German musicians to create an indigenous version of jazz with only modest success.[92]

As restrictions on live performances tightened, die-hard fans began to concentrate their activities around a handful of jazz clubs. The best-known was the Melodie-Club founded in Berlin in 1932. Even after the Nazis severely curtailed its actions, the club continued to issue news bulletins on a regular basis. These bulletins informed members not only about new records and where to obtain them but also about new American films and books. Less prestigious swing clubs emerged in various German cities. Most of these consisted of informal gatherings of high school and university students, yet in some cities they grew quite large, including Hamburg's Eisbahn Clique (Ice-Rink Clique), Frankfurt's Harlem and OK-Gang Club, and Karlsruhe's Cic-Cac Club.[93] These groups represented an alternative to the Hitler Youth, although their agenda was distinctly nonpolitical.

For most of their existence the jazz clubs kept a low profile and met in private homes rather than public places. But occasionally they organized "swing-festivals" which drew several hundred participants even during the war. Visiting one such festival in Hamburg in February 1940, a Hitler Youth official reported that "the dance music was all English and American. Only swing dancing and jitterbugging took place. At the entrance to the hall stood a notice on which the words 'swing prohibited' [Swing verboten] had been altered to 'swing requested' [Swing erboten]. The participants accompanied the dances and songs, without exception, by singing the English words. Indeed throughout the evening they attempted only to speak English; at some tables even French."[94] For these young people swing came to mean more than just a musical taste. Through the medium of American music, German youth defied their own country's traditional culture and political regime. Adoption of foreign cultures and languages became the vehicle for rebellion against the National Socialist repression of cultural freedom.

Although they succeeded in establishing a separate sphere in which they could express themselves more freely, these youths never turned their non-conformist behavior into active political opposition. Partly because of the non-political nature of the protest, Nazi officials conducted only a half-hearted anti-jazz campaign. They oscillated between phases of restriction and tolerance. Sometimes they even promoted jazz as a means to boost soldiers' morale behind the lines or to pacify the civilian population.[95] Jazz and swing thus became outlets for the dissatisfaction of the population without ever posing a serious political threat.

Jazz was the most prominent expression of Americanophile sentiment in Germany but it was not the only one. Germans read books by American authors, American newspapers and magazines as long as they were available in stores, at least until 1941. German popular magazines such as *Die Koralle* and *Westermanns Monatshefte* fashioned themselves after American models like *Life* and *Time*. Until the beginning of the war these magazines reported frequently on

American movie stars, reviewed the newest Hollywood movies as well as the latest best-selling American novels.[96] In fact more American monographs were translated into German in the 1930s than in the 1920s.[97] Young Germans in particular looked to America as the trendsetter for popular culture and mass entertainment.

The American movie industry turned out to be the biggest obstacle to establishing a nationalist folk culture in Germany. American films regularly scored higher box-office successes than domestic productions. Hollywood had begun its cultural conquest of the European market in the 1920s. Movies such as *It Happened One Night, Ruggles of Red Gap, Mutiny on the Bounty,* and scores of musicals including *Broadway Melody* and *Born to Dance* played in movie theaters in bigger cities until the middle of 1940. Walt Disney's cartoon character Mickey Mouse acquired such high popularity that it even appeared on the emblem of a German combat brigade during the war. Movie actors enjoyed similar popularity. Hollywood stars such as Clark Gable, Joan Crawford, and Katharine Hepburn regularly adorned magazine covers and advertisements.[98] German preferences in popular culture thus transcended national boundaries to embrace international trends.

American popular culture and its vast entertainment industry filled a void in Germany left by the regime's dour emphasis on völkische Kultur. Most Germans did not see a contradiction between shunning Americans as a people without a culture and being fascinated with its popular culture, especially music and films. The German term *Kultur* encompassed the culture of artists, writers, and composers, a distinctly artistic expression of high culture. Many considered American popular culture not part of Kultur but part of *Unterhaltung* (entertainment).

The United States also served as a model for the development of a mass produced German consumer goods industry. In their appreciation for American technology, Nazis again did not significantly change the patterns set during the Weimar Republic. Throughout much of the 1930s, Nazi economists sought to benefit from American expertise by promoting study tours to the United States. In 1937 alone a prominent German travel agency offered more than forty organized tours to the United States with various themes like agriculture, mining, and other industrial trades. Even Nazi organizations such as the DAF (German Workers Front) organized tours to the United States until shortly before the war.[99] The National Socialists' eagerness to emulate American technological success pointed to the Nazi regime's constant tension between modernism and antimodernism.[100] In fact, that tension mirrored the tension between Americanism and anti-Americanism. Whereas in the cultural realm Nazis wanted to return to an older German tradition of *Volkskultur*, in the technological realm they pursued the exact opposite: the rapid modernization of German industry up to and beyond the level of the United States.

Germans also followed the United States in the production of consumer goods. In the 1920s, Americans had taken the global lead in the mass production of household appliances and consumer goods such as radios, refrigerators, washing machines, and, above all, cars.[101] The radio had already become a permanent fixture in many German households during the 1920s, but the 1930s saw the introduction of ever more powerful receivers that allowed Germans to listen to worldwide broadcasts. In this area especially the Nazis' drive for technological advances clashed with their desire for cultural nationalism and cultural control. As these receivers internationalized radio broadcasting they also undermined the regime's effort to control information. The government could not censor foreign radio broadcasts.

Whereas National Socialists feared the independence of the listener, radio manufacturers used it as a selling point. A 1937 advertisement for the new Blaupunkt overseas receiver, for instance, featured an image of the Statue of Liberty emerging out of the radio. The caption read: "Here is America! Once you own the 'Blaupunkt Groß-Super 5 W 77' . . . , the delightful reception from the 'new world' will be a matter of course."[102] The use of this American icon of freedom and liberty sent an obvious message to German consumers: Owning a Blaupunkt promised the ability to subvert censorship in their own country and to tap into the sounds of the "land of the free."

The National Socialist promise to furnish every German household with a "people's car" was maybe the most obvious attempt to emulate the United States. The government promised the production of 100,000 Volkswagen cars for the market by 1940. Hitler himself promoted the development of what would later be known as the "beetle" and took a vigorous interest in its design. The German automotive inventor Ferdinand Porsche visited the Ford Motor Company in Detroit in 1936 before heading the mass production of the VW in Germany.[103] At the opening ceremony of the 1936 International Automobile exhibition in Germany Hitler hailed the mass production of German cars because, he explained, "the German people have the same desires as the Americans."[104] Even though the production of the Volkswagen on a grand scale did not commence until after the war, the expectations of ordinary Germans rose significantly. During the war years private ownership of cars rose faster in Germany than in Great Britain, although it still trailed far behind American figures. America's consumer society was the model for Germans; their desires and expectations mirrored those of their American counterparts.

Throughout the Hitler reign Germans were torn between a belief in their own cultural superiority and a desire to emulate the rest of the western world. This vacillation between nationalism and internationalism manifested itself above all in their attitudes toward the United States. Germans simultaneously emulated and condemned

American culture. They were drawn to the products of American popular culture, yet they scorned the apparent lack of high culture in the United States. They admired American advances in modern technology, yet they rejected the pace of modern American industrial society. These views about the United States did not differ significantly from those during the Weimar Republic. Even as Nazi anti-American propaganda increased during the war, its influence on German popular opinion remained elusive.

*   *   *

The debate in Germany between cultural nationalists and cultural internationalists mirrored to a remarkable degree the debate in the United States about Germany. The National Socialists' and cultural conservatives' idea of Germany as a superior culture corresponded to the American idea of Germans as a culture apart from western civilization, and in fact inferior to it. On the other hand German cultural internationalists found their counterpart in the likes of Dorothy Thompson and others who focused on the commonalities between Germany and the rest of western civilization. In these debates the cultural could not be separated from the political. Just as American and German propagandists used cultural arguments to explain the political hostilities between the two countries so did important factions in both populations insist on the persistence of a cultural affinity despite those political hostilities. These undercurrents of cultural affinity ultimately aided in the postwar political reconciliation between Germany and the United States.

For Americans the debate about the nature of the enemy did not end with the war. Yet as GIs moved into German territory in the fall of 1944 and encountered the civilian population face to face for the first time since the beginning of the war, they added a personal element to the rather abstract level of the debate. These personal experiences competed with and often contradicted their wartime images of the enemy. The wartime debates foreshadowed the postwar transformation of the personal, cultural, and political relationship between Americans and Germans. Only when taking into account the complex and volatile cultural aspects of this relationship is it possible to explain and understand fully the rapid postwar reconciliation between these two mortal enemies. Personal contacts between American GIs and German civilians played a crucial role in this reconciliation.

CHAPTER 2

Crossing the Border
The Breakdown of the Fraternization Ban

"Two years of war have built up an intense hatred among front-line troops for the Germans," Drew Middleton wrote in the *New York Times Magazine* on 8 October 1944. Having accompanied the First Army since it fought its way into Germany from Belgium in the middle of September, he reported that the American soldiers treated the civilian population with "a mixture of contempt and indifference and, in the case of many front-line outfits, hatred."[1] According to Middleton, the soldiers were adhering to the fraternization ban imposed on September 12 by General Dwight D. Eisenhower, the Supreme Commander of the Allied Expeditionary Forces.[2] Some would "give the husky blond children chewing gum and candy," he continued, "but most do not." Although Middleton's account of soldiers' attitudes was probably accurate for the troops he accompanied in the fall of 1944, soon after the publication of his article evidence of widespread fraternization abounded. In the early months of interaction between American soldiers and German civilians, troops displayed a wide spectrum of attitudes toward Germans, ranging from open hostility to a vague notion of cultural affinity. Yet it was the friendly relations between soldiers and German civilians that most troubled occupation officials. Those relations exposed the tensions between soldiers as private individuals and as agents of occupation policy. They became, over the course of the next year, the greatest internal challenge to the military government, eventually leading to the dismantling of the fraternization ban in October 1945.

As the first personal contacts occurred, policymakers in Washington were also finalizing their plans for the postwar treatment of Germany. Those plans were grounded in two basic presumptions: Germany's unconditional surrender and its collective guilt for the war crimes.[3] Unconditional surrender entailed Allied joint occupation of the country and complete control over Germany's political institutions, economy, and society. Collective guilt meant that all Germans, not just those in official positions, would be held responsible for the crimes committed in their name. Although there was some disagreement within the Roosevelt administration as to the extent of the changes necessary, all agreed that the Allies would have to transform Germany's political, social, and economic structure to ensure its inability to wage any future war.

Much of the initial work, such as the ousting of local political leaders, the removal of Nazi laws and customs from Germany's political, legal, and social institutions, and the dismantling of Germany's wartime industry, was in the hands of the soldiers and officers who had fought their way into Germany. Even though the advancing troops included a small contingent of civil affairs officials who were prepared to deal with enemy civilians, confusion prevailed as to the appropriate conduct of troops toward the local population.[4] In the early days of the occupation no firm guidelines existed concerning the conduct of troops toward the enemy population. The occupation directive, JCS 1067, was still undergoing revisions in September 1944.[5] Within this atmosphere of transition, Eisenhower's fraternization ban represented the only concrete manifestation for the soldiers in Germany of the American approach to the occupation, both conveying the message of collective guilt to Germans and serving as a security measure for the remainder of the war.[6]

The non-fraternization directive failed in part because by the fall of 1944 soldiers did not encounter many Germans characterized by the government's official wartime image of a monolithic people unified by their support for the war. Instead they found a defeated population devastated by the destruction of the war and rather desperate in its desire to make peace with the Allies. While Army pamphlets warned soldiers about "the German"—mostly in the masculine singular—soldiers saw a plurality of Germans, men and women, young and old, Nazis and non-Nazis, locals and refugees, perpetrators and victims. The lines that once had so clearly separated "us" from "them" became increasingly blurred. In fact, the war had demographically affected the German population leaving women, children, and old men behind while sending able-bodied men between sixteen and sixty into combat. The casualty rate among those men was so high that by 1946 women between the ages of twenty and forty outnumbered men 160 to 100.[7] This demographic shift eventually helped American soldiers to reconceptualize Germany as a feminized nation whose ability and will to wage war had been broken. That shift, which developed over the course of the occupation, will be discussed in the third chapter. Yet already by the fall of 1945 the enemy depicted in the pamphlets and propaganda films, the enemy who deserved a hard peace, had all but disappeared.

The gender imbalance was not the only factor inhibiting soldiers' willingness to enforce a harsh occupation policy. GIs also developed extensive friendships, primarily with German women. These relationships not only sexualized the concept of fraternization but also helped in depoliticizing the popular image of German-American encounters. As a result, military officials became less inclined to enforce the fraternization ban. Even though German women had participated in the war effort, GIs and their superiors held on to the traditional notion that warfare and political agitation were male domains and that women and children were largely passive bystanders. Except for a few highly publicized cases—such as Ilse Koch, the aptly named "bitch of Buchenwald"—few Americans blamed women for Germany's wartime atrocities.

The eventual breakdown of the ban signaled the demise of the idea of German collective guilt as a basis for U.S. occupation policy toward Germany. The story of the dismantling of the fraternization ban illustrates the reciprocity that existed between social and political relations. Just as American military officials could not prevent the emergence of mutual friendships between their soldiers and German women, so too policymakers could not hold on to a punitive directive in the face of the socio-cultural rapprochement in occupied Germany.

*   *   *

The concept of non-fraternization was not new to American military officials. After World War I when American, British, French, and Belgian forces occupied the Rhineland, a similar ban had been in effect. Enforcement of the post–World War I ban was a complete failure. The lessons from this earlier experience informed the planning for the new order. Military officials familiar with the earlier occupation recommended stepping up the public promotion of the order and tightening the punitive consequences for violators. Government films, guidebooks, and pamphlets, distributed to American soldiers prior to their entry into Germany, gave detailed characterizations of the German people and warned against personal contacts. However, what came to be known as the "non-fraternization directive" proved to be as unsuccessful as the earlier ban after World War I.

For military officials the fraternization ban served both as a security measure and a form of punishment for the German people. They expected not only fanatical resistance but also widespread subversion and espionage, fearing that shrewd Nazis could corrupt the minds of young and naive Americans and diminish their resolve in the campaign against Germany. In addition, military officials believed that if soldiers avoided friendly overtures toward the enemy, they would command greater respect among the population. Non-fraternization, they hoped, would drive home to the Germans their complete defeat and the superiority of the Allied forces. Another factor in support of non-fraternization was public opinion in the United States. Any evidence of friendly relations between American soldiers and German civilians could provoke negative reactions on the home front. Above all, however, military officials wanted to convey to both their own soldiers and the German population the principle of Germany's collective guilt. Believing that Nazism grew out of the peculiarities of German culture and society, the ban's architects planned to enlist each individual soldier in the effort to drive home to Germans the guilt and responsibility they shared for Germany's wartime aggression.[8]

The war department had prepared a simplified version of the non-fraternization rationale in the *Pocket Guide to Germany*. The booklet, prepared for distribution to GIs just prior to their entry into Germany, reflected the U.S. government's official view of Germany as a monolithic militaristic society. It not only told readers about the Germans' fanatical support for Hitler's policies but also sketched out Nazism's historical roots and the German people's major national characteristics. The objective of the guide was to overcome what many experts perceived to have been the major stumbling block after World War I: the soldiers' sense of cultural affinity with the German population.[9]

The *Pocket Guide,* in fact, used the failure of the policy after the last war as a negative incentive. The friendly relations between Americans and Germans after World War I, the booklet argued, were partly responsible for the outbreak of World War II. It reminded readers not to "forget that you are ordered into Germany now partly because your fathers forgot so soon what the war was about last time. They took it for granted that the friendly reception the Germans gave them after the Armistice in 1918 proved that Germany meant well after all. Our whole country let down its guard too easily last time."[10] American troops' naiveté in 1918, the rationale went, should teach GIs in 1944 a valuable lesson: German friendly gestures toward the victors could be seen only as an attempt to deceive the Allies yet again.

Since policymakers attributed much of the friendly interaction at the end of the first war to the apparent similarities between the two cultures, they called on troops to mistrust external signs of a common cultural heritage. Obviously addressed to American soldiers of Northern European descent, the booklet warned that "the German youth is a nice looking chap, much like the average fellow you grew up with back home. You may ask yourself how a guy who looks pretty much like one of us could believe and do all the things we know he believed and did. The difference is inside him—in his character."[11] The guide resorted to the image of the double-faced German to warn against any assumption of cultural affinity.

The guide also intended to convince soldiers of Germany's collective guilt. It asserted that Germans had learned since early childhood to use force, deception, and ruthlessness to "gain a position of dominance over all other peoples of the world." Germans' universal support for the Nazi regime, according to the text, demanded stern resolve and unwavering determination in dealing with the German people. Indifference toward any friendly overtures would remind Germans of their complicity in the regime's crimes. The guide warned soldiers that "however friendly and repentant, however sick of the Nazi party, the Germans have sinned against the laws of humanity and cannot come back into the civilized fold by merely sticking out their hands and saying—'I'm sorry.' " The German people had all read Hitler's *Mein Kampf,* the booklet asserted, so they knew Hitler's plans for world conquest and the elimination of racial minorities, and therefore shared the responsibility for the war crimes. Because of their complicity in the regime they all deserved the cold shoulder from Americans.[12]

The booklet played on stereotypes already propagated in such war films as Frank Capra's series *Why We Fight,* and *Your Job in Germany,* as well as newspapers and pamphlets on the home front. A cartoon in the *New York Times* in the fall of 1944, for instance, depicted a middle-aged, well-dressed, chubby man leaving a group of Germans to meet American GIs in a nearby jeep. His hand, extended to greet the conquerors, was dripping with blood. Puddles of blood on the ground were labeled Warsaw and Lublin. The Americans looked stern and angry; the caption read "No, Heinrich, it won't wash."[13] (fig. 2.1) The cartoon presented the ideal rather than the reality of the GIs' resolve in Germany, reminding readers of prominent known wartime atrocities.

Germany's historical record served as further proof of collective guilt. The booklet stated that Germany's aggression was the result of a peculiar cultural disposition rather than Hitler's leadership. It concluded that it was "a matter of History that there is nothing new about German aggression or desire for conquest. For centuries, this pugnacious spirit was able to operate only against Germany's immediate neighbors."[14] By pointing to Germany's historical predicament rather than to Nazism, the guide reflected the views of journalists and policymakers such as Emil Ludwig, Lord Vansittart, and Henry Morgenthau Jr., who argued that Germany's aggression preceded the rise of Nazism and was therefore rooted in its national culture.[15]

The guide also worked to dispel the idea that Germany's industrialization and modernization brought about civilization. To the contrary, it warned, "it was only recently, owing to modern inventions and the shrinking of the distances on the surface of the globe,

Fig. 2.1 The double-faced German. *London Daily Mail/New York Times,* fall 1944. Associated Newspapers.

that the German was able to contemplate realizing his dream of enslaving the world." In other words, modern technology in the hands of the wrong people brought destruction and enslavement rather than progress and civilization. This argument, too, is reminiscent of Morgenthau's theories that led him to suggest his plan for the de-industrialization of Germany. The authors of the guide hoped that the reference to Germany's errant historical path and its abuse of "modern inventions" would convince GIs to mistrust any superficial signs of commonalities with the Germans.

The booklet, however, remained ambiguous as to what kind of behavior constituted fraternization. The text, for instance, specified at the outset that "unless otherwise permitted by higher authority you will not visit in German homes or associate with Germans in terms of friendly intimacy, either in public or private." Yet it concluded with a language guide that provided the basic vocabulary for casual conversations with Germans such as "good morning" and "how are you?" Thus, while not allowing soldiers to interact with Germans on friendly terms, the guide provided the tools for precisely such encounters. The booklet also gave misleading advice to soldiers warning only that "marriage to a foreign girl is a complicated procedure. Before you get too romantic, remember that foreign girls do not automatically become citizens upon marriage to an American."[16] At the time, marriage to German nationals was not just a complicated procedure but banned outright. The confusing message of the booklet mirrored the confusion among rank and file as to the proper conduct of troops in Germany.

Because parts of the booklet conflicted with General Eisenhower's non-fraternization directive, it did not get into the hands of GIs until well after they had moved into Germany.[17] Eisenhower issued the directive to the Commanding Generals in the European Theater of Operation on 12 September 1944, the day the first troops entered German territory. How long it took for the order to reach down to the last private in the 12th Army group, the first to set foot on German territory, is unclear. The directive itself, however, was quite clear and specific about the soldiers' conduct toward the enemy population. The nine-page outline was designed to leave no loopholes for occupation troops. " 'Non-Fraternization,' " the directive stated, "is the avoidance of mingling with Germans upon terms of friendliness, familiarity or intimacy, whether individually or in groups, in official or unofficial dealings." "Avoidance of mingling" was specified as "the billeting of officers or men in the homes of the population"; "marriage with Germans or personnel of other enemy countries"; attending German-American church services; "visiting

German homes; drinking with Germans; shaking hands with them; playing games or sports with them; giving or accepting gifts; attending German dances or other social events; accompanying Germans on the street, in theaters, taverns, hotels, or elsewhere (except on official business); discussions and arguments with Germans, especially on politics or the future of Germany." Violators faced a sixty-five dollar fine and the possibility of a court martial.[18]

The extreme vigilance with which military officers prepared their troops for the entry into German territory illustrated two concerns. First, they feared that the soldiers' hostility toward the German people was of an ephemeral nature and therefore in danger of a quick turnaround once they personally encountered German civilians. Second, the military recognized the crucial role of regular troops in the occupation. Military analysts assumed that the breakdown of the fraternization ban during the American occupation of the Rhineland after the last war had contributed to the resurgence of the German problem. Thus, in order to ensure the occupation powers' complete control over postwar Germany, soldiers had to be firm with the people. Every friendly gesture toward German individuals, every act of communication or its refusal, assumed a political meaning. Success of the occupation effort thus appeared to hinge at least in part on the discipline of American soldiers in Germany. The nature of the war appeared to work in the Army's favor. Unlike World War I, there was no question in the minds of GIs as to Germany's responsibility for starting the war. Furthermore, Germany's brutal conduct during the war created more support within the Army for an enforcement of a policy of non-fraternization. Because of these circumstances, American military officials were more determined and more hopeful than ever not again to lose the peace after winning the war against Germany.

Yet, expectations clashed with reality as the first American troops advanced into Germany in the fall of 1944 (fig. 2.2). Off the

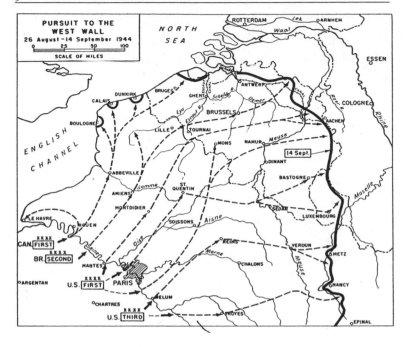

Fig. 2.2 Map of U.S. troop advances into Germany. August/September, 1944.
Courtesy United States Military Academy, West Point, New York.

battlefield, GIs encountered few Nazi soldiers, Hitler youth, or the
Volkssturm (local militias), but primarily women, children, and old
men. Furthermore, the reception of GIs in civilian communities
revealed a wide spectrum of sentiments among Germans toward the
intruders, ranging from poorly hidden hostility to sincere elation.
German reactions to Americans varied according to their age, gender, social status, and level of involvement in the Nazi party. GIs also
reacted in a variety of ways depending on their personal background
and their wartime experience. The earliest encounters between the
two groups thus brought to the surface the underlying ambiguities
with which Americans and Germans had viewed each other during
the war. These ambiguities undermined the official American por-

trayal of Germans as a monolithic entity and the assumption of Germany's collective guilt.

Prior to their entry into Germany Americans harbored some concerns about the enemy's conduct. These concerns, however, reflected fear of the unknown as much as expectations of violence. Reports of the formation of the Volkssturm—local militias stationed in every German town—reinforced the specter of deadly German resistance.[19] In the face of such expectations, the actual experience of soldiers in many German towns proved somewhat anticlimactic. Except for a few pockets of violent resistance, there was little opposition to the American advance. The first U.S. Armored Division's entry into the small town of Roetgen in September 1944 is illustrative. A *Time* correspondent, who witnessed the event, observed that "the Germans froze and stared. Then a German made a tentative V-sign. A woman started to cry. Finally, a 'Hausfrau' approached with an offering—a skirtful of green apples. Against orders, the GIs passed out chocolate. . . . Fear gave way to sullenness, and sullenness to little offers of assistance."[20] The reporter witnessed the full spectrum of emotions on both sides ranging from fear to relief.

The Army was greeted the same way in half a dozen other places, according to the article. Yet U.S. troops burned the nearby town of Wallenberg to the ground because its citizens fought the advancing troops.[21] The German military also vigorously defended Aachen and Stolberg on the border with Belgium. A *Newsweek* article described the spectacle at Stolberg as "typical of the tenacity by which the Germans attempted to turn every town and forest in their own country into another Cassino regardless of the damage or the casualties inflicted on the remaining civilians."[22] As soon as German Army divisions retreated, however, the civilian population offered little or no resistance to the invading troops.[23] In smaller towns the level of resistance to American troops depended less on a national plan of defense directed by Berlin than on local dynamics within the communities. Because of the unpredictability of the situation, any instructions soldiers received from their superiors were of limited use as they entered Germany.

The Army information campaign also did not prepare soldiers for the evidence of German atrocities they were to discover in the concentration camps of western and southern Germany. Those who participated in the liberation of the camps witnessed the most gruesome result of Nazi policy. Wartime intelligence had released only sketchy information about the camps. The soldiers' *Pocket Guide* contained not a single reference to their existence even though news agencies, military leaders, and political officials were well aware of them.[24] The scenes that awaited the liberators upon entering the camps—piles of starved and mutilated bodies stacked neatly like blocks of wood, living skeletons with hollow eyes, often only partially clad, revolting odors of urine, excrement, and putrefaction—confounded their expectations. It made, as historian Robert Abzug aptly described, "horrified believers out of the skeptics and brought a new and hideous sense of reality even to those who never doubted the worst."[25] After visiting the concentration camp at Ohrdruf in the spring of 1945, General Eisenhower ordered U.S. troops in the vicinity to visit the camp so that, in his words, those soldiers who did not know what they were fighting for, now at least, would know what they were fighting against. In addition, he cabled Washington to send official delegations to tour the camps, because, as he put it, "all written statements up to now do not paint the full horrors."[26] Neither the signs of friendly behavior in the small towns and villages nor the evidence of cruelty in the concentration camps fit the image of Germany that American army officials had tried to convey to their soldiers. GIs instead relied on their own experience to make sense out of sometimes contradictory signals, concluding that Germans were at once more barbarous and more benign than they had previously assumed.

Despite extensive efforts at publicizing evidence about the concentration camps many Americans only reluctantly accepted the reality of the atrocities. An Austrian-born American soldier commented that "my fellow G.I.'s, most of them American born, had no particular feeling for fighting the Germans. They also thought that any stories they had read in the paper, or that I had told them out of first-hand experience, were either not true or at least exaggerated. And it did not sink in, what this was all about, until we got into Nordhausen."[27] Personal experience thus had a much stronger impact on the soldiers' attitudes than anything they read in books, heard in lectures, or saw in films. Until the spring of 1945, however, the Allies had discovered only a few camps in southern and western Germany, France, and Austria, limiting the public exposure of the holocaust. American GIs' antagonism toward Germans thus concentrated on war-related atrocities such as Warsaw and Lublin rather than the mass exterminations in concentration camps.[28]

Among those heeding the Army's warnings about German duplicity was German-born Sergeant Stefan Heym, whose childhood memories made him extremely suspicious of Germans. Heym, who would later become one of East Germany's leading literary figures, was born as Hellmuth Flieg in 1913 in Chemnitz and emigrated in 1933, first to Czechoslovakia and in 1937 to the United States. He enlisted in the U.S. Army in 1943 and was among the first to enter Germany with the First Army. In a December 1944 *New York Times* article he dismissed German displays of happiness about the American arrival as false. He characterized them as arrogant and opportunistic, interpreting cordiality as subservience toward any form of authority. He asserted that after the disappearance of their Nazi masters, Germans simply turned to Americans as their new rulers. "We will have to deal with people whose backbone was broken 365 times a year for eleven years," Heym explained, "a people accustomed to be ruled by force, a people adoring force, a people which sees in lack of force a sign of weakness."[29] The last part of his comment served as a warning to American GIs never to let down their guard toward the Germans and to treat them with utmost firmness and resolve. British Brigadier General H. B. Kennedy, who had spent six years after World War I in the occupation forces in Germany, described the German people in much the same way. "The Germans, once they're licked, immediately begin licking the boots of their conquerors. They're so accustomed to being dragooned that they don't respect anything but authority."[30]

According to Clifton Daniel of the *New York Times*, GIs appeared to heed the warnings like those from Kennedy and Heym. He reported in December 1944 that Germans and Americans "pass on the streets without looking directly at each other. They manifest no hostility but they invite no intimacy. Under orders not to fraternize they speak only upon necessity. The barrier of language helps to enforce the non-fraternization rule."[31] Accounts like Daniel's conveyed the impression that this time around soldiers were prepared to adhere to the ban.

Army records, however, painted a far more complex picture of GI behavior in Germany. They revealed not only widespread disregard for the non-fraternization directive but also the Army's difficulties in enforcing the ban. Within five days of issuing the fraternization directive, General Eisenhower complained to General Omar Bradley of the 12th Army Group that "press reports and those from other sources indicate already a considerable extent of fraternization by U.S. troops with the German Civil population." He demanded that "this must be nipped in the bud immediately."[32] Washington policymakers showed equal concern over the lack of discipline among American troops. General George C. Marshall, then Army Chief of Staff, was especially troubled about press photographs of American soldiers fraternizing with Germans. Beyond asking Eisenhower to take steps "to discourage fraternizing by our troops" he demanded "that the publication of such photographs be effectively prohibited."[33] Marshall found that the display of evidence of fraternization in newspapers and magazines was as harmful as fraternization itself. Eisenhower immediately censored the issuing of all pictures or news items "which appear to indicate Allied troops are fraternizing with German soldiers or population."[34] Marshall's complaint and Eisenhower's swift action suggested that public opinion in the United States played a major role in issuing and enforcing the fraternization ban. If American military officials could not stop fraternization in the occupied area, they at least were determined to keep the American public from finding out about it. The portrayal of American resolve in the U.S. media was therefore the result of a deliberate campaign to suppress any evidence to the contrary.

De facto censorship of the press, however, worked only temporarily. In October 1944, *Time* magazine published an article documenting the friendly relations between GIs and Germans. Although "Allied leaders were prepared to be stern," the correspondent observed, "there was less certainty that U.S. troops would or could be as tough." A picture, accompanying the article, showed Germans sitting down at a table covered with Army rations and a group of smiling soldiers standing around watching them.[35]

The author of the article tried to generate some understanding at home for the troops' behavior. Quoting the British essayist C. E. Montague, who had participated in the Allied occupation after World War I, he asked, "how can you hate the small boy who stands at the door visibly torn between dread of the invader and deep delight in all soldiers as soldiers? It is hopelessly bad for your Byronic hates if you sit through whole winter evenings in the abhorred foe's kitchen and the abhorred foe grants you the uncovenanted mercy of hot coffee and discusses without rancor the daily yields of British and German milch cows."[36] The familiarity of the German socio-cultural environment had a disarming impact on the morale of American soldiers. They found it exceedingly difficult to hate people who reminded them so much of their own friends and family at home. Because of Army censorship, however, articles such as this remained an exception during the fall of 1944.

At the same time, however, reports poured into Allied Occupation Headquarters documenting the extent of fraternization. Those included Major Arthur Goodfriend, Chief of Information Branch of the Civil Affairs Division and editor in chief of the Armed Forces newspaper *Stars and Stripes,* who provided a detailed account of the conduct of troops in western Germany in the fall of 1944. Goodfriend had posed as an ordinary enlisted man of the 26th Regiment of the First Infantry Division that moved into the Aachen area in September. Based on his findings he asserted that "obedience to the non-fraternization order will be extremely difficult, perhaps impossible to achieve." He documented widespread disregard of the order. Yet he simultaneously excused the offenders by pointing to "the nature of the American soldier," which was "such that he tends to be kindly and generous in his treatment of other peoples, friend and enemy alike. [. . .] The tendency, indeed is to pick the opponent off the floor, carry him to his corner, dust him off, and shake his hand in the best sportsman's tradition."[37] The reference to good sportsmanship was problematic in this context because GIs encountered few of their opponents, German soldiers, face to face, but instead "picked off the floor" their wives, sisters, daughters, and mothers. Furthermore, later reports of rape and even murder demonstrated that sportsmanship was not always the rule.[38]

The soldiers' focus on women and children became clear in Goodfriend's account when he lauded the troops generosity toward the local population. He noticed that "soldiers helped German housewives with their chores, played with the children, and through other small acts of friendship made living more tolerable through the creation of a friendly atmosphere." GIs thus stepped into the roles vacated by the men who had left the communities to fight the Americans in the war. The absence of a soldier population in the German communities might have contributed to the GIs' lack of hostility toward their former enemies. In his report Goodfriend cited comments such as "these Germans aren't bad people. We get along with them okay;" or "these people aren't Nazis, they're glad to see us." One GI noted that "hell, these people are cleaner and a damn sight friendlier than the frogs [French]. They're our kind of people. We don't have any trouble getting along with them and they like us first rate." Goodfriend's GIs did not judge Germans on the basis of the Nazi past but their current experiences, including positive comparisons to other countries like Great Britain and France. They were above all interested in creating a pleasant social environment and found Germans to be more cooperative in that effort than any other people they encountered on the European continent.[39]

Goodfriend identified three major reasons for the soldiers' behavior. First he found that considerable confusion prevailed about Germans among GIs. Their experiences in Germany did not confirm the predictions of army pamphlets, lectures, and films. Another problem, according to Goodfriend, was "the indescribable loneliness of the soldier and his hunger for companionship, particularly the companionship of women." After months and years of combat duty in an all-male environment, many GIs longed for a return to civilian life. "The agreeable cleanliness and warmth of German farms and homes," Goodfriend continued, "are factors which tempt even the most principled and motivated men to seek, if only temporarily, sanctuary from the misery and indignity of living and fighting through a winter campaign." The third factor inhibiting success of the ban, according to Goodfriend, was the behavior of officers who through their own frequent violation of the rule set a bad example for their troops. Because their opportunities to associate with the civilian population were greater, they disregarded the non-fraternization order at least as, if not more often than ordinary soldiers.[40]

By the summer of 1945, fraternization with German civilians, especially young women, had become a major feature in American newspapers and magazines. "The GIs lounge around and fraternize as much as they dare," an American visitor to Germany reported at the end of the war, "and I haven't heard of any of them having any run-ins with the Huns." He defended their behavior by pointing out that they simply could not "help it with all the kids yelling for 'cheving goom' and 'chokolat', all the cute gals giving them terrific grins, and all the old men and women stopping to pass the time of day."[41] As GIs focused their attention increasingly on a particular segment of German society, namely young women and children, the battle over non-fraternization that had dominated the early weeks gave way to a tacit understanding between soldiers and military officials about acceptable forms of fraternization.

Especially after Germany's unconditional surrender on 8 May 1945, few soldiers and officers supported the military's insistence on the non-fraternization order. While the latter viewed the troops' abstention from contacts with Germans, or lack thereof, as an important aspect of occupation policy, GIs and officers in local detachments distinguished policy from personal relations. "In Germany fraternization is officially a matter of high policy," Percy Knauth of *Life* Magazine wrote. "But for the GI it is not a case of policy or of politics or of going out with girls who used to go out with the guys who killed your buddies. You don't talk politics when you fraternize. It's more a matter of bicycles and skirts waving in the breeze and a lonesome, combat-weary soldier looking warily around the corner to see if a policeman is in sight."[42] Unlike the military command, soldiers did not consider their personal relations with German civilians an infringement on their military duties.

Germans, too, were interested in separating the personal from the political. But for them it meant disassociating their own personal lives from the politics of the Nazi regime. Most Germans rejected the Allies' charge of Germany's collective guilt. Mathilde Wolff-Mönckeberg, the wife of a Hamburg University professor, expressed a common view when she complained in her diary in May 1945, that "all we ever hear on the wireless, all the news items in the shoddy little free newspapers we get concern the brutalities of the concentration camps with the lurid pictures and the ghastly details. W. [her husband] is angry, because our enemies accuse *all* of us, without exception, of being criminals, fully responsible for what has happened."[43] At the end of the war, the idea of collective guilt was unacceptable to most Germans.

Because many Germans had withdrawn from political life during the Third Reich, they now refused to accept responsibility for Nazi policies. Only a few gradually realized their own complicity with the government's actions. "We all have to share responsibility for these crimes and nobody should evade it," Wolff-Mönckeberg wrote only a few days later.[44] In this early phase of the occupation, Wolff-Mönckeberg's reflections on her own guilt were exceptional. Most of her compatriots were more concerned with the day-to-day challenges of procuring food and shelter and the uncertainty of their existence under foreign occupation.

When the inhabitants of the towns and villages of southern and western Germany saw the first American GIs in September 1944, they were not sure whether to welcome them as liberators or fear them as avengers.[45] Their reactions to the Allied invasion depended in large part on their experiences during the last weeks and months of the war. In many parts of the country, living conditions deteriorated significantly prior to the Allied invasion. Wolff-Mönckeberg wrote on 20 April 1945, shortly before Allied troops arrived, that everybody was "tired and shared the ardent desire for a rapid conclusion to this horrendous war. There was no hope of victory, not

the tiniest indication of hero worship for the Nazis."[46] In most cities
the last months of the war were marked by nightly bombing raids,
large-scale destruction, and the growing certainty, even among die-
hard Nazi supporters, that Germany was losing the war. By the
spring of 1945 most Germans had become thoroughly disillusioned
with their own country's war effort. The daily propaganda tirades
belittling the Allied Forces' strength and denouncing them as atro-
cious and ruthless barbarians largely fell on deaf ears. The general
hopelessness of the situation spurred many Germans' desire for a
quick end. While the population in the East feared the arrival of
Soviet troops, western and southern Germans considered themselves comparatively lucky to face British and American troops.
Most western Germans, therefore, awaited the arrival of American
troops with cautiously hopeful anticipation.[47]

Yet expressions of relief were tempered by an equally strong
sense of defeat and uncertainty about the future of Germany. After
British troops had occupied Hamburg, Wolff-Mönckeberg con-
fessed that, "however much we strain with every nerve of our beings
toward the downfall of our government, we still mourn most deeply
the fate of our poor Germany." Her joy over the end of the war was
tempered by "ineffable sadness which outweighs all the rest, about
our truncated, tortured, and tormented fatherland, our Germany,
which will no longer belong to us; and our once so proud and happy
free Hamburg, which will have to submit to English rule."[48] Wolff-
Mönckeberg, like most of her compatriots, separated Germany from
Nazism. In her description, Hamburg, and by implication Germany,
had been the victim first of Nazism and now of the British occupiers.
More importantly, by calling the developments "fate," she implied
that Germans had been powerless during the Nazi period and were
equally powerless to shape the postwar future. This view typified
the general passivity that occupation officials and observers noted
among Germans.[49] This apathy was not only a sign of resignation in

the face of foreign rule and seemingly insurmountable hardships but also served as a shield against the Allies' charges of collective guilt. The phrase "Was konnten wir denn tun?" (what could we have done?) became a blanket postwar rationalization for German inaction during the war.

Despite initial shows of enthusiasm and subsequent acceptance of the occupation as "fate," most communities had difficulties adjusting to the foreign presence, especially when the troops were nonwhite. Nazi war-time propaganda had saturated the German population with horrific stories of the barbarism of African-American troops. Older Germans also remembered when black soldiers from the French colonies had occupied the Rhineland after World War I. The French use of these troops had caused an international outcry in 1920 when a German women's organization charged them with the rape and murder of numerous German women.[50] At the time, the accusation of black troops raping white women provided enough incentive for Americans—whose troops in another part of the Rhineland included blacks—to protest on behalf of the Germans.[51] In 1920, only fifty-five years after the Civil War, white Americans were still apprehensive about the issue of blacks holding positions of authority over whites. Mindful of American attitudes, German accusations of rape focused on non-white soldiers from Africa, not on the small contingent of African-American soldiers who also served in the Rhineland occupation.

The experience with African troops after World War I provided fertile ground for Nazi propaganda during World War II and shaped German expectations of black troops' behavior. Maria Lorentz of Stuttgart recalled that in the fall of 1944 most people, including herself, were very much afraid of the approaching black troops whom they expected to take gruesome revenge on the German people.[52] Yet unlike the earlier occupation Germans this time expressed little public opposition to the presence of non-white soldiers. The fact that these soldiers were members of the United States Army and not from French colonial Africa certainly contributed to the difference in attitude.[53] African-Americans appeared in U.S. military vehicles wearing U.S. military uniforms. The U.S. colors gave them an air of authority that French colonial troops, who wore their own national uniforms, lacked.

German recollections of African-American troops were generally pacific. A resident of a small town in northern Hesse remembered that "whenever a Negro would meet a German kid, he would break into a smile. Dark hands patted blond hair, searched in the luggage or pockets and produced chocolate bars, for many children the first chocolate of their life."[54] The friendliness of African-American troops toward children most impressed Germans. Ernst Kuch of Heidenheim, south of Nuremberg, recalled that black troops "mostly spoiled the kids; they were given chewing gum and candy, whatever they wanted. In front of the Bergschule—that's where the reserve military hospital was stationed—sat a black guard, with his rifle pointed into the air. Every few minutes he would fire a shot into the air just to amuse the kids."[55] The emphasis of this and other reports on the black soldiers' friendliness with children indicated the transformation of a threatening stereotype—that of the crude barbarian into a non-threatening one—that of the good-natured man-child.

Most eyewitnesses to the American invasion remembered both the initial shock at encountering black troops and the subsequent amazement at their friendly and "civilized" behavior.[56] A collection of reports from towns and villages in the southwestern corner of Germany, commissioned by the state of Württemberg-Baden between 1948 and 1952, provides a glimpse of the broad spectrum of reactions to the arrival of the black troops. A retired schoolteacher from the town of Hofen recalled that "almost all of the troops that emerged out of the vehicles were Negroes, full-blooded and grinning, yet they were all good-natured and friendly."[57] He remembered that they gave chocolate and pralines to the kids, and cigarettes to the old. The population of Hohenstaufen near Göppingen was equally amazed at the courteous conduct of the black soldiers. The report concluded that no major disturbances occurred as a result of the stationing of black troops in the community.[58] Yet a fair number of reports also complained about the presence of black troops. Most complaints were phrased in moderate language, describing the troops' presence as "uncomfortable," or "not exactly pleasant." Yet a few went as far as accusing the non-white troops of rape and misdemeanors.[59] Part of the overall muted and sometimes laudatory nature of these accounts could be attributed to a conscious effort on the part of the authors, who compiled the reports between 1948 and 1952, to avoid accusations of racism and to separate themselves intellectually from the Nazi ideology of Aryan supremacy.

Yet even special praise for the conduct of African-American troops revealed the continued power of racism in German society. The language used to describe their behavior was infused with code words denoting crudeness ("grinning"), infantilism (playful behavior—"just to amuse the kids"), and animalism ("full-blooded"). Expressions of racism became more prevalent as popular attention shifted from the soldiers' interactions with children to their relationships with women. When reports addressed the issue of interracial liaisons, it was always with intense disapproval. One such report from the small town of Unterwilflingen in southwest Germany first confirmed that African-American troops in general behaved well but then immediately launched a vicious attack on women who were evacuated from the Rhineland and who appeared to have engaged in sexual relations with the black soldiers. Without explicitly mentioning the issue of interracial sex directly the report merely stated that "as the pastor alerted the women and girls to the dangers, those 'elements' reported his opinions straight to the blacks." The result,

according to the report, was that the women incited the black soldiers to retaliate against town officials by throwing rocks through
their windows and sending them anonymous letters, threatening to
set their houses on fire.[60] A report from neighboring Zipplingen read
much the same way: black troops had conducted themselves in an
orderly manner but young women who had been evacuated from the
Rhineland had behaved "indecently" toward them.[61] An October
1945 military government survey of black troops' behavior in Giessen, a town of about 30,000 north of Frankfurt, follows a similar
pattern. The town housed about 8,000 black and 2,000 white American GIs. The survey found that most Germans still had a positive
attitude toward blacks, in part because " 'fraternization' by Negro
soldiers in GIESSEN has not involved girls drawn from the community itself to any considerable extent. Most of the 'Frauleins' fraternizing in GIESSEN are transients passing through GIESSEN who are
approached at the Bahnhof (train station) by colored soldiers. In
addition, part of the 'fraternizing' done by Negro troops is with
Polish DP's."[62] The survey also revealed that most Germans disap-
proved of interracial sexual relations suggesting that Germans accepted the presence of black troops in principle but continued to
hold racial prejudices against blacks, particularly concerning miscegenation. By placing the blame on the women from outside the
community, the report challenged neither the community's moral
integrity nor the authority of African-American occupation troops.

Acceptance of the foreign presence increased among Germans if
they developed a sense of cultural or ethnic affinity with Americans.
One German woman who later married an American described this
affinity as a sense of "cousinship."[63] This ethnic bond often had its
origin in more than a vague notion of a shared cultural heritage.
Many Germans recalled a neighbor, family member, or acquaintance who had emigrated to the United States. By the same token,
many of the American émigrés or their descendants returned to

Germany as occupation staff. When German-Americans encountered German relatives they sometimes concealed their identity in order to avoid charges of preferential treatment. Frieda Berger recalled that she unknowingly met her cousin in the summer of 1945. As commanding officer in the district where she lived, he granted Frieda and her mother permission to stay in their house while American troops were billeted there. Throughout their encounter he kept his identity secret.[64]

Military officials faced a difficult dilemma concerning these German-American servicemen. While soldiers' family ties might jeopardize their resolve with the local population, they brought with them valuable language skills and knowledge of German culture and society. This dilemma produced contradictory political measures. In March 1945, a military directive banned all occupation personnel with relatives, such as siblings, parents, grandparents, aunts, uncles, cousins, or in-laws, from serving in Germany.[65] At the same time, some agencies were specifically searching for military personnel with a German background who could assist in communications and intelligence gathering. Within the Military Intelligence Branch, for instance, seventy percent of the German-speaking linguists had relatives in Germany. Enforcement of the directive would have seriously jeopardized the agency's effectiveness.[66] Military officials thus never enforced the ban.

Even without close relatives, German-American soldiers sometimes were overtaken by a diffuse sense of cultural affinity with Germans. When Sergeant Walter C. Krause served in the German town of Marburg between 1946 and 1950 he fell in love with the town probably, he mused, because "heritage permitted me to find something German in myself." At the end of his four years in Germany he concluded that he had formed a special bond with Germans: "I spoke German, and the lifestyle of the Germans was like my own family's. I was American, yet the German culture, which was supposed to be different, was much the same as I had found in my hometown."[67] A 1947 Army study on fraternization concluded that Krause's feelings were not unusual. According to the study, the first impression of many GIs, not just German-Americans, was that "the German people have many customs and standards in common with Americans. Thus many Americans felt themselves to be more at home in Germany than in the other European countries they had visited during their military service."[68] Once Americans thought of Germans as people just like themselves, it became much harder to enforce the non-fraternization ban.

Many Americans expressed their appreciation for German culture by resorting to familiar prewar stereotypes, such as their cleanliness, work ethic, and the Gemütlichkeit (coziness) of their homes. Noting these characteristics, a U.S. sergeant confided to a *New York Times* reporter that "these Germans are more like us than any people I've met over here. I can't be hard against these old people and women and kids."[69] Even critical observers acknowledged the similarities between Americans and Germans. "There is a 'reserve' about the Teuton that appeals to many Americans, because it parallels their own," war correspondent Julian Bach noted. "As they express it, many feel 'more at home' in Germany than they have felt since they went abroad."[70] Contacts with those Germans whose customs and homes reminded them of their own often served to alleviate homesickness.

GIs frequently contrasted German positive characteristics with negative depictions of the French. This juxtaposition led one critic to assert that the main reason for American sympathies toward Germans was that they had moved through France to get there.[71] Soldiers complained that "the frogs gyp the pants off you. Everything they sell you costs four or five times what it should. The Germans aren't that way—half the time they give you stuff for free. They're not out for the dough like the French."[72] GIs found the

French deficient in other areas as well. "GIs and officers alike deride the efficiency and fighting ability of the French Army," a *Newsweek* article observed in September 1945. American soldiers particularly complained that the French did not "work hard enough, that they spend their time staging parades and feeling sorry for themselves. And they contrast that with the ant-like energy of the Germans."[73] The apparently strong work ethic of the Germans, their eagerness to remove the rubbles from their cities and rebuild their homes appealed to many Americans.

Yet the sense of cultural affinity constantly competed with an equally strong sense of cultural alienation, especially among soldiers who personally witnessed the liberation of Nazi concentration camps. Jewish-American soldiers in particular were acutely aware of these contradictions in German culture and society. A fair number of GIs, posted to occupied Germany because they spoke German, were Jews who had fled Nazi Germany to the United States before the war. These soldiers were most reluctant to look for any similarities between Germans and themselves. Some had relatives who had disappeared in concentration camps, others felt a more elusive bond of ethnic and religious affinity. Meyer Levin, an American news reporter and writer, recalled an encounter with the Jews of Frankfurt at Passover, 1945. Out of the 40,000 Jews who had lived in the city before the Nazis took over, only 106 remained at the end of the war. "It was strange," he remarked, "how the Jewish GIs had already gravitated toward them. But according to military regulations, these Jews were German civilians and fraternizing with them was forbidden. So the GIs had left packages of matzoth for them on the doorsteps of the ghetto houses."[74]

For some Jewish Americans the assignment in Germany was as much a reaffirmation of their Jewish heritage as it was an apocalyptic confrontation with their intended extermination. Jewish GIs could not escape the thought that a mere chance of geography had saved them from the horrors their European kin had suffered. Yet German Jews did not always reciprocate the sense of ethnic affinity that American Jews expressed toward them. Levin was taken aback by the aloofness of a German Jewish woman whom he met in Aachen in the fall of 1944. She was the daughter of a wealthy old Aachen merchant family, "but married to an Aryan." He noted that he "had come with a prepared warmth, expecting an excited out-pouring from a person infinitely relieved, after years of hiding, to be able to speak openly at last to one of her own people. But the woman was carefully aloof, and made me feel rather that I was an invader, but that she would politely respond to my questions. It was an attitude with which I was to become quite familiar, among the Germans."[75] Levin's turnabout in this recollection, identifying the woman first as one of "his" people, and then as a German, indicates the internal confusion of both German and American Jews about how to reconcile their ethnic and national identities.

German and American reactions to each other differed according to their gender, age, status, and political convictions. Germans with the least political clout during the Nazi period, above all those whom the Nazi regime had persecuted for their ethnic heritage, political affiliations, or sexual orientation, doubtlessly regarded Americans as liberators. Conversely those who had staked their career on the Nazi state had most to lose from Germany's defeat and therefore responded to the American invasion with hostility. Most Germans found themselves somewhere in between these two poles. Relief over the end of the bombing raids meshed with grief over the extent of the destruction, the loss of loved ones, and the uncertainties of the future. American GIs reacted in similar ways to Germans, letting their own cultural and ethnic heritage as well as their wartime experience guide them in their approach to Germans.

In light of the diversity of the American experience in Germany, non-fraternization was doomed to fail. As GIs settled into the towns and villages of western and southern Germany preparing for a long-term occupation, military officials were losing the battle against fraternization. Even though the failure of the policy became clear almost from the outset, military officials were slow to doubt its validity. "There is no question but that the policy of non-fraternization is sound," a report from the Supreme Headquarters of the Allied Expeditionary Forces (SHAEF) stated as late as April 1945.[76] Instead of adjusting the rules to the realities in the field, the military command initially sought to reshape the soldiers' minds and lives.

The troops' widespread disregard for the ban, according to the SHAEF report, lay in the fact that "once the fighting is over the troops will no longer have the reminders of death and slaughter. They cannot help but feel the need for relaxation. They will forget much of what they have been taught and will feel the need for home comforts, an easier life and feminine society." The way to counter these desires, the report proposed, was first to step up the educational and informational campaign about the German character and Nazi atrocities. Second, the report suggested an improvement in the servicemen's living conditions to create a more hospitable environment within the Army compounds. If the Army provided entertainment and recreational activities, officials calculated, the soldiers would feel no need to spend their leisure time with the local population. The proposed measures included improvement of quarters, food, mail service, recreational facilities, increased offers of educational tours and leaves, stationing female auxiliary forces in the area, and the opportunity for wives and children to join their husbands in Germany as soon as the conditions allowed.[77] Although those measures served to distract the soldiers and provide some semblance of life in their home communities in the United States, they did not obliterate the biggest incentive for fraternization: sexual relations.

Throughout the fall and winter of 1944–45 SHAEF stepped up its campaign, utilizing every possible means of publicity to convince the troops of the need for non-fraternization.[78] Starting in January 1945, for instance, the War Department showed the film *Your Job in Germany* to occupation troops. The feature pointed to German history, its military tradition, and the apparent contradiction between the aggressive policies of the Nazis and the peaceful and tranquil home life of the average German.[79] Again and again military officials tried to evoke the image that behind the façades of the quaint little towns and the friendly faces of individual Germans lay the real nature of German militarism and authoritarianism.

SHAEF also created as many as seventy non-fraternization radio messages for the American Forces Network (AFN). These spots, airing between popular shows, reinforced traditional war-time stereotypes of Germany already familiar to GIs from magazine articles and films. One of them alluded to the image of the German fanatic: "Never trust a German. He's taught to sacrifice everything for the Fatherland. Stay away from all German civilians. Don't fraternize." Another alluded to the problem of GI relationships with German women: "Pretty German girls can sabotage an Allied victory. Don't fall for that booby trap. Steer clear of all German civilians. Don't fraternize." A third brought back the memory of the last war: "We did it before and we can do it again! Don't make that saying mean that 'we were fooled after the last war and the Germans can fool us again.' Nip their plans in the bud! Don't give Goebbels' henchmen a chance to work on you! Don't fraternize."[80] The radio ads were designed to increase the soldiers' distrust of any friendly gesture from Germans. Throughout the entire campaign, American military officials tried to carry over into the non-combat phase of the occupation negative war-time stereotypes of the German people. Especially by sustaining the image of the double-crossing German—fanaticism and authoritarianism hiding behind outward expressions of cordiality—the media campaign forced GIs to question any positive overtures on the part of Germans. Yet the ads, too, like the earlier measures, did not address the sexual appeal of fraternization. GIs were often quite willing to believe the negative stereotypes about Germans in general; but those did not keep them from fraternizing with women as individuals.

A more desperate and controversial avenue for military officials in their efforts to curb fraternization was to prosecute Germans for fraternizing with GIs. In early February 1945, four women stood trial in Stolberg for "acting in a manner prejudicial to the good order of members of the Allied Armed Forces." They had invited American soldiers into their house after dark and thereby, said the court, tempted them into violating the fraternization rule.[81] All four were acquitted because prosecutors could not present sufficient proof that the women were aware of the existence of the fraternization ban. The case aroused much controversy within the Army since it suggested that the military commanders needed German assistance to maintain and enforce discipline. In a SHAEF memorandum, Lt. Col. E. C. Woodall of the G-1 Division pointed out that "if we were to prosecute Germans for the mere fact of fraternization, they might well think that we were unable to maintain discipline and that non-fraternization was a policy forced by higher authority on an unwilling soldiery. Thus, the whole basis of this policy would be undermined, and at the same time discipline would tend to be weakened by a feeling in the soldier's mind that he was more sinned against than sinning if he responds to German advances."[82] Ironically, Woodall spelled out precisely the military's problem with fraternization, namely its inability to enforce the policy. But at the time SHAEF could not admit that. Instead, it released a directive to discontinue the prosecution of Germans for attempts to fraternize and ordered prosecutors to enforce the ban solely through internal "military disciplinary methods."[83]

After the abandonment of German prosecutions it became clear that neither persuasion nor coercion convinced GIs to refrain from friendly contacts with the population. GIs and military officials had developed fundamentally different understandings of the meaning of fraternization. For the creators of the policy it was a political act occurring within the context of the occupation. For GIs, on the other hand, fraternization was a leisure time activity that occurred outside the realm of their duties. These different attitudes toward fraternization also produced a different understanding of the concept of collective guilt. Most American soldiers held Germans collectively responsible for the war but absolved the Germans they knew from individual guilt. For them, collective guilt had become a vapid concept that applied to an abstract collective entity called Germany and not to individual citizens unless they had a direct role in the Nazi regime.

Enforcement of the fraternization ban became almost impossible once Germany surrendered on 8 May 1945, and security was no longer the main concern. While the official policy remained intact for some time, individuals within the military command began to voice their doubts. Assistant Chief of the Division for Control of German Information Services, Douglas H. Schneider, complained in a memorandum to his director, General Robert A. McClure, that protracted non-fraternization prohibited the Allied occupation from any participation in achieving the division's major objectives: the eradication of Nazi philosophy and the establishment of a peace-loving democratic spirit in Germany. "The fact remains," Schneider asserted, "that well contented and *well behaved* American troops are not bad ambassadors for our country and her ideals."[84] By supporting informal interaction between troops and German civilians, Schneider contended, the military government could actually help the process of denazification and reeducation. Schneider considered Germans susceptible to American influence. A necessary prerequisite for such a positive influence, of course, was the opportunity to interact freely with the enemy population.

Schneider's plan called for a complete reversal of the non-fraternization policy. Military officials were not prepared to make such drastic changes, but opted instead for a gradual dismantling of the ban. Sensitivity to American public opinion was of paramount importance in devising a strategy for relaxation as a secret note from General Eisenhower to Army Chief of Staff Marshall in June indicated. In this document Eisenhower reported on the problem of non-fraternization with respect to small children. "Ordinarily I would on my exclusive initiative take such steps here as I deem necessary to correct that situation," Eisenhower noted. "However, the most important thing at the moment seems to be public opinion in the United States and consequently I am forwarding herewith for your comment an order that I am considering publishing."[85] He submitted the proposed amendment excluding German children below the age of twelve from the order. Upon Marshall's suggestion Eisenhower replaced the specific age for a less specific "small children." When he announced the amendment on 8 June 1945, he insisted that it did not represent a relaxation but merely a qualification of the ban.[86] Small children, he reasoned, could not present a threat to the integrity of the American Army. Yet the exclusion of children marked a significant step toward the abandonment of the ban as well as a transformation of the German image in the American political mindset. The "qualification" symbolized the first crack in the American assumption of the German monolith.

The first sign of the actual dismantling of the order occurred a month later when Eisenhower permitted "contacts between personnel of this command and adult Germans on the streets and in public places."[87] The military government had realized its powerlessness in enforcing the ban. The expectation of an extended stay in one place also changed the dynamics of German-American contacts. An American Army officer observed at the end of May that although he supported non-fraternization in principle, "it will not be workable after our troops get settled in and particularly when they start to yearn for female companionship."[88] By the summer of 1945, not even its strongest supporters deemed the continuation of the fraternization ban practical or even possible.

The military government's open admission of its inability to enforce the order, however, would have led to severe criticism from civilians at home. Eisenhower therefore cited as the major reason for the relaxation the "rapid progress which has been made in the denazification and removal of all prominent Nazis from any part of German life."[89] This was only partially correct, however, since Americans had only just begun the long and arduous process of denazification.[90] Beyond being overly optimistic, Eisenhower's reference to denazification indicated a major shift in American attitudes toward Germany. Rather than assuming Germany's collective guilt, the military government began to distinguish between "guilty" and "innocent" Germans. Eisenhower's explanation suggested that fraternization with non-Nazis was permissible, at least to a certain degree. More importantly, the move reflected the dominant perception of American military officials concerning fraternization, namely that German women did not belong to the pool of Nazi sympathizers. On the basis of this assumption, military officials calculated, fraternization no longer posed a threat to the mission of the occupation.

On 1 October, policymakers terminated the non-fraternization order except for the billeting with German families and marriages with German nationals.[91] The cancellation of the ban not only removed one of the biggest sources of friction between occupation troops and the military government but also signified the transformation of the military government's attitudes toward the German people and its understanding of its own role in Germany. The gendered connotations of fraternization helped in diffusing opposition to the lifting of the ban. American soldiers' insistence on the apolitical nature of their contacts with *Fräuleins* ultimately overshadowed the military government's insistence on the political damage these relationships would do.

Yet there was no doubt in the minds of keen observers of the early occupation that the widespread informal interactions between GIs and German women would have broader political consequences. As early as the fall of 1944, as the first troops entered Germany, *New York Times* correspondent Clifton Daniel predicted, somewhat optimistically, that "the impact of these two groups on each other is the beginning of the process of German reeducation."[92] A few months later, a *Newsweek* article found that the large-scale contacts had produced a "growing sympathy of the Americans for the Germans." The article predicted that the political implications of this shift in attitude were "obvious and may become of great importance."[93] Exactly what those political implications might be was spelled out more clearly a year later in an *American Mercury* article by Saul Padover. Padover, a writer and officer in the Army's Psychological Warfare Division, asserted that when American GIs would return home from their service in Germany, they would "bring with them sympathy for German women, a sympathy that may well be translated into political terms of not being too harsh with the Reich as a whole."[94] In pointing to the link between American GIs and the home front in the United States, Padover pointed to the larger ramifications of the personal interactions. Fraternization in Germany could not be viewed in isolation from the larger questions of Germany's postwar treatment. What transpired between Americans and Germans in Germany had far-reaching repercussions in the United States as well. GIs functioned as cross-cultural mediators and interlocutors between the German and American population, just as their German contacts functioned as mediators between their own population and the American troops.

In October 1945, however, neither the military government nor the American public were willing to embrace the GIs' changed attitudes toward Germans. Opinion polls conducted In the United States in the fall of 1945 showed that a majority of Americans still opposed fraternization. They also revealed that opinions about fraternization split along gender lines. One survey asked participants whether they thought American soldiers should be allowed to have dates with German women. Seventy percent of the women yet only forty percent of the men under thirty years of age answered no.[95] The strong opposition among young women suggests that for them more was at stake than the weakening of American resolve in Germany. American women perceived the GIs' fraternization with German women as a personal affront. Their fears concerning German women were not entirely unfounded since by the fall of 1945 many GIs had already petitioned their commanders to marry German women.

Military officials in Germany were thus caught between demands for sternness by the American public and leniency by troops in Germany. Holding on to the fraternization ban meant alienating their own troops, and abandoning it meant alienating the American public. By gradually relaxing the ban and linking fraternization to the progress of denazification and democratization, military officials hoped to appease both sides.

* * *

The cancellation of the fraternization ban in October 1945 was not considered a major turning point in the American occupation at the time. Both Germans and Americans were preoccupied with issues of seemingly greater importance for the future of their relationship. In Nuremberg, preparations were underway for the first international war crimes trial ever, and Four-Power cooperation in the Allied Control Council showed the first signs of tension when the French declined to support an American proposal for the creation of an independent German administrative apparatus.[96] Yet even if it was overshadowed by the far-reaching questions of the first year of Allied occupation, the American decision to allow fraternization signaled the first indication of American political rapprochement with Germans. The softening of the American stance toward Germany clashed with the hardline positions of France and the Soviet Union in the Allied Control Council, both of whom were still opposed to Germany's economic and political reconstruction.[97] The shift in U.S. fraternization policy meant that American policymakers were either giving in to their soldiers' sensibilities or shared them.

Did giving up the fraternization ban mean that Americans were again losing the peace after winning the war, just as they had after World War I? Some Americans thought so. By not being able to control the social conduct of troops, the military government could not impose the rigid occupation it had outlined in the occupation directive. Yet others, among them high ranking military officials, came to doubt the wisdom of such a harsh occupation directive in light of the conditions in postwar Germany. These officials played a crucial role in overturning the fraternization ban and allowing GIs to interact freely with German civilians. For them, fraternization was an integral aspect of the social and political reeducation of Germany. They believed that the policy of non-fraternization was flawed not only in practice but in principle.

Thus the battle over fraternization in the first year of the American occupation involved more than sexual relations and the problem of discipline among a few hundred thousand war-weary troops. It involved the redefinition of America's assumption of Germany's collective guilt, it involved fundamental changes in American images of the German national character, and it involved a reorientation of American ideas about the meaning and the goals of the occupation. Americans no longer labeled Germans as political and social outcasts from the community of western nations. Instead fraternization opened the door toward reconciliation on the interpersonal level.

CHAPTER 3

Villains to Victims
The Cultural Feminization of Germany

"American soldiers pay no attention to German men," James P. O'Donnell wrote in *Newsweek* in December 1945. "To German women they do."[1] He reassured readers, however, that the GIs' interest in German women was outside the political scope of the occupation. Apparently, American soldiers' interactions with German women did not affect the way they thought about Germany, the war, or Nazi atrocities. O'Donnell's portrayal was indicative of the changing attitudes among many U.S. soldiers about the nature of their relationship with Germans. By the time the article appeared, the term fraternization had already become synonymous with sexual contacts between GIs and German women. *Life* magazine correspondent Percy Knauth found as early as July 1945 that fraternization had taken on this "brand-new meaning."[2] Postwar Germany appeared to be defined by "bare legs" and "skirts waving in the breeze" rather than Nazi soldiers and Hitler Youth.

The feminization of fraternization was central to the transformation of the American postwar image of Germany. This new image bore little resemblance to Germany's wartime demonization. Women played a crucial role in reformulating American conceptualizations of postwar Germany. Their perceived vulnerability as women became synonymous with Germany's political and economic vulnerability after the war. That vulnerability had very different manifestations: the image of the *Trümmerfrau* existed side by side with the more ambiguous one of the attractive and often deceptive young *Fräulein* in the American consciousness (fig. 3.1). Rather than punishing Germans for their atrocities during the war, American GIs became providers and protectors, first literally for the women they dated, and later figuratively for what they perceived to be an emasculated, starving population.

O'Donnell's observation about the American soldier's preoccupation with German women was actually not altogether correct. Less visible but more common, according to a 1946 military government survey, were contacts between German and American men.[3] The reason for O'Donnell's misjudgment lay in the distinctions drawn between official interactions and fraternization. American interactions with German men often concerned administrative and policy matters and occurred hidden from the public eye. American contacts with German women, by contrast, often occurred in public places, and focused on leisure time activities, with the exception of those women who worked for Americans in clerical or service positions. While American officials accepted the former as an integral part of occupation business, they viewed the latter as inimical to occupation policy (especially when reports of them surfaced in American newspapers). GIs, and with them *Newsweek*'s O'Donnell, however, regarded those relationships as private and innocuous.

Despite soldiers' assumptions, their relationships with German women had ramifications beyond the merely sexual. They ultimately undermined the original, punitive occupation policy not just through their early defiance of the non-fraternization directive but through the increasing compassion they showed toward the civilian

Fig. 3.1 Postwar images of German women: (*left*) The *Trümmerfrau* (Bundes-archiv, Bild. 146/74/152/16) and (*right*) the seductress (Bundesarchiv, Bild 146/75/98/27).

population. Just as Saul Padover had declared in 1946, this softening of attitudes eventually affected policymakers in Washington as well.[4] By that time, American officials, recognizing that informal inter-actions between soldiers and civilians were widespread, were en-dorsing such friendly contacts as a tool of the occupation. The grad-ual shift away from punitive occupation policies was completed by the announcement of the Marshall Plan in early 1947. The period of informal interactions between the fall of 1944 and the end of 1946 thus set the stage for the political reconciliation between the United

States and Germany and West Germany's political and cultural rein-
tegration into the western alliance.

*   *   *

In many ways soldiers' relationships with German women differed
little from their sexual exploits elsewhere in Europe and East Asia.
The desire for female companionship and sex often superseded the
question of whether the objects of desire were allies or enemies.
Writer and philosopher J. Glenn Gray, who served as an intelligence
officer in Europe during the war, was rather "astonished by the
soldiers' concentration upon the subject of women, and, more especially upon the sexual act."[5] For American GIs, fraternization at its
most basic level was sexual in nature. In fact, Gray suggested that sex
in the context of war often was a hostile act. "The conquest of the
sexual partner thus becomes very like the conquest of the enemy
who has forfeited the right to human status or equality."[6] The soldiers' sexual liaisons with German women could therefore be read as
an expression of their victory over a loathsome enemy as much as a
sign of personal attraction.

Some soldiers, especially those who saw their friends killed in combat or who witnessed the liberation of the concentration camps, regarded the "taking" of a German woman as a form of revenge. War correspondent Meyer Levin rationalized his own and other soldiers' desire to rape German women: "In war there is a reversal of the general code of the community of men. It is right to kill, and with this sanction comes a compulsion to reverse all other civilized injunctions: to steal, lie, blaspheme, and rape." Even though the army would try to control these impulses, Levin found, soldiers would commit minor offenses. "Thus theft is transformed into loot; rape in Germany was accomplished through the medium of a bar of chocolate, and was known as fraternization." His contempt for the German people was so deep that he could not contemplate any meaning of fraternization other than rape. Levin had come to Germany to cover the fate of Europe's Jews for the Jewish-American press. He had been among the first to visit Ohrdruf concentration camp. Together with his jeep mate, a French Jewish photographer whom he called only by his first name Erik, he searched for and found the latter's mother at Theresienstadt. Having witnessed the human suffering of the victims of Nazi atrocities, Levin candidly admitted that they both pondered the idea of rape as a way to release their hatred. "We were no different from the others," he explained. "Erik had infinitely greater motivation for revenge; my own bitterness was general—a bitterness for what the Germans had done to my people; Erik's was personal, for what they had done to himself and his family." Yet the problem, as Levin saw it, was that the soldiers' desire for rape was met by "the lustful eagerness of the German girls to fulfill their roles as conquered women." Thus, fraternization, in Levin's eyes, signified German women's willingness to pay the price for their defeat, for "to pay, in this way, was indeed a kind of vindication of the very morality under which they had lived and fought and worshipped."[7] Levin inverted the meaning of rape by asserting that even if a woman is willing, a man commits rape as long as he is motivated by the desire to rape.

Contrary to Levin's assumption, most fraternizers, German and American, were motivated by factors other than revenge or defeatism. Nor did all German women enter voluntarily into sexual liaisons with American GIs. Many rejected the sexual overtures by the foreign army; some were sexually assaulted. According to official records, rape allegations in the American-occupied area rose dramatically in the early months of 1945. While only eighteen cases were reported in January, and thirty-one in February, the number of complaints rose dramatically to 402 in March and 501 in April. In May, the month of Germany's surrender, the cases declined to 241, to sixty-three in June, until leveling off at forty-five for the rest of the year. Of those cases, between a quarter and a half were brought to trial and again between a third and a half of those ended in convictions: three in January, five in February, sixty-nine in March, 128 in April, eighty-five in May, seven in June, and "only a scattering thereafter," according to the official report.[8] The incidents of rape were so pervasive in early 1945 that *Stars and Stripes* war correspondent Leiser, who was accompanying the Ninth Army into Germany wrote a concerned dispatch to his headquarters in Paris. He noted that "numerous officially reported cases of rape in the newly-occupied Rhineland present an ugly new angle today to the non-fraternization problem." He assumed that "the actual number of rape cases was considerably higher than the reported eleven, four of which ended in murder."[9] Not surprisingly, the news dispatch was suppressed by the Public Relations Division of SHAEF.[10] Yet even at the height of rape incidents, in May 1945, Americans did not reach the level of sexual abuse attributed to Soviet soldiers.

Recent scholarship has provided ample evidence that Soviet troops frequently resorted to rape in their zone, particularly in the immediate aftermath of hostilities.[11] Norman Naimark's study of the

Soviet motivations to rape German women in April 1945 confirms at least part of Gray's and Levin's theses, namely that rape served as revenge and a way to humiliate the enemy. Yet the fact that women in the Soviet zone were far more reluctant to enter voluntarily into sexual liaisons with Soviet soldiers disproves another aspect of Levin's thesis, namely that their Nazi education had taught them to accept their fate in this way. Other factors contributed to this discrepancy, such as the relative poverty of the Soviet troops stationed in Germany and traditional German prejudices against them as uncivilized and barbarian—especially those from the eastern part of the Soviet Union. At least for German women, cultural and economic factors played a much larger role in their response to the soldiers' sexual advances than any sentiment of defeatism that Levin detected.

Most GIs who sought the company of women at least initially did so for sexual rather than social reasons. Because of this connotation GIs rejected the military government's claim that such contacts imperiled the occupation effort. In July 1945, a soldier complained to *Life* correspondent Percy Knauth, "I think this non-fraternization is just plain stupid. What I mean is, it's going against human nature."[12] Most soldiers simply did not distinguish between allies and enemies in their search for female companionship. The *New York Times* put it more bluntly: "It's a case of boy meets girl, and the ranks of Allied armies are in favor of it, whatever the home fronts may think."[13] By reducing fraternization to basic natural instincts, supporters were able to divorce it from the larger political concerns of the occupation.

The abandonment of the fraternization ban in October 1945 legitimized but did not significantly alter the pattern of interaction between GIs and Germans. American-German couples still faced significant restrictions on meeting each other in public or private places. In the early phase of the occupation German women, for instance, could not join GIs in their entertainment clubs. Army officials might have tolerated the reality of American-German affairs but they refused to facilitate them by opening American social clubs to German nationals. GIs frequently violated the rules by simply pretending their dates were displaced persons. In Mannheim, Lia Parker often attended events at one of the American clubs by claiming Polish nationality. "They knew better," she recalled, "but let us come in anyway."[14] The exclusion of women from Army social clubs proved to be just as unenforceable as the non-fraternization ban itself.

By early 1946, the Nuremberg-Fuerth Enclave of the American military government was experimenting with the plan to issue social passes to "desirable" members of the German population. Those passes would allow Germans to attend American social functions. Conceived by the commanding general of the International Military Tribunal, Brigadier General Leroy H. Watson, the plan considered only women as recipients of these passes. Reasons for rejection of applications included "unfavorable or unclean personal appearance, false statement in the questionnaire or during the interrogation, undesirable political or social background, criminal or venereal disease record, under eighteen years of age." By limiting access to German women, occupation officials not only adjusted to the general pattern of fraternization but also perpetuated the traditional assumption that contacts with women were somehow less harmful to the occupation effort than contacts with German men. The Nuremberg model became official policy in the entire zone in September 1946, thus legitimizing the gendered preferences of the soldiers as part of the official occupation policy.[15] The new rule relegated German men to the status of second class citizens by limiting their opportunities to interact with occupation forces. The introduction of social passes, however, met with uneven results, causing resentment in some areas from both German women and Americans.

Thus in November the order was rescinded, leaving the regulation of fraternization in the social clubs up to the local commanders.[16]

As American clubs opened their doors to German women, Army compounds continued to remain off-limits. Yet soldiers and officers frequently violated that rule as well. German women regularly stayed overnight in Army compounds as guests of officers, a well-known practice unofficially accepted by the military government. In early 1946, a British woman complained about this laxity in a letter to the editor of *Stars and Stripes*. She exposed the double standard within the military ranks, yet could not do much to change the situation. Since commanding officers themselves frequently violated regulations, the military government faced strong opposition in its effort to enforce discipline. The article caught the attention of a *New York Times* reporter who wrote about it in the United States. The publicity in the United States led to immediate sanctions within the military government. Whether or not these new regulations were enforced, however, remained doubtful.[17]

It was the public aspects of fraternization, however, that gained the most attention in the United States. GIs and German women strolling arm in arm along rubble-filled streets were common sights in the American zone. Dana Adams, a correspondent for the *New York Times*, described a typical weekend in an American-occupied city: "It is Saturday afternoon, and the soldiers are still there with their fräuleins. In every park they are thick with couples and in groups on the grass."[18] The presence of German-American couples had become an integral part of urban everyday life.

As American soldiers settled into towns and cities for a long-term occupation, the opportunity and temptation to meet and date German women increased exponentially. Some relationships evolved from official contacts, especially through work. After the end of the war, employment of Germans in U.S. occupation facilities rose significantly. By the middle of July 1945, the Seventh Army had hired over 1,000 German civilians. By November, the figure had risen to 25,000.[19] Employment opportunities for Germans ranged from unskilled technical support to service and clerical work. In the latter group well-educated women who could speak English predominated. When Kaethe Schmidt heard in the summer of 1945 that the Americans in Berlin-Tempelhof—close to where she lived with her parents—were looking for a translator and secretary, she immediately applied. The provision of two meals a day in addition to the regular salary attracted her to the position. Upon acceptance she also received a *Lebensmittelkarte* (ration card) and, "at least for several months, my meals at lunch and supper."[20] The free meals allowed Kaethe to save her personal food rations, which in turn improved her family's daily diet.

Maria Higgs, assigned to wash dishes at an American base, thrilled to the idea of eating leftover breakfasts. "None of us could remember when we had last seen so much food—and it was all for us," she explained. "It didn't matter that we all threw up afterwards. Our stomachs just couldn't take it."[21] Maria's and Kaethe's jobs were among the most coveted because they provided access to extra food rations. In most other jobs, the military government went to great lengths to prevent the provision of meals from Army stocks to German personnel.[22]

Women who worked for occupation agencies were actually under less material pressure to seek relationships with American soldiers than others. For them, access to food was not dependent on personal relationships with individual GIs. Ann Schade, who met her future husband while working for the military government, insisted that her relationship evolved out of "mutual respect and genuine feelings for each other" rather than material considerations.[23] In fact, intimate relationships with officers sometimes jeopardized a woman's employment at an American agency. Kaethe Schmidt observed that her female German colleagues who had become involved with U.S. officers often lost their jobs once the affair was over. She was therefore initially quite reluctant when Don Sears began courting her.[24]

If not always the decisive factor in the evolution of a relationship, food and other material benefits nonetheless played a major role. Don Sears, Kaethe Schmidt's future husband, supplied her family with soap, food, and other scarce goods. In return Kaethe's mother washed his clothes and ironed his shirts. Ann Schade's relationship with her future husband began when he offered her occasional rides home, reducing her commute from one-and-a-half hours to fifteen minutes. "Since I had lost all of my belongings in the war and was unable to return to my parents (the iron curtain had already come down)," she explained, "it was natural that I should cling to Philip, who was so kind and good."[25] Liese-Lore Spreen's future husband brought a turkey to their first date.[26] Food had replaced flowers and jewelry as the most common instrument of courtship.

Because Americans possessed commodities German women lacked and needed, they were willing to strike bargains. Some women received food in return for domestic services. Maria Reed met several Americans through her mother's private laundry business. For her services she received cigarettes, coffee, soap, and other scarce items. "This way she could trade cigarettes for potatoes etc., and our life was better," Maria explained.[27] American PX rations of food and cigarettes also sustained the black market.[28] A few cigarettes bought GIs cuckoo clocks, valuable carpets, or Nazi souvenirs. A female customer of the black market explained: "Old Reichsmark coins, which weren't valid anymore because of their silver content—we weren't supposed to have them anymore—and party badges—all badges from Hitler's time, Hitler Youth badges—with those we went to the [American] barracks, and in the barracks we got cigarettes. And the cigarettes we exchanged for food at the farmers."[29] A good wrist watch could yield as much as four pounds of butter, ten one-pound cans of American meat rations, or three cartons of cigarettes.[30] The German underground economy depended to a large extent on American GIs' interest in exchanging food and cigarettes for luxury items.

Women also used their bodies as bargaining chips. The borderline between love affairs and prostitution became blurred because nearly all GIs supported their German lovers with food and material supplies. Women often could not escape the charge of prostitution, no matter what the nature of their relationship with an American. "There was a lot of 'trash,'" Ann Schade complained, "who sought the alliance with Americans for the 'benefits' such as food and candy and cigarettes."[31] Thus even women who excluded themselves from the charge of material opportunism were quick to accuse others.

Some women resorted to prostitution to save themselves and their families from starvation. For others it became an additional source of income. A Neuss social worker reported in 1947 that "young single women whose husbands were war prisoners, missing, or dead, engage in irregular relations with truck drivers [who had access to the supplies they were transporting], foreigners [i.e. Allied soldiers or displaced persons who had better food rations], in other words, with those who could supply them with natural goods." Some mothers even sent their teenage daughters—in one case the girl was allegedly twelve—into DP camps, or areas occupied by American soldiers, in order to obtain food and cigarettes in exchange for sex. Still others simply fell in love with GIs and regarded the material benefits of the relationships as secondary.[32] Whatever the original motivation, food had become a central aspect of American-German interactions. Whether as a friendly gesture of goodwill or as payment for services, this informal system of food and material aid established a pattern that would later recur in official American aid programs such as the Marshall Plan and the Berlin airlift.[33]

The military government produced only rough estimates of the actual extent of fraternization between soldiers and German civilians. Occupation officials had no doubt, however, that the end of hostilities triggered a significant rise in fraternization. Internal polls from several regiments about the soldiers' fraternization between V-E Day and the end of September 1945 produced widely differing results. They ranged from fifteen to twenty percent of the 4th Armored Division to all members of the 53d Quartermaster Base Depot.[34] One indicator of the extent of sexual relations was the dramatic increase in sexually transmitted diseases (STDs) during the early occupation. Throughout the spring of 1945, according to an USFET report, the VD rate among U.S. combat troops in the European theater had hovered around five percent. Yet after V-E day the rate shot up dramatically peaking at nineteen percent in August. The same report alleged an infection rate as high as eighty-nine percent among African-American troops.[35] Yet a medical survey of about 123,000 soldiers with VD between 6 July and 21 December 1945 showed that more than half the cases occurred outside Germany (table 3.1) Even though the total number of infections remained fairly stable throughout the remainder of the occupation, *Newsweek* still noted with alarm in September 1946 that unless some drastic measures were taken, three out of ten GIs would be infected by the end of the year.[36] Among Germans, one in two hundred were infected with gonorrhea and one in five hundred had syphilis in 1946. Among women the figure was still higher: one in 166 had contracted gonorrhea and one in 433 had syphilis. The total figures represented a twofold increase in gonorrhea and a threefold increase in syphilis since 1934, the last year any systematic data was collected.[37] This dramatic increase presented a public health problem that demanded

Table 3.1: Geographical Distribution of Contacts Resulting in
Venereal Disease

Country	Cases	Theater (by percentage)
France	56,320	45.8
Germany	43,988	35.8
Belgium	10,268	8.4
England	4,685	3.8
Austria	3,328	2.7
Czechoslovakia	2,115	1.7
Luxembourg	657	0.54
Netherlands	585	0.5
Italy	415	0.3
Denmark	289	0.2
Switzerland	207	0.2
Norway	69	0.053
Sweden	9	0.007
Total	122,953	100.0

Source: *Fraternization with the Germans* 77.

cooperation between American and German health officials. As a result, Americans began treating not only GIs but infected Germans as well, giving them for the first time access to the new drug penicillin. The joint treatment of Americans and Germans gradually reduced the rate of infection among both groups.[38]

The threat of venereal disease became the most compelling tool for the military government to discourage fraternization. The American Army newspaper *Stars and Stripes* led the campaign by conflating the problem of VD contagion and Germany's Nazi past. The paper created a cartoon character, "Veronica Dankeschön," who spent her days trying to seduce innocent GIs (fig. 3.2).[39] The cartoons suggested that Veronica was not only infected with VD but also with Nazi ideology, and that she set out to pass both on to her ignorant American lovers.

Another quantifiable indicator of the nature and frequency of

Fig. 3.2 "Veronica Dankeschön." *Stars and Stripes,* 1946.

contacts was the steadily rising figure of so-called Besatzungskinder (occupation children), children born from liaisons between German women and occupation soldiers. Births out of wedlock peaked in Germany at sixteen percent of all births in 1946; one-sixth of those were believed to be Besatzungskinder.[40] Unofficial estimates placed the number of American-German babies at roughly 94,000 over the course of the occupation. This development prompted some Germans to joke that if America ever got into another war in Europe, it would not be necessary to send any troops—just the uniforms.[41]

Women had no legal recourse to force American fathers to provide child support. Military government regulations stipulated that "no individual in the military service will be required or requested to admit paternity but in a case of voluntary admission on his part and a specific expression of desire to furnish financial or other assistance to the woman involved."[42] In addition, military authorities would take no action aiding foreign courts in obtaining child support from a member of the U.S. Armed Forces. Ruth Haas therefore pleaded in vain for military government cooperation in December 1948.[43] Military authorities informed her that if the father of her child, a sergeant in the U.S. Army, did not voluntarily acknowledge his paternity, the military government would not exert pressure on him to do so.[44] American GIs thus carried no legal responsibilities for their children in Germany or any other foreign country.

Military regulations not only facilitated GIs' escape from paternal responsibilities, they in fact obstructed the efforts of those who actively sought custody. A legal quagmire prevented most American GIs from adopting even their own children. Since American military courts could only try criminal cases, American servicemen would have to bring their adoption cases before German civil courts. Military law, however, prohibited American citizens from appearing before those courts.[45] As a result, American GIs had no legal means to gain custody of their children. Occupation officials' willingness to lift the fraternization ban thus did not translate into a positive attitude toward American-German formal relations. To the contrary, the military used every possible means to prevent such efforts.

The army's obstructionism extended to marriages as well. As early as 1944 GIs began to petition the military government for permission to marry German women. At this time the fraternization ban still prohibited GIs from even speaking to Germans. After the official termination of the non-fraternization order in October 1945, marriages remained prohibited for another fourteen months.[46]

When the military government relented and allowed marriages in December 1946, applicants still had to follow an elaborate bureaucratic procedure that included medical and moral exams for the German fiancée.[47] These hurdles came in addition to the general procedures developed for war brides from Allied countries. The dramatic increase in the number of foreign spouses of American citizens seeking admission to the United States compelled Congress in December 1945 to pass the so-called War Brides Act, allowing alien wives and children of American members of the armed forces to enter the United States outside the regular immigration quota. In June 1946, Congress passed another bill, known as the "sweetheart bill" to allow fiancés and fiancées of Americans to enter the United States for the purpose of marriage.[48]

American requests to marry German women emerged even before the military government lifted the fraternization ban. *Newsweek* reported as early as September 1945 that "a growing number of American soldiers have applied for permission to marry Germans."[49] It would take at least another year, the article quoted a Welfare Department official in Berlin, before the military government would permit such marriages. Some GIs simply refused to wait that long. Russell W. Horton and two fellow GIs decided to take their requests to the highest order. They petitioned President Harry S. Truman in 1945 to allow them to marry German women. When Truman failed to respond, Horton decided to marry anyway.[50] He proceeded to do so in October 1945. To his mother in Elmsford, New York, he wrote: "You can't put love on a political basis. It's nature. You can fight nature for 50 years, but you won't win. I'm going to have my Trudy!"[51] Horton's attitude exemplified the friction between his personal and official interpretations of his relationship with a German woman. While he saw his marriage as a statement of affection for an individual who happened to be of German nationality and therefore an act outside the political context of the occupation, his superiors saw it as a political act undermining the goals of the occupation.

Because of the political ramifications, military officials were determined to punish marriage offenders. In the summer of 1946 they decided to remove Herman R. Kaplan, a driver for the Central Headquarters of the United Nations Relief and Rehabilitation Administration (UNRRA), and James J. Powell, an UNRRA dispatcher, from Germany because they had married German women without official authorization.[52] The case received public attention when *Stars and Stripes* reported that the two Americans had discovered a loophole in Army regulations that excluded employees of international organizations such as UNRRA from the general orders of the theater commander. Underscoring his determination to be with his wife, Kaplan told the paper that "I took the chance of remaining the rest of my life in Germany with Isa. I weighed the possibilities and decided I would share my future with Isa whatever the U.S. decided about shipment of German wives to America." Powell was willing to give up his Florida dairy cow breeding farm to be with his wife. "The farm must be running down," he worried, "but my wife comes first."[53] More and more Americans were prepared not only to defy Army regulations but even to forfeit their right to return to the United States in order to marry German women.

Many Army veterans with wedding plans in Germany had returned to the United States before they could get married. The letters that some of them wrote to General Joseph T. McNarney in his capacity as Commanding General in the European Theater offer a glimpse of their grievances, their attitudes toward Germans, and the occupation in general. E. L. Northcutt of Manchester, New Hampshire, appealed to the General for help after trying unsuccessfully for more than nine months to obtain permission to marry a German woman. "I think my attitude toward the girl has been proven unquestionably sincere by my efforts, in the face of such discouraging obstacles, to make her my wife," he pleaded. "That alone if one is to believe the teachings of Democracy and Religion, is enough to justify the decision."[54] Northcutt's reasoning was typical in its emphasis on the personal rather than political implications. He assumed that the sincerity of his commitment should be enough to convince the general to change his ruling. For occupation officials, however, the larger political symbolism of a German-American marriage weighed far more heavily than any personal circumstances.

From the GIs' perspective, the harshness of the rules rewarded those who disregarded them. War veteran Joseph Carl Korber, who returned to the United States without his German bride, felt betrayed because the military government punished him for working within the system. "I find that it really does not pay, because there are fellows who married German girls while in service, and now are living contended [sic]."[55] Richard Graham of San Francisco provided extensive details on his own and his bride's impeccable moral character in order to show the benefits of this German-American union. "I am trying my best to send her necessary things she needs very bad," he explained, "a little at the time, because I promised I would do that for her when packages are permitted to go there and they are as you know."[56] Graham's concern for his bride's physical well-being was indicative of a larger shift in interpretation of the American role in Germany. Even though he saw his duty to his German girlfriend primarily in private terms—as that of a male provider for his dependent wife to be—his sense of private responsibility developed during, and had fused with, his former public role as a representative of the U.S. occupation force.

The persistence of GIs slowly undermined the military government's resolve concerning marriages. Yet even as Congress and the military government relaxed restrictions, German-American couples had to overcome numerous obstacles.[57] The December 1946

Circular 181 on marriages, which officially lifted the marriage ban, still required Americans belonging to the U.S. Forces in the European Theater to obtain military government approval to marry. Soldiers could submit applications only "from six months to three months prior to the date that a) applicant is scheduled to leave the European Theater upon completion of overseas tour, or for discharge, or b) applicant is scheduled to be placed on terminal leave for discharge in the European Theater in the case of military or naval personnel, or c) applicant will cease to be employed by, accompany, or serve with the U.S. Forces, in the case of civilian personnel."[58] Occupation officials would not approve a marriage until three months after an application was first submitted. Concurrent with the submission of the application a German fiancée or fiancé had to apply for a military exit permit at the nearest military government office. Only with a valid exit permit would the commanding officer of the American individual approve the marriage. Another hurdle to overcome was the investigation of the moral character of the German fiancée. "Commanding officers," the circular stated, "will make such local inquiry or investigation into the character and moral background of the German fiancée or fiancé as they deem advisable. This inquiry will include an interview by a chaplain with the applicant and with the fiancée or fiancé."[59] In many cases the time between eligibility to apply for permission to marry and its approval was too short, and the American had to leave before the couple could get married. If that happened fiancées had to apply for entry into the United States under Public Law 471, which allowed alien fiancées of members and former members of the Armed Forces entry into the United States for the purpose of marriage.[60]

In the case of Robert J. Maylie and Lucie von Kettler, the time from application to approval took almost seven months.[61] Between January and July 1947 the two went through countless bureaucratic procedures and humiliating examinations before they finally

Fig. 3.3 U.S. Constabulary Thomas L. Garner marries Heidi Rink in Berlin, 1947. Bundesarchiv, Bild 183/R90871.

obtained permission to marry. This occurred only after Maylie's commanding officer had confirmed that "the proposed marriage will not bring discredit upon the Military Service,"[62] and a chaplain had testified that their union would not "be contrary to public interest."[63] In the context of the occupation the act of marriage assumed public and political significance far beyond the concerns of bride and groom (fig. 3.3).

Military officials had designed the complicated and tedious procedure in part to discourage German-American couples from planning marriage in the first place. Yet by June 1947, within the first six months after the fiancée law took effect, the OMGUS Combined Travel Board had already processed 2,515 exit applications under Public Law 471 and 2,984 were still pending.[64] Not all of those applicants would receive permission to travel to the United States, yet by June 1950, 14,175 German wives, six husbands, and 750 children of "citizen members of the United States Armed Forces" had entered the United States. Only Anglo-American marriages exceeded that figure, with more than twice as many British wives (34,944), nine times as many husbands (53), yet fewer children (472), moving to the United States. Another 1,862 Germans entered the United States between 1947 and 1949 as fiancées. Germans accounted for twenty-two percent of all fiancées coming to the United States under the provisions of the Fiancée Law, more than any other single country. By contrast, Japan sent only 758 war brides and five children to the United States.[65] Racial and cultural differences between Americans and the Japanese can at least partially explain this stark contrast.

The growing number of German-American couples applying for permission to marry signified a shift in attitudes on both sides of the encounter. As more American soldiers held closer ties to the local population, their perceptions about their role in Germany began to change. Their interactions with German women sensitized them to the food shortages and material hardships these women and their families endured. By the same token, their experiences desensitized them to the wartime atrocities of the German population. In fact, they perceived wartime and postwar Germany as two different worlds. Gender differences invited the separation of these worlds. German men dominated these soldiers' wartime images of Germany whereas women shaped their postwar images. The ruthless fanaticism of the war period contrasted sharply with the postwar desolation and apathy in the midst of hunger, material hardships, and desperate living conditions.

The perception of a feminized Germany was at odds with the demographic profile of those Germans who interacted with Americans. A 1946 occupation survey found that "Americans have not come into contact with all types of German people equally." While most Americans stationed in Germany knew at least one German, two-thirds of the German population never made the acquaintance of an American, according to the survey. Those who did profess to know Americans were more likely to be younger, better educated, and of higher economic status. Among women between ages twenty and twenty-nine, forty-two percent responded that they knew an American, yet only six percent of women over seventy did. Among men between twenty and twenty-nine, fifty-three percent knew Americans. The survey concluded that Americans "meet those people who, from some points of view, can be said to be the 'better' Germans—better in class, social position, occupational status, and education."[66] Whether they really constituted the "better" Germans remains questionable, yet the report accurately observed that Americans were not meeting a representative sample of the German population.

Most of those better-situated men met Americans through official occupation business. On occasion, official interactions offered the opportunity for informal exchanges as well. One of those friendships evolved between Prince Louis Ferdinand, the grandson of the last German emperor, Wilhelm II, and an American officer, Captain Merle A. Potter, the military governor of Bad Kissingen. The two founded the first German-American club in 1946, a club dedicated to the advancement of German-American understanding and cultural exchange. Membership in this and similar clubs all over the American zone was initially restricted to men.[67] The Prince's aristocratic heritage and Potter's military rank illustrated that those clubs served the political, social, and military elite in both countries rather than average GIs and German citizens.

For most American soldiers the observation of the *Newsweek* correspondent held true: they did not pay much attention to men and focused on young women instead. By the time it became legal for them to meet German women in public, most of the combat troops had been replaced by young men who had not fought the Germans. The new soldiers were less inclined to approach the German population with a personal sense of resentment. Nonetheless, most GIs still regarded their assignment in Germany as a hardship and envied their compatriots who could return to a civilian life of rising prosperity, marriage, and family.[68] In this general mood of low morale, soldiers began to look to German women not only as sexual objects but as embodiments of the civilian life to which they longed to return. Some would even move in with girlfriends, leading a life that on the surface resembled that of their married compatriots at home. In Army slang, those belonged to the "shack-up" category of fraternization, to be distinguished from the "pick-ups" according to Saul Padover. Pick-ups were women who hung out around train stations and other public places, ready to spend a night with an American GI. "They are not, it should be stressed, professionals" Padover explained.[69] The longer Americans stayed in Germany, the more likely they were to find a steady girl friend, Padover found, because the loneliness and the yearning for female companionship weakened even the most upright young American.

The German women who became these soldiers' companions often followed similar motivations. They saw the relationships with soldiers as an opportunity to recreate the culture of domesticity they had envisioned for themselves during the war. Both German social traditions and Nazi ideology had pressured young women into marriage and motherhood. In a speech to the National Socialist Women's Section (NSF) in September 1934, Hitler declared: "If the man's world is said to be the State then it may perhaps be said that the woman's is a smaller world. For her world is her husband, her family, her children, and her home."[70] Nazis expected women to make the home and the family a thriving place for Nazi ideology.[71] Even women who wished for a more active role in the Third Reich were barred from positions of authority. A case in point is the career of Gertrud Scholtz-Klink who headed the Women's Bureau, the umbrella organization for Nazi women's groups during the Third

Reich. While Scholtz-Klink commanded an empire of approximately thirty million women in Germany, her ability to influence national policy remained negligible.[72]

During the war National Socialists tried to balance their need for female laborers with the ideology of female domesticity. They called on women to move into the labor force to fill the jobs vacated by male draftees. Although the drive fell far short of Nazi expectations and industrial needs, women increasingly assumed the roles of breadwinners and providers for their families. The German government pressured women into leaving their traditional household roles yet insisted that the ultimate goal was the preservation of that tradition. Propagandists made sure that women regarded their work not as a departure but as an "extension of their roles as mothers and housewives."[73] Their labor on the home front would assure the survival of the Aryan ideal of the family and the strength of Germany's future fighting men. Yet despite the massive propaganda effort German women were reluctant to take jobs outside the home, especially if they had a family to care for. Because of this reluctance to perform public duties for the regime many of them escaped the denazification procedures of the American military government.[74]

The low visibility of women as active players in the Third Reich contributed to the assumption among American GIs that relations with German women occurred outside the political context of the occupation. Since women had not driven the Nazi policy of extermination, or fought in the war and killed American GIs, contacts with them could not possibly obstruct occupation duties. The Nazi policy of relegating women to the sidelines of the regime thus benefited them after the war. They encountered less hostility from the occupying forces than their male compatriots and at most faced criticism for their blind acceptance of the Nazi state.

German women themselves fostered this stereotype. In December 1945 the female author of a *Frankfurter Rundschau* article chided women who "only too willingly and blindly repeated what their husbands had told them, and thereby cast the biggest guilt upon themselves."[75] By asserting that women had the tendency to believe smoke and mirrors (Bluff und Tand) the author succeeded in at once indicting and exculpating German women. Their only crime apparently lay in their political gullibility and their willingness to follow their husbands, the real culprits of the regime.

Women's distance from Nazi politics, whether by choice or by force, facilitated their postwar adjustment to the occupation forces. Their wartime retreat into the domestic sphere had rendered them largely immune to the radical social changes of the regime. Unless they were Jewish, married to a Jewish man, or belonged to one of the other groups of non-Aryans, Nazi policies did not significantly change women's place within German society. The regime's emphasis on women's roles as mothers and housekeepers built on traditions dominant throughout the Weimar Republic. This emphasis on the domestic sphere also helps explain why German women remained reluctant throughout the war to join the workforce.[76]

After the war, women continued to do what they had done during the war, namely secure food, prepare meals, and keep house. Yet as the focus shifted from the battlefront to the ruined domestic landscape, women's work moved to the center of the national consciousness. Because of the food and other material shortages of the early postwar period, ordinary household chores became Herculean tasks. Families often relied on women to appropriate food from scarce sources, while German community leaders relied on them to clear the rubble from the streets and contribute to the reconstruction of urban housing.[77] In the immediate postwar period, the daily food rations barely sufficed to sustain the population's well-being and declined in some areas of the American zone to an all-time low of 800 calories a day during the winter of 1946–47. Families often relied on women to organize food on so-called *Hamsterfahrten* (hoarding trips) into the countryside. Farmers in rural areas usually exchanged food for material goods such as clothes, jewelry, and other luxury items.[78] In the postwar economy, farmers quite possibly were the only population group within German society whose living standard actually improved.

War casualties forced more women into the position of main provider for their families. They bore the brunt of social and economic reconstruction, because many German men had died in the war, were interned in POW camps, or had returned physically or psychologically maimed. In the age group between twenty and forty, women outnumbered men by a ratio of ten to six. Young women faced not only increased responsibilities for their families but also the possibility of remaining single for the rest of their lives. Ann Schade who worked for the American military government in Frankfurt recalled, "I never met a German man during the three years I was in Frankfurt, a fact that might have predisposed many of us who eventually ended up marrying foreigners."[79] This demographic imbalance not only led German women to seek out potential husbands among the occupation forces but it also warped American perceptions of postwar German society. If German men had been the main instigators of Nazi war crimes, then their low visibility in public life after the war eliminated one of the perceived major threats to Allied security.

The shortage of eligible bachelors among the German population threatened the ideal of marriage and motherhood. A 1949 article in a German women's magazine spoke of the panic that took hold of young women who faced fierce competition in their search for the right partner. "A kingdom for a Man" was the main premise, "no matter what he is like."[80] In these circumstances, American soldiers presented an attractive alternative to their German counterparts. Ilse Welli Holzhäuser, who witnessed the arrival of American troops near Stuttgart, noticed the difference between GIs and German men. "Here [among American GIs] you didn't see starved faces furrowed by strain and exertion anymore, but soldiers who appeared extraordinarily rested and well-cared for."[81] Anneliese Uhlig, a German actress who later married an American serviceman, also recalled the favorable outer appearance of the GIs. "They had beautiful teeth, they were so healthy, clean, well fed." It had been long since she "had seen a man who wasn't crippled in some way."[82] Hilde Robichaud of Vienna remembered that she was "fascinated by these young men [American GIs]; they seemed so carefree, happy, and well-fed, friendly, gentle with children and animals." Upon observing them sitting in outdoor cafés reading "funny books" and drinking coke from a straw, she wished she could "erase all the sad memories of the past and act as young and spirited as they did."[83] Contacts with GIs enabled young women to tap some of that material abundance and carefree leisure time.

Material hardships in Germany not only made GIs more attractive to German women but also gradually pushed soldiers into a role they had not originally envisioned for themselves, that of providers for an impoverished population. Food allocations in postwar Germany did not suffice to sustain the population's well-being. Germany's urban population was especially hard hit because there were fewer opportunities to supplement the meager supplies with home-grown food. Unable to provide for themselves, Germans looked to Americans for help. Military government opinion surveys of Germans indicated that by 1946 the majority of them expected the United States to provide food aid. Worse yet, when food rations declined during the harsh winter of 1946–47, Germans blamed Americans for the shortages.[84] In the context of American-German relationships, the dependent-provider relationship became gendered as American men provided for their German girlfriends.

These women found themselves in a rather paradoxical position assuming the role of provider for their own families, and that of dependent in their relationship with American GIs.

American soldiers' appropriation of the role of providers in Germany mirrored the emergence of the new "domesticity" in the United States. After the social upheavals of the Great Depression and war, many Americans looked forward to return to a life of security and stability. Public pressure increased on American women to give up their temporary wartime jobs and return to hearth and home. Even though the reality of women's lives looked much different—many women continued to work outside the home—the new culture of domesticity restricted women's choices and shaped men's as well as women's expectations.[85] Whether voluntary or not, many American women gave up their hard-won economic independence for dependence on a male breadwinner.[86] For the majority of German women economic independence was neither an option nor an ideal, especially among those without a male breadwinner in the family and with scarce economic resources.[87] These women looked to Americans to fill the vacuum, offering companionship and sex in return for American army rations.

Among the soldiers who filled that vacuum were 30,000 African-American GIs. Many of them, particularly those from the American South, experienced for the first time in their lives the freedom to date white women without fear of retribution. At a time when lynching was still all too common in the American South, Germany appeared, especially to those who grew up in the South, like a haven of racial tolerance. The major black news magazine *Ebony* announced in bold headlines in October 1946 that black soldiers found "more friendship and equality in Berlin than in Birmingham or on Broadway." After researching black troops' lives in Berlin, where between six and eight hundred black soldiers were stationed, the author found no evidence of racial discrimination and over-

whelming evidence of racial tolerance among the Germans. He concluded that "democracy has more meaning on the Wilhelmstrasse
than on Beale Street in Memphis."[88] The article devoted much attention to the fraternization between black GIs and German women as
well as to the clashes that occurred between black and white GIs as a
result of these relationships.

One such incident occurred at a dance at the enlisted men's club
in Asberg, Bavaria. According to the article, five white soldiers, identified as mostly Southerners, objected to African-American GIs
dancing with German women. "One of the whites, T5 Floyd D.
Hudson, who is from the South," the author related, "threw a beer
bottle into the center of the dance floor. Angered members of an
anti-Aircraft battalion, who were staging the dance, armed themselves with .30 caliber carbines and went gunning for the whites.
During the ensuing battle, Hudson was fatally shot in the side and
his four companions were all wounded." As a result three black
soldiers were court-martialled and sentenced to death.[89] The article drew a sharp contrast between the racial tolerance of German
women and the prejudice of white American troops whose sometimes violent opposition to interracial relationships exposed the
contradictions of the American effort in Germany: to eradicate the
Nazi ideology of Aryan supremacy from the German consciousness
while still upholding the American system of racial segregation. This
hypocrisy did not escape African-American soldiers serving in Germany nor their black compatriots in the United States, where articles documenting the racial tolerance of Europeans including Germans multiplied.[90] In fact, the purpose of the *Ebony* article was not
so much to hail Germany's progress toward equality and tolerance as
to expose the shortcomings of race relations in the United States.
From the African-American perspective, Germany thus ironically
became a model for domestic race relations in the United States.[91]

The report stirred such controversy in the United States that

Newsweek commented on it in its 16 September 1946 issue. Before quoting extensively from the article, *Newsweek* wrote that "the European's racial tolerance had posed a problem for Americans that will not be forgotten with the war or with the return of Negro soldiers from service overseas."[92] According to *Newsweek,* not American racism but European racial tolerance was the problem facing Americans. The acceptance of interracial relationships in Germany fueled concerns among white Americans about the potential effect of these soldiers' experience on the civil rights struggle in the United States.

A young reporter for the *Pittsburgh Courier,* William Gardner Smith, used his own service as an occupation soldier as the basis for a fictional account of the life of a black sergeant in Germany. The plot revolved around a group of black GIs who were stationed first in Berlin and later in Bremburg, a fictionalized town in the Rhine-Main area near Frankfurt. The main character and narrator of the story, Hayes Dawkins, comes to Germany with an open but critical mind. On his first date with Ilse, a German woman, at a lake resort near Berlin, he is surprised to find many black GIs with white women sharing the beach with white couples. The paradox does not escape him. "Here, in the land of hate," he ponders, "I should find this one all-important phase of democracy. And suddenly I felt bitter."[93]

Throughout the novel, various protagonists contrast the positive experience in Germany with the discrimination they suffer in the United States. One black GI actually defects to the Russian zone in order to avoid shipment back to the United States. On the eve of his departure, he explains his decision: "What kinda goddam job you think I can get in Georgia? Diggin' ditches? I don't want to go back there . . . I like this goddam country, you know that? It's the first place I was ever treated like a goddam man . . . You know what the hell I learned? That a nigger ain't no different from nobody else. I had to come over here to learn that. I hadda come over here and let the Nazis teach me that."[94] Smith's fictional account captured the general mood of black soldiers in Germany after the war. John Stevens of the 761st Tank Battalion, an all-black combat unit, recalled that "we were treated better by the civilian population than we were treated in America. See, in our country we couldn't buy a hot dog when we were in uniform, had to ride in the back of the bus when we were in uniform—you were nothing in uniform. But over there, you were treated like a king."[95]

Yet African-Americans were wrong if they assumed that racism had vanished from German society. For every German woman who engaged in sexual relations with an African-American, there were several who would not because of racial prejudice. These prejudices became more pronounced with the emergence of the *Mischlingskinder* or mixed blood children, born of the liaisons between black soldiers and German women. Estimates placed the number of these children between two and three thousand over the course of the military occupation, out of a total of around 94,000 occupation children born in all four zones combined.[96] Their fate in Germany after the war demonstrates Germans' conflicting attitudes toward interracial relationships. A poll conducted by the magazine *Survey* in 1949 found that German mothers treated their Mischlingskinder considerably better than their counterparts in England and Japan. The authors of the poll declared that while most English mothers had placed the children in orphanages and some Japanese mothers had even resorted to infanticide of occupation children (both black and white), German mothers remained devoted to their non-white offspring. The report stated that "in Germany not only is infanticide unthinkable but even separation is rarely considered."[97] On these grounds the survey concluded that few German women held any racial prejudice against the black troops from the United States. The fate of the Mischlingskinder, who were no older than five years at the time of the survey, was still uncertain in 1949 since they had not yet entered the public school system where they would encounter increasing prejudice.[98]

The article also presented a sociological profile of the mothers. While a plurality of the 600 interviewees were clustered at the lower end of the economic and educational spectrum, women from different walks of life in different situations entered into relationships with black GIs against the prevailing prejudices among their own compatriots and those of their occupiers.[99] Some of the women profiled in the article expressed the hope of marrying the father of their children and moving to the United States, presumably to escape the prejudices they feared their children would have to endure within Germany. Yet, besides being wrong about the belief that the United States would be more tolerant toward mixed-race couples, these women often underestimated the opposition to miscegenation that existed even within the Armed Forces. Military officials were much more likely to reject black GIs' marriage applications than those of white GIs.[100] As a result, many black soldiers' promises of marriage remained unfulfilled.

Among Germans, opposition to interracial relationships was often coupled with a general disapproval of fraternization with foreign soldiers. This opposition most often manifested itself in the form of verbal abuse against the women. Those who went out with American GIs often acquired the label "Ami-whore." Discrimination also occurred in more subtle ways. Frieda Berger remembered how the local baker's wife refused to serve her because she was dating an American and pointed out that she could get her food from her American lover.[101] Such hostility grew out of both jealousy and moral outrage, reflecting the internal dilemma Germans faced concerning the occupation. While they envied the material privileges women gained from contacts with American GIs, they scolded their association with the former enemy as a national humiliation.

In some areas opposition to American-German love affairs became more aggressive. In Bavaria placards publicly denounced individual women for allegedly "selling themselves for cigarettes, sugar, and chocolate." The posters often threatened reprisals.[102] German ex-soldiers and disillusioned former Hitler Youths frequently cut off women's hair or physically harassed those they believed associated with American men.[103] Clashes with GIs over women increased and led an Information Control Division (ICD) report to conclude that "the GI and the German Fräulein is Germany's primary social problem."[104] German men perceived the women's apparent preference for GIs as a humiliation further magnifying their symbolic emasculation as a result of the military defeat. Not only had they lost the war and had to endure a foreign occupation, but they were also losing their women to the victorious troops.

Sociologist Daniel Glaser in a 1946 article rather uncritically described women as objects of intercultural rivalries. Glaser had conducted a study of American soldiers' sentiments toward Europeans and saw contests over women as a major source of friction between Americans and Europeans. He postulated that rivalry existed whenever two groups sought "identical objects" and identified women as the most commonly fought over "objects." "Generally," he concluded, "the Americans, with their tobacco, candy, and money, held the advantage."[105] Both Americans and Germans thus interpreted women's preference for one man over another as a signifier of power of one nationality over another.

While GIs in occupied Germany became more and more intimate with the former enemy, anti-German and anti-fraternization sentiment persisted in the United States for quite some time. Leading experts on Germany continued to fuel the idea of Germany's historical pathology. Brigadier General Edwin L. Sibert, who had worked in Germany as Assistant Chief of Staff of Army Intelligence, reminded Americans of Germany's historical record. The Prussian King Frederick William I, he argued in 1946, "created the basis of a

Prussian civil service which in the end produced the type of 'little man' who elected Hitler, the type which Hitler represented." He compared that type to a "human robot" without any will of his own and "bred quite as carefully" as the "special breed of seven-footers whom Frederick William 'grew' for his guard regiment, or the special breed of greyhounds that his son Frederick the Great grew for his pleasure."[106] Germans, he contended, operated like machines in response to commands and lacked a moral and ethical conscience. According to Sibert, Germans were people of subhuman qualities, existing beyond the understanding of the western civilized world.

One way to explain the discrepancy between GI and American sentiments toward Germans was to portray the average GI as a goodnatured yet simpleminded fellow. This is precisely what Richard Joseph did in a *Reader's Digest* article in 1946. Joseph had spent some time as a staff sergeant in France and Germany. He was attached to a French division as an interpreter and cryptographer when the U.S. Seventh Army invaded Southern France in 1944. Titled "Why So Many GIs Like the Germans Best," the article acknowledged the remarkable transformation in attitudes among GIs toward the Germans. Joseph reported that among soldiers returning from Europe, four out of every five declared in a Red Cross survey that they liked the Germans better than any of their Allies.[107] The main reason for this favorable attitude, according to Joseph, was that "from the moment he crossed the border he was submerged in a sea of willing Fräuleins." The end of the fraternization ban a year later eliminated the tension, "and the GI discovered that the Germans were the friendliest people in Europe." Joseph viewed this new attitude with much concern since from his own experience he had learned, he declared, that "your average German is a two-faced coin." The friendly behavior of the Germans was not much more than propaganda to regain power. GIs, "open and unsuspicious by nature," according to Joseph, were now bringing their favorable yet wrongheaded attitudes with them to the United States. "He," the soldier, "will soon be organized. His associations will lobby in Washington and support politicians who think as their members do. On international issues the veterans will take stands in accordance with the impressions they brought back with them from Europe." In short, Joseph predicted that the returning GI could soon tilt the political mood in Washington decisively in favor of Germany, leading to an abandonment of the existing policy of punishment. These soldiers "could help a defeated, humiliated, desperate, vengeful Germany rise from its ashes for a third try at world domination." Joseph's doomsday scenario certainly exaggerated the power returning GIs would have on deciding Germany's future treatment, yet it articulates two crucial issues. First, it showed the persistent view, at least among some Americans, of a monolithic Germany whose only goal was world domination. Second, it indicated that the personal interactions between GIs and Germans not only changed the dynamic of the occupation but also had longer-term and farther reaching social and political repercussions in the United States.

One of the most persistent stereotypes of those critical of fraternization was that of the gullible, naive GI. Many Americans feared that instead of Americans denazifying Germans, pretty German girls were nazifying Americans. One soldier's mother blamed Army officers for the widespread fraternization in Germany because they had failed to convey to the troops the reasons for the American presence in Germany. "Our boys never did understand why they were fighting and they never did understand the enemy." She also accused German women of taking advantage of the Americans' lack of understanding. "Because a particular German girl is pretty and willing," she charged, "too many American soldiers feel that the German war crimes and concentration camps could not have been really German, but the work of only a few Nazis. If they believe that, it is because the Nazi girl agents have succeeded and Army educators have failed."[108] In her opinion German women fraternizing with GIs epitomized the Nazi ideology's continued power. Her complaint can be attributed, at least in part, to the widespread concern about soldiers' infidelity when stationed far away from home. Army wives, who began arriving in Germany in 1946, also objected to having to share the dance floor with an increasing number of German women in the Army clubs. "If some of the officers who fraternize could only know how we abhor 'rubbing shoulders' with their 'shack jobs' in our local night clubs," one wife wrote, "they might confine them to their shacks."[109] She was one of approximately 35,000 wives of U.S. officers who were encouraged to join their husbands in Europe in order to stem the tide of widespread fraternization with German women.[110]

Concerns about GI gullibility and German women's cunning-ness were the subjects of a popular movie, *A Foreign Affair,* produced in 1947 under the direction of Billy Wilder. The Film, Theater, and Music Branch of the Information Control Division of USFET had asked the Austrian-born director in the summer of 1945 to produce a motion picture about the occupation of Germany. In a memoran-dum to the Headquarters of USFET, Wilder revealed the purpose of the feature: "Now *if* there was an entertainment film with Rita Hay-worth or Ingrid Bergman or Gary Cooper in Technicolor if you wish, and a love story—only with a very special love story, cleverly devised to help us sell a few ideological items—such a film would provide us with a superior piece of propaganda."[111] When the film was finally released in 1947, it had become an anti-fraternization film. The plot depicted the moral cleansing of American Army Cap-tain John Pringle, played by John Lund. Pringle had become "in-fected" with the virus of postwar German immorality represented by his sexual liaison with the nightclub singer Erika von Schlütow, played by Marlene Dietrich. Pringle eventually is rescued by Phoebe

Frost, a career-oriented American congresswoman who undergoes a remarkable re-feminization over the course of the movie.

Wilder's portrayal of Erika von Schlütow, the only three-dimensional German character in the film, reveals the fundamental mistrust many Americans still harbored toward the German people during the early postwar period. Yet the choice of a woman to personify the German national character already signified Germany's postwar status as a weakened, essentially feminine, yet still dangerous, power. In *A Foreign Affair* Germans are threatening not militarily but in their power to corrupt naive Americans. However, more than a judgment on the moral integrity of occupied Germany, the movie serves as a parable of the rescue of America's soul from the seductive power of foreign entanglement. As the historian Emily Rosenberg pointed out, the film reflected the domestic American debate between internationalists and isolationists.[112] The re-feminization of Phoebe Frost, her turning away from a career as a politician to that of a wife and potential mother, mirrored the postwar desire of most Americans to return to more traditional forms of gender roles. Captain Pringle's life also undergoes a transformation away from sexual promiscuity represented by his relationship with Schlütow toward a life of social and moral responsibility. Pringle's eventual decision in favor of Phoebe Frost underscores the conclusion of *Newsweek* correspondent James P. O'Donnell, namely that "Yanks fraternize one way but think in the other direction." Both O'Donnell and Wilder's movie assured Americans that GIs still blamed the Nazis for the war and that they continued to have strong feelings about German ideas of racial superiority, their quest for Lebensraum, and their concentration camps. Fraternization, O'Donnell explained, did not change American opinions on these issues.[113]

Yet by the time the movie appeared in theaters in the United

States in 1947 fraternization was no longer prohibited and attitudes toward Germans had changed considerably. The longer American soldiers stayed in Germany, the more they felt responsible for the people they were supposed to police, and the more likely they were to have a positive attitude toward Germans.[114] This concern extended to political circles in Washington as well. President Truman himself was shocked by the material and human devastation in Berlin when he arrived for the Potsdam Conference in July 1945. "A more depressing sight than that of the ruined buildings," he wrote later in his memoirs, "was the long, never-ending procession of old men, women, and children, wandering aimlessly along the autobahn and the country roads carrying, pushing, or pulling what was left of their belongings. In that two-hour period I saw evidence of a great world tragedy, and I was thankful that the United States had been spared the unbelievable devastation of this war."[115] Truman's description of this scene revealed his compassion rather than resentment toward the people whom his country held responsible for the war. He saw not former Nazi soldiers and administrators but victims of the regime. Their gender and age mitigated their complicity in the Nazi empire's war crimes. The tragedy of the war, as Truman saw it, struck women and children, whether German or not.

Upon his return from Potsdam, Truman ordered special envoy Byron Price, former director of censorship, to study relations between American occupation forces and the German people.[116] Price's report pointed to a direct correlation between American experiences in Germany and political considerations in Washington. He stated that "the entire structure of Military Government in Germany, including the Potsdam Declaration, should be re-examined in light of experience and new conditions." He told the president that the same Germans who first greeted Americans as liberators had become disillusioned and depressed about America's punitive policies. Furthermore, Price reported that "fraternization, which has come about naturally and inevitably, has made some friends, particularly among the young children who are the hope of the long future." He did not mention the Fräulein problem which would have cast fraternization in an unpopular light. Instead, he emphasized that the American soldier was "the world's best salesman of democracy."[117] Informal relations and cooperation between occupation troops and the local population, he intimated, could thus speed Germany's democratization.

Price's report signified a turning point in the administration's thinking about its role in Germany. Barely a month after the lifting of the fraternization ban, Price advocated the utilization of fraternization as a means of democratization. Barely three months after the Potsdam Conference, he advocated the abandonment of punitive policies. According to Price, America's job in Germany should not be to punish the Germans but to gain their trust and their cooperation in their own political reorientation and economic reconstruction. While the report included statements on every aspect of occupation policy including a critical assessment of the progress of denazification, Price began his deliberation with a vivid description of the critical food and housing situation in Germany. Those conditions prompted him to call for a significant effort toward economic reconstruction. Referring to the Potsdam Declaration which stipulated that Germany was to be treated as a single economic unit, Price unleashed a barrage of criticism against the French, whose "rigid opposition" in the Allied Control Council "amounts, to speak plainly, to the economic dismemberment of Germany." Price saw economic reconstruction as a panacea for the dismal material conditions as well as a way to convince Germany of the benefits of democratization.

This document suggests that the Truman administration began to think about a shift in U.S. policy toward occupied Germany based on conditions within Germany itself rather than on any shifts in the geopolitical power configuration. Nowhere in the report did Price express concern that Germans could turn toward communism if material deprivations persist. Nowhere in the document did he suggest that Soviet occupation authorities were obstructing the joint governance of Germany. To the contrary, the major threat in Germany, according to Price, lay not in a potential shift to the left but a resurgence of Nazism. And the most powerful tool to prevent such a resurgence, he suggested, was not punishment as stipulated in JCS 1067, or Germany's economic dismemberment, as the French apparently advocated, but economic reconstruction coupled with positive and personal re-education.

Price's depiction of Germany was a far cry from the image of the fanatical, authoritarian Nazi state Americans had known during the war. Price's Germany consisted of victims rather than villains. As victims, all Germans, not only women and children, were in need of material aid and spiritual encouragement rather than punishment. This new image of Germany invited Americans to conceive of themselves increasingly as providers and role models rather than stern avengers. Price believed that the practices of thousands of soldiers in occupied Germany held more promise for Germany's democratic reorientation than any measures imposed by the punitive occupation directive. He proposed that more control should be placed in the hands of the Military Government to determine policies of denazification, democratization, and economic reconstruction.

Increasingly compassionate reports in the United States about hunger and material deprivations in Germany began to affect attitudes at home. While opposition to fraternization remained strong in the fall of 1945, some groups in the United States—especially those in the German-American community—began to press for relief efforts to Germany. The first organization to receive permission to provide aid to Germany was CRALOG (Council of Relief Agencies Licensed to Operate in Germany) in April 1946. Shortly afterward, in

June, the Co-Operative of American Remittances to Europe, better known as CARE, began operating in Germany. In 1946 CRALOG provided almost 10,000 tons of relief. In 1947, the figure had risen to 13,000 tons, and a year later relief peaked at 30,000 tons. CARE packages rose even more dramatically, from 320,000 packages in 1946 to almost 1.9 million a year later.[118] CARE enabled private citizens to donate relief packages to individual addresses in Europe. By 1947, sixty percent of all CARE packages went to Germany, suggesting a high level of personal connections matched by an equally high level of compassion toward Germans.[119] Americans of German descent often sent parcels to their relatives in Germany. Others sent relief packages to addresses provided by their friends and relatives who were stationed in Germany. GIs often connected potential donors with beneficiaries. This trans-Atlantic transfer of goods strengthened Americans' sense of themselves as providers for needy Germans.

The unofficial provision of food and material aid alleviated Germans' reservations about the presence of American troops on their soil. Although many continued to condemn relationships between women and GIs, they frantically searched for personal connections to Americans. The revival of correspondence with a "long-lost uncle" in America promised material relief. Beginning in November 1947, the International Red Cross in the American Zone offered to help Germans in their search for relatives in the United States.[120] Within a few months thousands of families requested the services. Family ties to the United States further strengthened the sense of cultural affinity between the two countries. Yet above all these connections promised material relief, the single most important incentive for Germans to reestablish contact with American relatives. By the same token, family ties to Germany became a major incentive for Americans to contribute to the German food relief.

Even though volunteer organizations donated food and other

essential goods at an unprecedented level, the food situation continued to deteriorate in the fall and winter of 1946–47. Fearing widespread starvation, General Lucius D. Clay, then deputy military governor of Germany, called on Washington to send relief supplies. As Price had done earlier, Clay linked his appeal for a more benevolent treatment of Germany to political goals. He later reasoned that "we could not hope to develop democracy on a starvation diet."[121] Clay found a welcome ally in former President Herbert Hoover. In early 1947, Hoover traveled to Germany and Austria as an envoy of the President to survey the food situation there. When Truman asked Hoover to make the trip he acknowledged that "a serious food situation still exists in certain areas, particularly those in Europe occupied by our forces and for which we therefore have a direct responsibility."[122] After visiting Germany, Hoover became convinced that American policy toward Germany had to become more supportive of economic reconstruction. General Clay recalled that during his visit Hoover, like Truman, believed "that there was no place for starvation where the American flag was flying and that with the raising of the flag we accepted the responsibility to maintain human values."[123] Upon his return, Hoover, like Price a year and a half earlier, stressed the need for economic reconstruction in Germany. Like Price he fused humanitarian concerns with practical ones, advocating increased production in Germany as a way "to relieve American and British taxpayers from their burden in preventing starvation in Germany."[124] Yet unlike Price, Hoover in early 1947 began to add the rhetoric of anti-communism to the humanitarian and practical arguments for economic recovery. By 1947, the cold war provided the final argument with which American military and political leaders could justify the policy change that political advisers like Byron Price had suggested as early as 1945.

Yet even within the increasingly tense environment of U.S.-Soviet relations, personal exposure to conditions Germany proved to be the most powerful argument in support of U.S. aid. Clay recalled receiving a skeptical delegation of Congressional representatives in 1947. The legislators had come to Germany to assess personally the needs of the German population. He remembered Representative John Taber as "a difficult man to convince when the appropriation of federal funds is involved. However, he listened attentively to our presentation, visited the Ruhr, and was convinced that our needs were authentic. He and his companions, Clarence Cannon and Richard B. Wigglesworth, returned home to support our program to the last penny." According to Clay the legislators "were touched by the conditions they saw and their post exchange rations usually found their way into the hands of German children." In order to underscore the urgency of U.S. aid Clay's remarks in his memoirs were accompanied by the photograph of an emaciated German child in a Berlin hospital. The caption read that this child was not expected to live.[125] By convincing the congressmen of Germany's physical devastation, Clay had cleared an important hurdle toward an official aid policy for Germany. The delegation's mission and Clay's assessment refute the dominant assumption that Congress agreed to aid Germany only as a means to fight communism. If Clay's recapitulation of the visit is correct, the congressmen searched for and found evidence of Germany's need rather than a communist threat. They apparently had already accepted America's responsibility to meet such a need, if it should exist. By 1947, then, Germany had, in the eyes of these policymakers, assumed the status of victim and the United States that of provider and protector.

Two years after the end of the war, most Americans conceived of Germany the way American soldiers had first viewed German women: as victims of the harsh material conditions brought about by the war. The hard-working self-sacrificing Trümmerfrauen, as the women who cleared away the rubble in the cities were called, became icons of postwar Germany's fate.[126] Americans began to treat them as victims, just as they treated Germany's former internal and external enemies as victims of Nazi brutality. Current conditions in Germany assumed a larger importance than former atrocities, thus spurring changes in American policy toward Germany. As a result, policy toward Germany came to differ little from other countries that had been U.S. allies during the war.

Germans fostered the image of themselves as victims of a harsh occupation policy and dependents of the United States. As they increasingly relied on American food relief, they also increasingly blamed the military government for shortages. An opinion survey by the ICD one year after the end of the war concluded that Germans expected the United States "to appear as a sort of political, economic and social Santa Claus."[127] As the food and fuel shortage worsened in the winter of 1946–47, Germans increasingly blamed the occupation troops for the situation.[128] The population adopted the role of a juvenile or feminine dependent to a parental or masculine provider. Germans had accepted their helplessness and transferred responsibilities to the occupation authorities.

The embrace of powerlessness went hand in hand with a pervasive mood of political apathy. Since the beginning of the occupation American officials complained about the lack of German participation in the political reconstruction of the American zone. Even before the first troops entered German territory, Americans anticipated difficulties concerning Germany's political reconstruction. *New York Times* correspondent James P. Warburg predicted that "we shall find the German people tired, sullen, and apathetic, more concerned with questions of food, clothing and shelter than with ideas of political reconstruction."[129] In the fall of 1945, Lewis F. Gittler of the Psychological Warfare Branch of the Army found "the same mood of selfishness and apathy" among the German people everywhere he went.[130] Material concerns thus appeared to overshadow any German interest in re-establishing a democratic system in their country.

Germans in fact increasingly made the material improvement of their lives a condition for political reform. This attitude became obvious at a press conference for the departing military governor McNarney in March 1947. German journalists bluntly asked the General whether the military government had realized how difficult it was to teach democracy to a starving people.[131] Apparently agreeing with the question's basic premise, McNarney assured the press that the United States and Great Britain were doing everything within their power to assure an improvement of the food situation. By linking their own democratization to the improvement of material conditions, Germans were able to gain some leverage in the reconstruction of their own country.

McNarney's reaction to the testy German question reflected the changes in the military government's assessment of its task in Germany since the end of the war. In 1945, he might have responded with a curt reminder that Germany's victims had suffered and were still suffering at least as much economic deprivation and that Germans themselves were to blame for their situation. By 1947, however, images of hungry, cold German women and children had overshadowed the aggressor-images of Nazi soldiers, increasingly pressing American officials into the roles of providers and protectors. What had begun as GIs' informal food aid to German women and children grew into an official program of American food and material aid and culminated in the Marshall Plan in 1947. At the same time, the military government issued a new occupation directive, JCS 1779, which emphasized German-American cooperation and economic reconstruction.[132] Both the Marshall Plan and JCS 1779 marked not only the beginning of a new policy direction for Americans but also the culmination of a cultural transformation of American-German relations that had begun with the first advance of American troops into German territory in the fall of 1944.

*   *   *

Within two years of the end of the war, American soldiers, Washington policymakers, and the American public had transformed their image of Germans from villains to victims. Fraternization played a crucial role in this transformation. For a short period in the immediate aftermath of the war, Americans saw in German women the embodiment of Germany's national fate.[133] The Trümmerfrau removed not only the visible reminders of the war from the urban landscape but also the image of the Nazi storm trooper from the American consciousness. With the onset of the cold war and growing anti-communism in the United States, Americans conceived of Germans as victims not only of material shortages but a looming communist takeover as well. By 1947 Americans had concluded that Germans no longer posed a threat to their European neighbors but instead required protection and guardianship. And the United States was eager to provide both.

The informal relationships between GIs and German civilians illuminate the social and cultural dimension of American postwar involvement in Germany. On its surface, fraternization appeared to have occurred outside the political realm of the occupation. Yet even if soldiers themselves conceived of their actions as apolitical, these actions nonetheless had far-reaching political consequences. The social interactions between Americans and Germans bridged the divide between politics and culture in postwar American-German relations.

CHAPTER 4

Selling Democracy
GIs and German Youth

"Youngsters," a U.S. military government report asserted in May 1946, "have become at the same time the hope and the problem of the German people." Arguing that juvenile delinquency threatened the already fragile social order in Germany, the report placed Germany's youth at the center of the country's political rehabilitation. "The treatment of this all-important age-group," the report continued, "will determine whether they will become the nucleus of a future nationalistic group 10, 15, or 20 years hence, or whether they will develop into the strong basis of a democratic and peaceful Germany."[1] The military government's increased focus on Germany's youth beginning in the spring of 1946 was indicative of a subtle shift in American occupation policy. It signaled the departure from the punitive policy of denazification and demobilization toward a rehabilitative policy that emphasized re-education and democratization.

German youth served a dual purpose in this process of rehabilitation. First, they promised the greatest success in the military government's re-education effort since young people were considered more receptive to new political and ideological concepts. Second, youth focused American attention on a part of the German population whom many already regarded as the victims of the regime and the war, thus facilitating a move toward a more compassionate and sympathetic approach to the occupation. German youth, like German women, thus formed an important pillar in the reformulation of America's image of postwar Germany.

The military government's concern for Germany's youth manifested itself above all in the creation in the spring of 1946 of the German Youth Activities (GYA), a program designed to bring together American GIs and German children in sports and recreational activities at specially created youth centers.[2] The direct American involvement in the re-education of Germany's youth reinforced the paternal role that American soldiers had already adopted toward German women. GIs who participated in the initiative increasingly assumed the role of Ersatz-fathers primarily to German boys just as they were assuming the role of Ersatz-husbands to the women they dated. Yet the GYA program went a step beyond the informal and initially illegal interactions between American men and German women by officially accepting, even encouraging fraternization, albeit in a highly structured environment and with a particular population group. By integrating fraternization into OMGUS's re-education program, military officials hoped to overcome the sexual connotations of the term.

The focus on the democratization of Germany's youth furthermore allowed the military government to reconcile one of the most profound paradoxes of its mission: how to impose democracy on another people through essentially undemocratic means. By concentrating on youth Americans were able to create an image of Germans as infantile citizens who had to be taught how to use the power of citizenship morally, responsibly, and democratically. Youth education could thus serve as a model for the democratization of the rest of the German population, turning Americans into schoolmasters and Germans into students of democracy.[3]

The metaphors of political infancy and maturity had already been used in classical political writing, such as Alexis de Toqueville's

Democracy in America. Toqueville warned that infantile citizenship could turn democracy into despotism when the leaders represent an "immense protective power which is alone responsible for securing [men's] enjoyment and watching over their fate. That power is absolute, thoughtful of detail, orderly, provident and gentle. It would resemble parental authority if, fatherlike, it tried to prepare its charges for a man's life, but on the contrary, it only tries to keep them in perpetual childhood."[4] Toqueville's observations had direct relevance for the American re-education mission in Germany. The objective of the German Youth Activities Program in particular was to prepare its overwhelmingly male charges for life as responsible citizens in a future democratic Germany. Yet at the same time the program's emphasis on material aid and recreational activities risked leaving these youth in what Toqueville termed "perpetual childhood." In other words, Americans in Germany walked a thin line between encouraging independent political thinking and perpetuating material dependence on the United States. The nature and reception of GYA, its effort to link material aid to the transmission of democratic values, illustrated the constant dilemma between the two poles.

Ironically, GI-youth interaction proved to be as difficult to control as the soldiers' interaction with German women during the fraternization ban. In fact, as had occurred during the battle over fraternization, GYA organizers often followed the soldiers' lead in the field. They increasingly justified the emphasis on material aid as a means toward the end of democratization. Yet while material aid entailed concrete practical results and could easily be measured, democratization remained a rather elusive goal whose success or failure was not immediately apparent.

* * *

In the eyes of American officials, the young generation was least responsible for Germany's aggressions but at the same time most in need of ideological re-orientation.[5] The early postwar period, however, saw more contradiction and confusion in the area of re-education policy than any other occupation policy. Early guidelines concentrated on negative measures, such as suspension of all teachers affiliated with the Nazi regime, removal of Nazi textbooks, and American control over the German educational system.[6] These measures removed one ideology without offering an alternative. Early on, officials largely relied on Germans to re-educate their youth. With non-fraternization as one of the occupation's central doctrines, American officials were reluctant to involve American servicemen directly in the process of Germany's ideological conversion.[7] Only after the dismantling of the fraternization ban did OMGUS actually acknowledge that American-German interaction could aid re-education (fig. 4.1). Yet it took until April 1946 for occupation officials to utilize it as a tool of re-education in the GYA program. The new program formed part of a general shift toward the exculpation of Germany's youth, which also included a general amnesty from the denazification procedures for anyone under twenty-seven years of age in June 1946.[8]

The inception of the youth activities program in April 1946 occurred at a time when the relationship among the occupying powers became increasingly volatile. In the previous month Winston Churchill had declared in Fulton, Missouri, that an "iron curtain" had descended across the European continent separating the East from the West.[9] Already by the fall of 1945 cooperation among the four powers in the Allied Control Council had become increasingly difficult. The French were the first to dig in their heels by refusing to agree on certain economic and reparations measures.[10] Yet by the beginning of 1946 the Soviets, too, became more intransigent. They were expanding their authority in Eastern Europe and tightened control over political institutions in their zone by forcing a merger between Social Democrats and Communists into the new Socialist

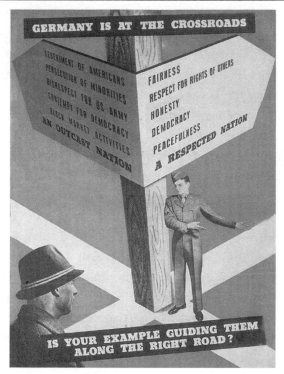

Fig. 4.1 The GI as re-educator. OMGUS poster undated. Bundesarchiv, Bild 4/4/10.

Unity Party (SED). While Americans were able to exert considerable pressure on the French, their relationship with the Soviet Union deteriorated, curtailing the chances of a unified allied policy toward Germany.

In addition, American policymakers were themselves becoming ambivalent about the desirability of a unified Germany. By the spring of 1946 they moved toward the economic consolidation of their zone with the British irrespective of French and Soviet objections.[11] Even though this consolidation signified the U.S. and British willingness to move toward unification it also decreased the

possibility of accommodations with France and particularly the Soviet Union, since the creation of the economic bizone followed the
western capitalist model rather than the state controlled socialist
model favored by the Soviets. The friction among the Allies and
mixed messages from Washington created some leeway for local
military administrators to chart an independent course for their
troops' role in Germany.[12]

Within this context of increasing estrangement among the Allies,
the German Youth Activities Program served as a testing ground for
the political merits of closer American-German cooperation, allowing soldiers to become more involved in Germany's social, cultural,
and political reconstruction. Occupation officials hoped that ordinary GIs could instill in German youth a new sense of purpose and
belief in democratic values.[13] With the creation of the youth program the military government also hoped to regain control over
fraternization by integrating it into the occupation's official agenda.
Between October 1945 and April 1946 the authorities' position had
thus moved from grudging acceptance of the existence of fraternization toward active encouragement of it in the field of youth
activities.

The transformation of American official attitudes proceeded in
stages. The first was the realization that juvenile delinquency was not
an exclusively German problem but one that hampered American
occupation goals in Germany as well. If Americans wanted to reform
German culture and society, they could not ignore the problems of
the nation's youth. The second stage marked the military government's realization that the corrective policy of terminating Nazi
youth groups needed a complementary policy of offering alternative
democratic institutions. The third stage marked the gradual acceptance of fraternization as a tool of re-education. Occupation officials thus adopted the position of several earlier critics of non-
fraternization, who had advocated the use of American soldiers as

"ambassadors of democracy."[14] Having been forced to accept the reality of fraternization, military officials were determined to turn its existence into an asset.

By the beginning of 1946 both Germans and Americans had grown alarmed about the dramatic increase in juvenile delinquency. They feared that the country's youth was sliding into moral decay and ideological nihilism.[15] A Munich newspaper article warned that the trend required special attention in the effort to reconstruct the German nation.[16] The traumatic experience of war, death, and forced relocation seemed to have driven many youths to the point where they believed in nothing and mistrusted everybody.

Homelessness, poverty, and the loss of one or both parents took a heavy toll on Germany's youth. Among the 15.5 million youth who by 1950 were twenty years old, 1.25 million had lost at least one parent. 250,000 had lost both parents. Over 1.5 million children were among the expellees from the eastern parts of Germany ceded to Poland and the Soviet Union, and 740,000 of those lived in temporary camps.[17] Many homeless and orphaned youngsters drifted among the occupation zones in search of relatives and better living conditions.

Indicative of their plight was the fate of a sixteen-year-old boy, identified only as A., whom the Munich police arrested in 1946 for stealing a jacket. His mother had died in an air raid in his hometown of Essen-Oberhausen two years earlier. His father had not returned from Russia. After his mother's death the boy lived with an aunt in Dortmund until German authorities evacuated him and other children to East Prussia to escape the advancing western front. In Danzig the army trained him as an assistant in the air force. Shortly afterward the Red Army captured him yet released him a few months after the war's end because of his young age. He made his way to Berlin where he searched for his married sister. Unable to find her house in the ruins of the city, he moved to Bavaria because, as he related to the Munich police, he had heard rumors that Bavaria had the highest food rations. Another juvenile delinquent, Anneliese E., seventeen, told the police after she was picked up that she had been held by three black GIs in a Villa outside Munich and raped repeatedly over the course of one week. She later recanted, admitting to having sought relationships with black GIs.[18]

Most homeless youth drifted toward metropolitan areas. Protected by the anonymity of large cities, teenage girls often resorted to prostitution in order to make a living. Others eked out a meager existence through petty theft and break-ins. Yet the largest source of income for these youth was the black market. Robert J. Havighurst, who visited Germany in the fall of 1947 for the Rockefeller Foundation, estimated that around 20,000 youth regularly engaged in black market activities.[19] In the early months of 1946 the Munich Juvenile Court handled over 700 criminal cases, most of them related to theft or black market activities.[20] The German prison system, overwhelmed by the high number of delinquents, did not have adequate facilities to house youth in separate correctional facilities. Three private organizations, the Verein Kinderschutz (children's protection agency), the katholische Jugendfürsorge (Catholic youth welfare), and the evangelische Jugendhilfe (Protestant youth aid), made initial attempts to stem the tide of criminality, yet their capacities were equally limited.[21] German institutions, themselves debilitated by the war, proved unable to cope with the crisis on their own.

German as well as American observers believed that the rise in juvenile delinquency and prostitution stemmed from a general decline in moral and ethical values within the young generation. The *Frankfurter Rundschau* warned that nihilistic tendencies were spreading among the nation's youth.[22] Even though the majority of youngsters had rejected the ideals of the Third Reich after its collapse, they also appeared to reject any democratic political ideals for the future. Tania Long of the *New York Times* warned that German youths were "floundering in a morass of hatred and cynicism."[23] Having fallen for a false ideology once, Germany's young generation seemed too disillusioned to accept another.

The complete lack of faith in politics posed enormous problems for the democratization of Germany's youth. How could American occupation officials convince these youngsters that their political promises deserved more trust than Hitler's did? Why would they rely on their former enemies if their own government had deceived them once so badly? Long noticed a decidedly negative attitude among the youths toward any idealistic concept. "We have been fooled once," she paraphrased their views, "if this democracy we hear so much about is the real thing, if it brings us work, food, comfortable living, and above all, security, well, then we'll support it. But, meanwhile, we'll wait and see."[24] According to this statement, material security rather than idealistic political concepts would provide the strongest incentive for the adoption of the American democratic way.

The military government only gradually assumed a role in the fight against juvenile delinquency and disillusionment. An early USFET (U.S. Forces European Theater) directive on youth activities merely established that German youth organizations had to gain approval of the U.S. Group Control Council before re-convening.[25] OMGUS eased regulations in October 1945 to give blanket approval for the formation of all independent non-military and non-fascist youth groups. The directive also encouraged the formation of youth committees in every district (Kreis) to coordinate activities.[26] The relaxation of restrictions revived many organizations that the Nazis had dissolved, such as the Boy Scouts, Protestant and Catholic youth groups, the YMCA, and the YWCA.

The October directive signaled a subtle shift in the military government's youth policy. Occupation officers had reached a consensus that re-education required the involvement of American forces in order to succeed. "The more thoughtful type of German youngster," a military government report noted, "looks anxiously, expectantly, sometimes even desperately, for a type of leadership that can teach new ideas and ideals." It would therefore be "the task of the Military government, of the occupation troops, and of the German civilian authorities and youth leaders to see that this vacuum is filled with constructive, positive, and democratic ideals in order to direct the youth of Germany toward a new future."[27] German children, the military government concluded, lacked leadership in two areas. First, the removal of Nazi leaders left a void in the administrative structure of youth activities. Second, the break-up of many families, compounded by the death of many fathers weakened parental guidance. Under the new program American GIs would help fill those voids.

It took until April 1946, however, for the military government to enlist officially the help of American troops in German youth affairs. Under the GYA program, "each major command is to appoint a mature officer to devote his entire time to liaison work with German youth agencies." Furthermore, "troops qualified to work with youth groups will assist the local youth committees and groups in the various ways that such committees may request."[28] Rather than relying on voluntary initiatives from various detachments in the zone, youth activities now became a regular full-time assignment for some GIs.

The new directive elevated to an official level what had already existed before, namely the informal interaction between American soldiers and German children. As with the fraternization controversy, occupation authorities adapted to a situation they could not change. Ever since they had set foot on German territory, American officers and GIs had interacted with German youth on a personal basis. "As much as you might hate the Nazis," Sergeant Giles explained, "you can't hold it against a bunch of innocent children. All of us give them candy and gum we get in rations and whatever else we can pick up."[29] As early as July 1945, however, a substantial number of GIs went beyond candy and gum to establish informal youth groups, organize sports activities, and sponsor other events. Those activities had taken place without official support and until October 1945 in violation of military government regulations.[30] The April 1946 directive thus merely resolved the discrepancy between official regulations and unofficial practice.

The creation of GYA followed practical considerations as well. The program marked a conscious effort to regain control over the process of interaction between Americans and Germans. The first Education & Religious Affairs report after GYA's inception acknowledged that these "youth activities gave an excellent opportunity for 'guided fraternization' in a constructive meaning of that ill-used term."[31] The military government embarked on a campaign to redefine the meaning of the term "fraternization" in an effort to redirect public attention away from American-German sexual relations toward less controversial forms of social interaction. American officials sought to re-invent "fraternization" as a concept denoting the inculcation of Germans with democratic values and thereby deemphasize its sexual connotations.

The earliest American efforts at youth re-education dated as far back as the war. The U.S. military launched the first such initiative at a special youth camp within the German POW camp at Compiegne in France. Boys between the ages of twelve and seventeen received lessons in arithmetic, biology, English, American history, geography, German reading and writing, and other subjects. The teachers were "carefully screened non-Nazi German prisoners of war."[32] Re-education efforts at Compiegne and elsewhere relied on German personnel rather than involving Americans directly. The GYA program differed from these earlier initiatives in two ways. First, it committed large contingents of American officers and troops, rather than Germans, to the task. Second, instead of lecturing youth on the benefits of democracy, GYA favored providing material aid and organizing physical activities such as the donation of athletic equipment, food, and toys, and the development of recreational programs. The shift in the curriculum away from ideological education toward social activities reflected the military government's increasing conviction that in the impoverished environment of postwar Germany, the physical well-being of children was a necessary prerequisite for the success of the re-education program.

German and American youth officials unequivocally confirmed their commitment to this approach at a conference in Wiesbaden in September 1947. Participants concluded that the goal of democratization "is more efficiently served by way of practical acting than by theoretic explanations of democratic principles and mere verbal instruction." Even though they acknowledged the need for ideological guidance, youth officials agreed that it should be limited "to presenting American ideology and the ways of American democracy so as to help German youths to develop their own form of democratic life." Material help, on the other hand, would be "bound to have a rather valuable moral effect."[33] Youth officials were determined to reform the nation's youth through practical aid rather than the moral force of the democratic message alone.

After observing the educational system in Germany for the Rockefeller Foundation, Robert J. Havighurst came to essentially the same conclusion. He asserted that the solution to the youth problem in Germany had to include above all "an economic improvement which offers some promise of a decent living in return for hard work." The creation of a "program of education for democracy in the schools and in adult organizations" should come second. Havighurst's third suggestion included an "immediate program of supplementation to family influences in the rearing of children, wherever family life has become inadequate."[34] This last point referred to the absence of fathers he had observed in many German families. He estimated that about a third of the younger school children were living without a father. Even though some of the fathers would eventually return from captivity, Havighurst saw this lack of paternal guidance as a problem, especially for boys. The GYA program appeared to implement all of Havighurst's requirements, even though the report itself makes no mention of it. It provided material aid to alleviate economic hardships; it created centers of re-education and democratization; and most importantly, it utilized young American GIs as surrogate fathers to the young boys who attended the program.

Athletics formed the biggest part of the American program. Beginning in the spring of 1946, the U.S. Army donated sports equipment and other surplus materials to German youth groups. In the month of May alone, the Bavarian Education & Religious Affairs Division turned over to youth groups several thousand skis, ski poles, jackets, trousers, knapsacks, bathing suits, belts, and 800 kilograms of leather for shoes. A report justified the transfer of goods by linking the widespread disillusionment and despair among the younger generation to the economic hardships in Germany. "The economic situation affects the population generally, and until it has been corrected for the country as a whole, it will not have been corrected for German youths."[35] Following the same pattern as the relaxation of the fraternization ban, Americans focused on material relief to children and youth before embarking on a general relief policy aimed at Germany.

Material assistance assumed priority throughout the American zone. In Berlin, troops released sports and camping equipment as well as opened playing fields and gymnasiums.[36] The military government of Württemberg-Baden underscored the centrality of "the role of the Army in providing material assistance to German youth."[37] As a result of U.S. Army donations, German athletic clubs, which had shut down operations toward the end of the war due to the shortage of sports equipment, were able to re-open. It would be years before German manufacturers would resume production of athletic equipment.[38]

Military officials saw material aid and recreational activities as the best vehicle toward the youth's democratization. Local organizers, who enjoyed a high level of autonomy in shaping youth activities, however, increasingly treated the material aspect of the program as an end in itself. Their emphasis on food and other material aid grew out of their daily experiences in the German communities. They witnessed all around them the vast differences between the German living conditions and their own. While GIs received a daily ration of 4,000 calories which included meat, vegetables, and sweets, the average German daily intake in the summer of 1946 amounted to less than 1,200 calories.[39] Begging children in front of PX stores served as especially powerful reminders of the inequities in living standards between Germans and Americans.[40] The distribution of food and material goods on occasions such as children's festivals served as much to alleviate the soldiers' latent unease about their privileged position as to show the benefits of the American way of life.

Even in the United States popular attention focused increasingly on the material deprivations of Germany's children. In early December 1946 a New York-based German language newspaper, the *Staatszeitung und Herold,* published an appeal to collect money for "the rescue of German children." The funds would be used to buy clothes, food, and medical supplies to be distributed to German welfare organizations under the auspices of CRALOG. The paper's campaign constituted the first private money drive for Germany officially sanctioned by the American Treasury Department. The *Staatszeitung* underscored the urgency of the need for help because "America's hopes for a democratic Reich are threatening to collapse because of the hunger of its people."[41] The paper, too, alluded to the reciprocity between democratization and material well-being. In fact, it suggested that democracy in Germany could thrive only if its citizens escaped material deprivations.

American involvement, however, went beyond material assistance to German children. GYA operatives launched an extensive effort to acquaint German children with American sports, above all baseball and football. The motivation behind this athletic re-education campaign was not solely based on offering youth an alternative to hanging out in the streets. Military officials saw a direct connection between America's athletic traditions and the American democratic spirit. James K. Pollock, special adviser to the American group in the Central Control Council, remarked on the educational potential of football in his diary. Upon watching a game in the Berlin Olympic Stadium in the fall of 1945, Pollock imagined "how the empty seats might have been filled with Germans who could have been given several good lessons arising out of the great American game." He later continued: "If the Germans could understand its contributions in giving us some qualities the Germans have always lacked, their younger generation might be improved. I wonder why we have not made an effort to explain football to the young Germans who seem to be eager to learn about American ways."[42] Pollock unfortunately did not specify which qualities football could teach Germans. Nevertheless, in all its vagueness, Pollock expressed a common American sentiment that would guide American youth officials in their design of the GYA program.

In their emphasis on the educational merits of athletic programs American occupation officials followed the lead of early twentieth-century education reformers in the United States. In 1911 Luther Halsey Gulick, a founder of the New York Public Schools' Athletic League, credited athletics, especially team sports, for developing "the idea of corporate, of inter-institutional morality." Athletic activities in an organized setting, advocates believed, would foster social cooperation, fairness, merit, and opportunity.[43] American re-education officials might have turned to baseball in particular because of its reputation for order, organization, and non-violence. Ronald Story argued that the sport appealed to young men in the latter half of the nineteenth century because it provided security and order in a period of "disorderly, destabilizing mobility and insubordination, particularly as evinced in the brawling cities and experienced by boys in the city streets."[44] American youth officials must have seen the situation of German boys in the early years in much the same way as observers of urban industrializing America in the second half of the nineteenth century. Whether or not baseball actually helped stabilize these youngsters or even gave them a glimpse of democratic culture in America remains questionable. American GIs might have resorted to the game as a way to provide a sense of security, stability, and familiarity for themselves in an otherwise chaotic and volatile foreign environment.

The Berlin detachment of the military government launched its sports campaign on 14 August, 1946 with a sector-wide sports day. American officers and enlisted men gathered on various playing fields to teach German children softball, football, volleyball, and other popular American sports. By organizing such a sports event, American officials hoped to attract enough youth to create competitive leagues and play on a regular basis. According to the American-sponsored German newspaper *Die Neue Zeitung*, German youth took up American games with enthusiasm.[45] The paper even published a series called "Little Course in Baseball" in order to familiarize young Germans with the sport (fig. 4.2).[46] Each article explained rules and techniques of pitching, catching, and batting but also took great pains to explain the history of the American ball game and its place in American national culture. A little prematurely, perhaps, the paper heralded baseball as the new German pastime. "Specially trained American servicemen," the article announced, "are in the

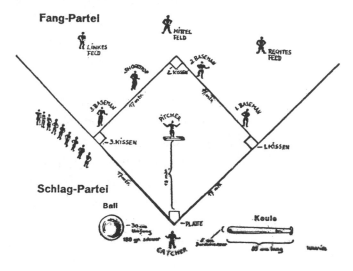

Fig. 4.2 Baseball instructions for German youth, *Die Neue Zeitung,* 1946.

process of letting the German youth in on the secrets of the new game."[47] There appeared to be no question in the author's mind about the future popularity of baseball and, by association, the success of the American way of life among German youngsters. Though more guarded than the *Neue Zeitung,* other German papers also reported on the popularity of baseball, suggesting that German children were eager to learn the American pastime.[48]

By the fall of 1946, American soldiers had formed youth baseball leagues all over the zone. In Berlin, the "Bears," "Tigers," and "Mickey Mäuse" regularly competed against each other. The city alone claimed 5,000 converts to the American national sport.[49] Even in smaller towns like Bad Kissingen near Frankfurt youth formed baseball teams under the guidance of American GIs. Equipped with bats and gloves donated by the Army, the *New York Times* reported, they "now frequently play teams from other towns in matches that have begun to steal the German crowd from the usual Sunday soccer games."[50] The competition between baseball and soccer for players and spectators served as a metaphor for the competition between American and German culture for the hearts and minds of the young generation.

U.S. organizers continuously stressed the correlation between American sports and democracy. According to one observer of the Bad Kissingen youth activities program, representatives of the U.S. Army hoped that teaching German children how to play baseball and football would "help replace militarism and racism with democratic ideals of peaceful fair play." Furthermore, they hoped that their "plan will make it less likely that there will be new generations of wistful young men on crutches throughout the world."[51] Ernest O. Hauser of the *Saturday Evening Post* also saw sports activities as the best tool of re-education. He observed that young people in Germany mistrusted every printed word as propaganda. Practical activities, like ball games, on the other hand could teach a valuable lesson in democracy. "If we can teach German kids how to take a beating and how to give a beating, we'll have got our money's worth."[52] American ball games had assumed the difficult task of teaching Germans about American democracy. The emphasis on these particular sports activities revealed the predominance of male youth in the re-education effort. Consistent with the wartime assumption that German men were primarily responsible for the atrocities of the Nazi regime and women were largely passive bystanders, Americans took for granted that German boys were in greater need of supervision and re-education than girls. They also expected to find the future leaders of a new Germany among the nation's male youth.

The enthusiasm with which the American media heralded the

victorious march of baseball and football through Germany stood in stark contrast to some comments by German participants in the program. Children often complained about the ethnocentric focus of the American sports program. An eleven-year-old boy from Bamberg in Bavaria complained that Americans were interested in showing German children only American sports. He charged that Americans "don't know anything about our own favorite game, soccer, only football, which is something completely different than soccer."[53] A sixteen-year-old girl from Bayreuth recalled that her brother, who for a short time had participated in the Army baseball program, was not enthusiastic about the game. The Army shortly afterward discontinued the practice in that area because of a lack of interest among the local youth.[54] These surveys indicated that the enthusiasm for baseball and football among German children was not as widespread as news reports would have their readers believe. The material advantages of joining American sports programs could not always overcome the cultural barrier that still separated U.S. soldiers from German children.

Criticism of the sports program came from other sources as well. A *New York Times* article in early 1947 mocked that "in the field of athletics, concentration appears to be principally on teaching the young Germans baseball, perhaps on the theory that if they learn the game popular in a democratic country they will become democratic."[55] Arthur Kahn, an occupation official, also questioned the effectiveness of the program. "In an almost desperate attempt to teach German children democracy, we put most of our emphasis on baseball, hoping for a carryover from baseball to politics. Despite our noble efforts (reinforced with Coca-Cola and chewing gum), German children still prefer soccer and cannot be considered democratized."[56]

Another criticism originated from the Soviet command in Germany. In September 1946 Soviet officials charged that through their athletic activities Americans were promoting the re-militarization of Germany's youth. They accused Americans of violating the inter-allied regulation prohibiting certain athletic disciplines as military training.[57] This regulation had referred primarily to such sports as parachuting and glider flying. Whether the Soviets feared the success of the program as a tool of re-education or were genuinely concerned about its military implications remains unclear. Yet their criticism also served as a reminder of the Nazi youth athletic programs that functioned to prepare the nation's youth for war. Among the Allied powers, the Soviet Union was the only one with a similarly activist approach to youth affairs. Like the United States, the Soviet Union saw the country's youth as the key to Germany's future ideological course. Both were also more determined than Britain and France to implant in Germany their respective ideological principles. In their occupation zone the Soviet Union created the Freie Deutsche Jugend (FDJ or Free German Youth) shortly after the termination of the Hitler Youth which became the official youth organ of the SED.[58]

The criticism of American journalists, German youth, and Soviet occupation officials exposed the shaky foundation on which the athletics-democracy link rested. Yet while the sports program's moral and ideological impact remained subject to vigorous debate, it succeeded in establishing a forum for interaction between occupiers and occupied. Through contacts on the playing field German children befriended American soldiers and became acquainted with American culture and customs. The influence was reciprocal, however, leading to a change in American perceptions about postwar Germany as well. These personal encounters further solidified the relationship between them as providers to dependents, teachers to students.

If military officials found it difficult to defend the athletic program as a tool of political re-education, they were on even shakier ground concerning the countless children's and youth festivals they organized in their zone. These special events included games and competitions as well as plenty of food and candy. The organizers accentuated charitable aspects above all else by showering participants with small presents, candy, and various other food items. The American initiative in this area further served to enunciate the primacy of material aid and the continued fuzziness of its political reorientation program.

The Coburg Kinderfest in July 1946 epitomized the recreational nature of the American efforts. In this northern Bavarian town, members of the Sixth Constabulary Squadron staged a festival for over 1,000 German boys and girls.[59] The soldiers began the day by chauffeuring the children around the city in Army jeeps. On the fair grounds the youngsters then competed in various games and received food as prizes. For their participation in the day's events the organizers rewarded them with chocolate bars and candy.[60] The event focused entirely on entertainment and food and resulted in little more than bringing American soldiers and German children together.

Americans organized similar youth events all over the occupation zone. The *Neue Zeitung* reported that soldiers in Berlin frequently organized youth events like the one in Coburg for the approximately 127,000 youth between the ages of ten and eighteen.[61] The Office of Military Government for Württemberg-Baden promoted youth activities in its region through booklets and brochures. The caption to a picture showing German children engaged in a potato-sack race read: "Into this merry picture stepped personnel of headquarters of OMG Württemberg-Baden with 750 candy bars and sundry other good things to the delight of 750 German children of Stuttgart and vicinity at the close of their one-month summer vacation." Besides handing out candy bars for the children American GIs also targeted parents by offering such prizes as soap and coffee.

Americans used all the modern trappings of advertising to sell their brand of consumer-democracy to the German people.[62] Yet rather than using ideas and ideals to sell a particular product, Americans used products to sell an idea.

According to the Education and Religious Affairs branch of the military government, these programs found great resonance among the population. A survey of cities in Northern Baden showed a dramatic increase in participation and spectatorship between December 1945 and the spring of 1946. In Karlsruhe the number of youth participants in sports activities rose from 1,300 to 31,700 by April 1946, and spectators rose from 21,000 to 131,400. Other youth activities attracted 4,000 participants in December 1945. By April of the next year that number had risen to 13,060 children. Those youth received instructions in a total of 590 classes. The report concluded that the figures in Karlsruhe and elsewhere indicated "not only a rising interest in sports activities, considerably above the normal increase to be expected with the improvement in weather during spring, but also a steady and enthusiastic growth of support given to leisure-time activities of every variety."[63] Whether the programs aided in the youth's re-education remained less clear.

American charity events culminated in a flood of aid parties during the 1946 holiday season. The outburst of generosity among soldiers coincided with a general shift in the Army youth assistance program. As the program became more established, GYA concentrated more on cultural and educational activities that could be carried out indoors. As part of the cultural program, Americans introduced German children to American holidays such as Halloween and Thanksgiving.[64] These holiday activities culminated in the organization of countless Christmas parties all across the zone in December 1946. According to a *New York Times* article, Christmas parties that year increased tenfold over the previous year, a powerful indicator of the increasing compassion among American service-

Fig. 4.3 An American Santa Claus comes to German children. Bundesarchiv, Bild 146/85/99/2.

men toward the German population but also of the support within the military government for the charitable contributions of the occupation forces. The article announced that American soldiers were planning to assume "the Santa Claus role" for approximately half a million German children. In order to be able to provide all those children with Christmas presents, organizers had collected money, toys, and candies from fellow GIs. They bought oranges, figs, and nuts in Italy; socks, handkerchiefs, and gloves in Belgium and Luxembourg; and children's shoes in Czechoslovakia. They sent home for small gifts, and even made toys themselves in Army workshops. PX stores set up boxes for donations of sweets and other foodstuffs.[65] The enthusiasm with which American soldiers played the Santa Claus role for German children epitomized the changing perceptions of their role in occupied Germany (fig. 4.3). They saw themselves no longer as occupiers of a hostile country but as paternal providers for a people ravaged by hunger and deprivations.

In the midst of the Christmas frenzy for German children, few heeded the fate of the children of displaced persons, the victims of the Nazi regime. The *New York Times* noted with alarm that only fourteen dollars had been collected for displaced persons' Christmas by mid December, noting that the neglect of DP children in occupied territory has "added a drop—rather more than a drop—of gall."[66] The previous year GI holiday parties and gift donations had benefited almost exclusively children of displaced persons. The radical shift in focus exposed the transformation of attitudes among GIs over the course of the year. The Christmas season in particular emphasized the common cultural and religious heritage of Christian Americans and Germans. Most of the displaced persons, on the other hand, were of Jewish heritage, exposing a deepening cultural gulf between most American soldiers and DPs.[67] As opportunities for interaction between young Germans and GIs increased, DPs remained ghettoized in camps and thus isolated from both the German population and the American occupation forces.

Opportunities for informal contacts multiplied as a growing number of American-operated youth centers opened their doors to German adolescents inviting them to join GIs in recreational activities, handicrafts, and casual conversations. Many of the 250 Army Officers and 600 enlisted men who worked full-time for the GYA Program staffed these community centers and provided the physical environment for informal interaction and potential re-education.[68] The youth centers soon became popular meeting places for young Germans. In the fall of 1946, the Education & Religious Affairs Division of Berlin-Zehlendorf donated a house for the exclusive use of 800 registered members of the Klub der Jugend (Club of the Youth). The fourteen rooms of the villa included a workshop in the basement, a photo lab, a reading room stacked with American newspapers and magazines, and a music room with a piano, record player, and American records. Members of the club could sign up for English-language classes and twice a month the club organized dances for the general public. A reporter of the local *Tagesspiegel* observed that most of the children preferred to spend their entire free time in the clubhouse, less because they enjoyed the programs offered by the American GIs, but because "at home it is cold and dark anyway."[69] Thus, even as Americans were emphasizing educational over material aspects of their youth program, they continued to attract German youngsters primarily for material benefits, including such basic amenities as heat and electricity.

Most of the youth centers opened their doors only to a preselected group of children. In Zehlendorf, young people had to become members of the Klub der Jugend before they could use the facilities. In Vegesack, near Bremen, children also had to be affiliated with one of the registered local youth organizations to gain access to the youth center.[70] In Bremen, Army Sergeant Patrick J. Moriarty organized the "Bremen Boys Club" by choosing 165 out of a pool of 7,000 boys who applied for membership (fig. 4.4). In addition to food and a warm place to stay the club offered lessons in democracy. Moriarty had developed an elaborate concept of self government in which members elected their own officers, drew up a constitution, conducted open debates, and decided on all their activities in democratic fashion. In an interview with *Life* magazine, Moriarty acknowledged that many of the boys joined the club because of its material benefits, but he insisted that they stayed because "they are learning to like these strange new democratic ways.[71] Moriarty's club offered not only exercises in democracy but games, recreational activities, and occasional dances to which girls could be invited as well. According to the article, Moriarty and his staff blended educational with recreational activities to keep the youth engaged. Considering the total number of about 64,000 youth in the Bremen Enclave, however, the club's impact on the re-education of the city's youth appeared minimal.[72]

Fig. 4.4 Sergeant Moriarty and members of his boys club in Bremen. Walter Sanders/TimePix.

Sergeant Moriarty received additional publicity through his father, Joseph, a judge of the Eighth Judicial District of Minnesota. The elder Moriarty, who had ties to the Washington political establishment, visited Germany in early 1948 to survey conditions there. He made a passionate plea in a letter to President Truman to extend the "financial and moral support" to the youth activities program, "which it is entitled to. This institution," he continued, referring to the GYA, "must be established on a sound basis entirely under the Army or as a separate unit of the Department of State, with proper facilities for full-scale operation with trained and competent personnel and adequate financial support and without delay, or America will lose one of its greatest means to elevate Germany to a truly democratic nation."[73] By 1948, Germany's youth was commanding the attention of Washington policymakers, assuming center stage in the program of the country's process of political and moral rehabilitation. By 1948, too, Germany's political recovery became increasingly bound up with the growing anti-communist sentiment spreading in the United States. Moriarty himself invested considerable space on the topic of communism in Germany in his letter to the President, arguing that Germany held a central role in the balance between American democracy and Russian communism. "The movements of Germany," he warned, "are and will be a determining factor in throwing the balance to one end or the other, and such shifting in all probability may determine the future fate of civilization."[74] The American GIs who worked with Germany's youth, like his son, in Moriarty's eyes, thus performed an invaluable service in saving not just German but world civilization.

Most of the American youth clubs catered to boys, perhaps in an effort to obviate the charge of facilitating sexual liaisons between GIs and young German girls through the youth program. German parents, too, were understandably reluctant to let their teenage daughters join American-sponsored activities. The arrival in late 1946 of female dependents in the American zone, however, offered the opportunity for a separate girls' division of the youth activities program. Together with members of the Women's Army Corps (WAC) these women became instrumental in creating a female youth affairs program. By the spring of 1947 OMGUS had appointed a member of WAC to almost all GYA staff in the zone.[75] In May 1947, 250 women attended the first zone-wide training conference in Berlin. According to a military report, the average monthly participation of female dependents in youth activities between May 1947 and April 1948 was about a thousand, led by thirty-two full-time WAC officers. The agenda of the female volunteer section of the GYA included activities such as sewing, handicraft, music, dancing, home nursing, and discussions.[76] With the exception of discussions, all activities reinforced female behavioral and work patterns. The American assistance program for girls thus did little to diminish the inequality between the sexes within German society. To the contrary, it prepared girls for lives as housewives and mothers, a prospect that could not materialize for all of them in light of the female surplus in the German population.

Only few female versions of the boys' clubs emerged in the American zone. One example was the "friendship house" in Munich. A personnel officer of the American general consulate, Julia M. Curry, had selected twenty American and sixty German women between the ages of sixteen and twenty-five to participate in her club. The group's primary agenda was to increase the cultural understanding between Americans and Germans and to provide a "good time" for its members. In fact, according to a 1949 article in a German youth magazine, the girls did not intend to solve the ominous problems of this world but instead "wanted to be together what they most like to be: happy young girls with the heart in the right place."[77] The article further stressed the remarkable similarities between American and German girls: "It is simply impossible to separate the Germans from the Americans among all the cheerful civilians. Once the dividing uniform disappears, one thing becomes clear: young girls are alike in all nations."[78] The club's avoidance of any political discussion of the Nazi past or Germany's progress toward democracy not only underscored the dominant assumption in both countries that women's realm was outside the political sphere but also allowed the participants to level all differences between their respective cultures, celebrating an international "girl-culture" rather than showcasing their national differences.

When the GYA Program celebrated its third anniversary in April 1949, one month before the end of the military occupation and the creation of the Federal Republic, it pointed to some impressive statistics. American officials had blanketed the American zone with youth centers. An estimated 600,000 German youths were using these facilities each month; 275 military personnel and 1,000 trained German employees worked full-time, and about 1,500 military and civilian personnel worked voluntarily with the youngsters in 300 youth centers. Membership in the U.S. zone, according to GYA records had risen from 200,000 in its first year to almost 1.4 million. This did not necessarily mean that 1.4 million German children participated in the activities since youth might have held dual or multiple memberships in various activities. Nonetheless, German youth were actively participating in American sports, went to summer camps, played with toys donated by American GIs, and congregated in buildings requisitioned by the military government.[79]

Yet it remained doubtful whether these activities had any impact on the participants' ideological disposition. For one thing, the GYA program both assisted and competed for the youth's attention with several indigenous youth programs that re-emerged after the war. Two years after V-E Day approximately thirty-nine percent of the 2.3 million youth in the American occupation zone, including Berlin and Bremen, were organized in youth groups. By far the greatest number of these youth, about forty percent, were affiliated with church groups. Another thirty-two percent belonged to German athletic clubs.[80] The only advantage GYA had over these groups was its superior material resources. German athletic clubs especially lacked equipment. Although the military provided material for some of these clubs on a loan basis, it transferred most of the equipment and space to GYA for the creation of separate athletic programs.[81] By keeping German sports clubs short on equipment, Americans hoped to attract more children to their own activities.

Despite the material advantage, the youth program had difficulty gaining recognition among German youngsters. Not even half the zone's youth knew about the program and even fewer participated. An April 1947 poll by the Opinion Surveys Branch of the OMGUS Information Control Division (ICD) found that among 1,000 German youth between ten and eighteen years of age, only forty-three percent were aware of the existence of GYA.[82] In the four cities covered by the survey—Frankfurt, Kassel, Heidelberg, and Munich—less than twelve percent were well informed about the program. Another thirty-two percent had heard something but not much about GYA. When asked whether they had taken part in any of the GYA activities even fewer children answered affirmatively. In all cities more boys than girls had participated.[83] This lack of awareness of the program's existence inhibited the success of the GYA mission from the outset.

Most children who participated in the activities of the youth program openly admitted that they did so for "bread and circuses." The survey found that forty percent of program participants attended because of candy and food. Sports and games came in second with twenty-six percent. Almost as many youth, about twenty-three percent, participated in the program in order to show Americans "what Germans really were like."[84] Only a little more than six percent of the children referred to the chance to learn about democracy as the main reason for attending. These results must not have come as a surprise to officials who sought to court youth precisely through material allurements.

The children's overall evaluation of the program varied greatly among the four cities that took part in the survey.[85] These differences can in part be attributed to local variations in the youth programs but also to the differences in material conditions in these cities. Food, fuel, and housing shortages plagued citizens of Frankfurt more than Munich or smaller cities like Heidelberg and Kassel. Poor living conditions increased the likelihood that these children would look to Americans for relief. Thus, refugee children and those of lower class background were more likely to support the GYA program than middle and upper class youth. Religion also played a role: Catholic areas appeared to be less supportive of the American youth activities than Protestant.[86] In conversations with nine girls and six boys between the ages of eight and eighteen in Frankfurt, ICD interviewers found that most youths wanted Americans to help them with some form of material aid such as clothes, shoes, food, and toys.[87] The fact that at the time of the interviews Germany was experiencing one of the coldest winters in its history probably made the need for material aid even more urgent. Yet even in areas less affected by wartime destruction youngsters attached practical rather than ideological meaning to the existence of the American youth program.

The goal of democratization was not completely lost on the children who participated in the youth program. A military government survey in the Bavarian town of Gunzenhausen, southeast of Nuremberg, asked twelve children what, in their opinion, the Americans expected from the youth program.[88] Four of them answered that Americans wanted to educate German children in the democratic mold. Another two assumed that they wanted to win over the German children. One child asserted that Americans wanted to create cannon fodder against communism, another that they wanted to bring the children together, whereas four had no opinion. While not exactly representative, the survey indicated at least some awareness of the program's intentions.

Democratization obviously was far more important to the military government than to the program's participants. Indeed, considering the fact that between eighty-seven and ninety percent of the

German youth in the American zone never took part in any of the activities, the GYA program's contribution to the democratization of the German youth was negligible. Yet among those who did participate, most acknowledged to Army interviewers that they had gained a better understanding of democracy after attending American youth activities.[89] However, the Army survey failed to define the term "democracy" for the children, leaving wide room for personal interpretation. In addition, because most participants knew about the American goal of democratization, many likely told the interrogators what they thought they wanted to hear.

To the extent that the program shaped children's ideas about democracy, its emphasis on material aspects made them more likely to associate democracy with attributes like prosperity, abundance, and recreation than freedom and self-government. The youth's conflation of democracy with materialism was actually not too far removed from American postwar postulations about the meaning of democracy. Even though most Americans, when asked, might have defined it in abstract terms such as liberty and self-government, they saw capitalism and consumerism as concrete manifestations of democracy. In fact, by 1950, anti-communists in the United States openly hailed American consumer capitalism as the ultimate expression of freedom and juxtaposed it with the material deprivations in communist regimes. Young Germans conceptualized democracy and freedom in exactly those material terms—by contrasting the practical benefits of the American youth activities with what their compatriots in the East found under communism.

While German children embraced GYA for its material benefits, their parents approved of it for its discipline. Neither valued democratization as a particularly important part of the program. An extensive 1946 Army survey, in which trained German interviewers questioned 3,400 persons in 175 localities, revealed that among parents and guardians of children eighteen years of age and under, fifty-four percent had a favorable opinion of the GYA program and would permit their children to participate. Among the well educated, the figure was eighty-four percent.[90] Most parents liked the program because it kept children off the streets and gave them something to do in their spare time. This concern reflected one of the most imminent problems parents faced in the early postwar years: most able-bodied adults were required to work outside the home leaving children without adequate parental supervision after school. The prospect of outside adult supervision appealed to parents particularly in light of the rising rate of juvenile delinquency. Understandably, perhaps, most adults viewed criminal actions of the young as a far more pressing issue than their political reorientation.[91]

Parents' faith in the American ability to supervise their children was not universal. In Gunzenhausen in early 1947, five out of twelve parents would not let their children attend any GYA events. Only one of the five, however, had reservations directly related to the American sponsorship of the activities, noting that "I want to keep the children at home because he [the American] is still the enemy."[92] The others objected to any form of organized youth activities that removed the children from parental control. The discrepancies among the various surveys might have been the result of uneven profiles of the parents questioned. Small towns like Gunzenhausen had fewer problems with juvenile delinquency than metropolitan areas. In addition, women in rural areas faced less pressure to work outside the home because food provisions were better and the level of destruction was far less severe than in major metropolitan centers. In rural Catholic Bavaria, church officials were particularly inclined to register public disapproval of GYA. Some saw the program as an unwelcome competition for their own youth groups, others objected to the activities themselves, especially those that did not separate the sexes.[93] In general, Germans appeared to be most open to American efforts wherever occupiers filled a vacuum in their own social structure and more likely to reject them if no such vacuum existed, or if the activities undermined established local social codes of behavior.

Among those most likely to welcome the youth activities were single mothers of adolescent boys. Many of them saw the program as a way to compensate for the lack of paternal discipline and guidance in the home. Mothers hoped that GIs could discipline the boys, engage them in ball games, and teach them practical and technical skills. A widow and mother of four in Bayreuth whose husband had died in the war appreciated the youth program as a meaningful way for her children to spend their free time. She worried that she could not keep her three sons, ages eight, thirteen, and fifteen, and her ten-year-old daughter off the streets and out of mischief's way. She hoped that the American program would turn the children into diligent and upright citizens, "contrary to the youth education of the Nazi period."[94] For many single parents the youth activities program thus complemented, if not replaced, parental supervision.

Germans accepted the American youth activities because of their usefulness for German purposes, not so much because they intended to change radically the social structure of their society but because they hoped that the American youth program could help them regain control over their children and bring order and stability into their lives. One Bayreuth mother articulated a common concern when she expressed the hope that the American youth program would not "alienate the children from their parents as during the Nazi period, but teach them obedience toward their elders."[95] This view was reminiscent of a Wilhelmine ethic of authoritarian education rather than an American model of democratic guidance.[96] The American military, ironically, was more likely to encourage than alleviate those tendencies within the German population since it was organized along hierarchical lines with an emphasis on obedience toward military superiors.

To the dismay of both German and American juvenile supervisors, the American influence on German youth was most striking in an area not particularly fostered by either of them: American popular music, dance, and movies. Jazz in particular found a receptive audience among Germany's youth, continuing a trend begun in the Weimar period. Young Germans saw jazz not only as a way to relate to postwar American popular culture but also as an opportunity to connect to the German cultural vivacity of the Weimar Republic.[97]

Since Nazi officials had been only partially successful in suppressing jazz, a skeletal network of jazz clubs and fans remained in place ready to revive the jazz scene after the war. During the occupation, however, white American youth officials and cultural diplomats were reluctant to advance jazz as an American cultural icon, because of its African-American roots.[98] Officials therefore faced the dilemma of witnessing the adoption among young Germans of a part of American popular culture they did not necessarily want to export. Yet they had little recourse in suppressing this trend because American GIs themselves demanded to hear jazz and swing on American Forces Network programs and in Army dance clubs. Half a decade before the emergence of rock'n'roll as the quintessential music of youth, jazz set the stage for the creation of a separate youth culture that transcended national boundaries. For young Germans, the wholesale or even partial adoption of an international youth culture offered an escape from the burdens of the Nazi past. Age would thus become a more important factor than nationality in defining their cultural and social identity.

In the dismal physical environment of the early postwar period, young Germans appeared to have an almost insatiable appetite for popular entertainment and music. Heinrich Küpffer, a young student in the American zone right after the war, remembered that swing and its successors jitterbug and boogie-woogie dominated

German dance floors.[99] New jazz clubs organized performances, sold records, and offered fans a forum for discussion. Küpffer remembered the proliferation of jam sessions and the occasional performance of famous Big Bands and musicians, among them Louis Mitchell's Jazz Kings, Duke Ellington, Louis Armstrong, and Cab Calloway.[100]

While AFN blanketed the American zone with the sound of American jazz, American cultural officials tried to introduce German audiences to American "high culture." Steeped in the European cultural tradition, these officials tried to popularize such composers as Aaron Copland and Samuel Barber, albeit with only limited success. They had to compete for audiences with a strong European classical contingent of composers like Beethoven, Mozart, and Schubert. Jazz, swing, and the American musical, on the other hand, filled a niche in the postwar music scene by appealing to a younger generation of music fans, who especially in Germany, were eager for a radical break with their country's cultural traditions.[101]

Like popular music, American motion pictures also enjoyed wide popularity among young Germans after the war. While they had been a formidable presence in Europe in the interwar period, the physical destruction of movie studios in France and Germany combined with the censorship of German filmmakers, afforded American producers the opportunity to sweep the European market. American Information Control officers were eager to utilize film as a tool of re-education since film was arguably the most powerful medium by which Americans could shape foreign perceptions about their own culture and society. Yet this power did not necessarily work in the producers' favor since occupation officials were interested in projecting a particular image of the United States abroad. They placed tight controls on the release of U.S. productions to German audiences, banning a number of motion pictures that presented the United States in a less than favorable light. Among the censored films were ones about the depression such as *The Grapes of Wrath*, gangster films like *Key Largo*, and even such blockbusters as *Casablanca*.[102] Despite these restrictions, American movies provided a major part of German youth entertainment in the postwar period and contributed significantly to the shaping of their image of the United States.

The embrace of American popular culture products represented as much a symbolic break with the Nazi past as an embrace of American values and ideology. Young Germans used American music and dance as a vehicle to distance themselves from the traditional culture of their elders, and at the same time to reach beyond the national confines of their own country toward an international community of youth. If not as a means to democratize Germany's youth, American popular culture succeeded at least in reopening the dialogue between young people in the United States and Germany.

*   *   *

The success of jazz and the failure of baseball in Germany demonstrated that Americans could not dictate which aspects of American popular culture Germans would adopt or how they would integrate them into their own cultural framework. Popular music and mass entertainment found a niche in the German cultural spectrum and therefore enjoyed wide popularity. Baseball, on the other hand, had to compete with the indigenous game of soccer which already accomplished for German boys what baseball promised. Acceptance or rejection of American cultural artifacts, customs, or institutions thus followed its own dynamic, regardless of American occupation policies. The GYA program thus succeeded best in areas where it filled a vacuum in the children's social environment.

Because GYA officials so closely hinged the re-education effort to the economic assistance program, they fostered the image among young Germans of the United States as a prosperous and materialist country. For Germany's youth, democracy and materialism were inextricably linked. By rejecting the traditional ideologies of right and left and instead choosing material recovery and economic prosperity as the new political pillars of postwar Germany, these youth appeared to have captured, maybe even defined Germany's postwar spirit.

But the GYA program accomplished more than instilling in German children an image of American wealth and abundance. It also laid the groundwork for at least the exposure to American culture by creating a forum of interaction between young Germans and American GIs. American soldiers came away from this interaction with a new definition of their relationship toward postwar Germany. They saw themselves increasingly as providers and protectors, as surrogate fathers to stranded German boys just as they had become surrogate husbands to German women.

German children even more than women invited the image of Germans as victims rather than villains. Youth were innocent as well as malleable. The American focus on Germany's youth helped in overcoming the negative image of the Nazi past and directing attention instead to their postwar plight and their potential for rehabilitation and renewal. The extent to which Americans had internalized the victim image of Germany's youth is illustrated by the recollections of Doris K., a young woman born in 1924 who had been an ardent supporter of Nazism to the end of the war. When she appeared before a Jewish-American occupation official for her denazification hearings he released her with the words: "The worst crime was committed on us, but the second worst crime was committed on you."[103] Her youth—she was nine when Hitler came to power—fostered in him an image of victimhood despite clear evidence of her participation in and support for the Nazi state. Even though she admitted to having been an ardent believer in Nazism he saw her as an innocent and naive victim of Nazi propaganda, lifting the terrible burden of complicity off her shoulders for the sole reason of her youth during the Nazi era.

Germany's postwar rehabilitation could work, however, only if the process of democratic maturation worked. The ideological aspects of the GYA program were designed to accomplish just that. By teaching young boys to assume the role of decision-makers in a democratic Germany while teaching girls to assume responsibilities as mothers and wives in democratic households, Americans projected their own postwar model of an ideal society onto Germany. Just as conservatives in the United States pushed men to reassert their roles as father figures and breadwinners and encouraged women to leave the workforce for more traditional duties as mothers and housewives, so too did American GIs in Germany assume the roles of surrogate fathers and breadwinners for a dependent population.[104] For the time being, this postwar social model created a sense of security and order in a world of chaos and uncertainty.

CHAPTER 5

Forging a Consensus
Americans, Germans, and the Berlin Airlift

On a Saturday in the early summer of 1948, the commandant of the American sector of Berlin, Colonel Frank Howley, received a visit from his medical officer who reported that the Russians had cut off the milk supply to the western sectors. The embargo followed the Colonel's earlier refusal to give in to the Soviet demand that western trucks pick up the milk directly from the East Berlin farms rather than having it delivered to the sector border, as had been the custom from the beginning of the occupation. "Unless we get that fresh milk," the medical officer warned, "six thousand German babies in our sector will be dead by Monday." Howley later recalled that "the news appalled me. I am a family man and I could share the anguish of the German mothers and fathers who were faced with this dreadful calamity. As commandant of the American sector of Berlin I could not let this happen."[1]

At the time he grudgingly gave in to the Russian demands, Howley wrote, but when the blockade started a few weeks later he was prepared. "No longer were the German babies in my sector in danger. I had brought in 200 tons of condensed milk and 150 tons of powdered milk. When the Russians screamed to German mothers over the radio that the Americans couldn't feed their babies, I fought back over the air and in the newspapers with a special formula using prepared milk as a substitute for fresh milk. Not one of *my* babies died!"[2] By focusing on the plight of West Berlin's infants, Howley magnified the vulnerability of the population, the ruthlessness of the Soviet action, and his own assumed role as a father figure not only for the babies of the western sectors but for the population as a whole.

Howley's recollection illustrates the larger significance of the airlift for the changing relationship between Germans and Americans. The massive transport of vital goods into Berlin over an eleven-month period consolidated American images of themselves as providers and protectors of victimized Germans. What had begun in the fall of 1944 as a punitive occupation of an enemy country had by 1948 turned into a protective occupation of a dependent people. Germans, too, saw the airlift as an expression of their changed relationship with Americans. Material aid, particularly food, had been a central element of that relationship from the earliest encounters. The image of soldiers giving candy, especially chocolate, to German youngsters had become as much a staple of German recollections about American GIs as the reception of CARE packages from the United States. With the airlift these informal charities turned into a massive relief effort that sustained the viability of the entire population of West Berlin.

For eleven months hundreds of U.S. C-47s and C-54s and British cargo planes brought vital material, including food, clothing, coal, and medical supplies, from five airports in the western zones through three air corridors, each twenty miles wide, to three airports in West Berlin (fig. 5.1). Military officials had calculated that in order to sustain the population, planes had to carry a minimum of 4,000 tons of material a day. By December the daily average exceeded 4,500 tons. In April 1949, "Operation Vittles" reached its peak capacity by flying 13,000 tons of material into Berlin within a twenty-four hour period

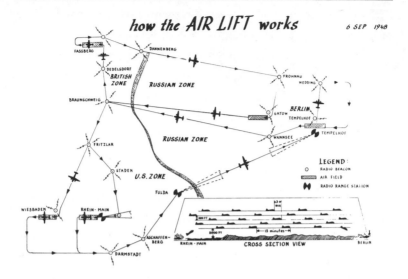

Fig. 5.1 The Airlift in operation. Photo: Landesbildstelle Berlin.

(fig. 5.2).[3] This dramatic undertaking more than anything illustrated the swiftness and extent of Germany's political rapprochement with the United States.

The story of the Berlin airlift has usually been told within the framework of the deteriorating relations between the United States and the Soviet Union. The 1948–49 showdown over the city was the first serious conflict of the cold war. The American defense of the city, cold war historians asserted, formed part of the U.S. commitment to the containment of the Soviet Union. West Berlin was the prize the Soviet Union wanted to extract from the West in exchange for the creation of a separate West German state, a prize the United States was unwilling to relinquish. Germany served as the locus for the unfolding of the great power rivalry.[4]

Yet in the context of the previous four years of informal and formal American-German rapprochement, the Berlin airlift emerges as a very different story, one that moves the relationship between

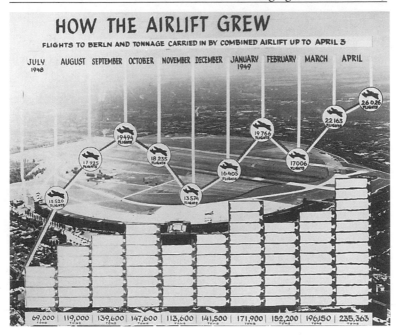

Fig. 5.2 Monthly Airlift deliveries. Photo: Landesbildstelle Berlin.

Americans and Germans to center stage. While the change of focus does not negate the traditional cold war interpretation of the Berlin crisis, it highlights the cultural environment in which the cold war unfolded. The Soviet threat to West Berlin did not change the U.S.-German relationship but allowed both countries to redefine it as a geo-strategic necessity. The Soviet threat was a justification rather than the cause of the changed relationship. Germans used it to distance themselves from the legacy of the Nazi crimes and to re-invent themselves as victims not only of harsh material circumstances but also of a possible communist takeover. Americans used it to justify their embrace of postwar Germany and legitimize the program of democratization. American-German relations improved not just because by 1947 Americans saw the Soviet Union as the greater evil but because Americans and Germans had reached a consensus over the meaning of their relationship. In the economic realm they agreed on the central importance of consumer-capitalism for Germany's democratization. In the cultural realm, they both accepted the transformation of America's role from conqueror to protector and provider and Germany's role from aggressor to victim. In the political realm they achieved a mutual understanding, despite evidence to the contrary, that the process of Germany's political rehabilitation was complete. The airlift brought together these disparate strands of the consensus by deflecting German and American attention away from Germany's Nazi past toward an anti-communist future.

* * *

At the core of the Berlin crisis of 1948 lay the nexus between economics and political reform. In their own zone of occupation, American military officials had for some time operated on the premise that Germany's political democratization was intricately interwoven with its economic recovery. As a result they increasingly emphasized both material relief and the revitalization of German industry as key pillars of Germany's political re-orientation.[5] But more than an economic means to a political end, Americans regarded the revival of a consumer capitalist economy as an essential component of the American system of democracy. The creation of the bizone in 1946, which united the economies of the British and American zone; the adjustment of the level of industry plan, which raised production in the western zones to much higher levels than had been agreed upon by the four occupation powers in 1945; and the Marshall Plan in 1947, all paved the way for the emergence of a consumer-capitalist society in western Germany.[6]

The most important step, however, came with the currency reform of 20 June 1948 in the three western zones of Germany. The new German Mark promised financial stability, renewed competitiveness in the international market, and the prospect of prosperity modeled after that of the United States.[7] It also promised to integrate Germany's economy firmly into the western capitalist market economy, thus further diminishing Soviet control over the country's economic and political destiny. The western Allies' currency reform in their zones both aided West Germany's unification and accelerated its partition from the Soviet zone. As it consolidated and revived the economy of western Germany, it destroyed any prospect of unity with the eastern zone.

The economic plans of the three western powers were antithetical to those of the Soviet Union, which envisioned an economic system based on centralized control and government planning. More importantly, the Soviets shared with the French the concern that a re-unified and economically powerful Germany could again pose a military threat to the rest of Europe.[8] France had refused to join the Anglo-American economic union in 1946 and agreed to participate in the currency reform only under pressure and at the last moment.[9] While the United States was able to bring France in line with its policies—largely because of its strong economic leverage—the Soviet Union was determined to follow a different course.

The western Allies' decision to introduce a new currency also exposed the precarious status of Berlin. Because goods and currency flowed freely among the various sectors of Berlin, a new currency in the three western sectors would inevitably affect the eastern part of the city and the surrounding Soviet zone. The geographic location of Berlin in the middle of the Soviet zone ensured that the two opposing economic systems would clash. By the spring of 1948, efforts by the Allied Control Council to come to an agreement over the currency issue had failed.[10] While American policymakers insisted on introducing the Deutsche Mark (D-Mark) in the western part of Germany, they realized that its distribution in Berlin would force the Soviet Union to respond since the D-Mark would undermine Soviet economic and political authority in East Germany.[11] Americans faced a precarious dilemma between ensuring West Berlin's economic and financial integration into West Germany and maintaining a working relationship with the Soviet Union. They ultimately opted for the former.

Initially western occupation officials were willing to heed Soviet reservations and exclude West Berlin from the currency reform. Yet even this small gesture of compromise toward the Soviet Union incurred vigorous opposition from Berlin community leaders. Ernst Reuter, the designated Social Democratic mayor of the city, argued that the currency reform in the western zones would only prompt the Soviets to carry out their own reform in the eastern zone.[12] He was sure they would include Berlin thus forcing the western sectors into the economic orbit of the Soviet zone.[13] Even though Reuter was aware that the introduction of a separate currency in West and East Berlin would effectively doom the unity of the city, he strongly supported it because, as he asserted, those who have the currency have the power.[14] In 1945 this kind of statement would have elicited concern among the Allies, but in the tense atmosphere of the summer of 1948 Americans were more likely to interpret Reuter's quest for "power" as a positive sign of his commitment to western economic and political integration. Reuter calculated correctly that inclusion in the western currency reform not only guaranteed West Berlin's participation in the western zones' economic revival but also committed the western Allies to stay in West Berlin.

Reuter's view was noteworthy considering his personal history as a former communist who had spent time in the Soviet Union after World War I. He had been one of the founding members of the German Communist Party but moved to the SPD in 1922. After his return from exile in Turkey after World War II, he became one of the strongest critics of Soviet policy in Germany. The Soviets, in turn, refused to accept his election as mayor of Berlin in 1947, leading to the assumption of the post by his deputy Louise Schroeder.[15] Reuter's disaffection with Soviet policy was shared by many German Social Democrats who placed Germany's economic and democratic recovery above ideological dogmatism. For Reuter, the choice was not anymore whether Germany would risk economic and political division, but whether West Berlin would become part of the western or eastern German political and economic sphere. Indeed he used the specter of a Soviet monetary takeover of the western sectors as leverage to extract a commitment from the western Allies even before the blockade had begun.

American policymakers heeded the mayor's concerns after a last half-hearted effort at negotiations with the Soviets failed.[16] On 22 June, Clay discussed the Berlin situation with the Soviet delegate Vassily Sokolovsky. The latter insisted that only the eastern currency—introduced in the Soviet zone and the Greater Berlin area that same day—should circulate in Berlin. "It is clear to everybody," he wrote in a note to Clay, "that the introduction of two currencies in Berlin would not only undermine the economy and currency circulation in the area of Greater Berlin, which is located in the Soviet zone of occupation and economically forms a part of that zone, but it would also undermine the economy of the Soviet zone, and this cannot be allowed by the Soviet occupation authorities in virtue of the obligations placed upon them by international treaties."[17] Alarmed but not surprised about the Soviet move to claim Berlin for its currency, Clay introduced the D-Mark in West Berlin with a special "B" stamp the following day. The Soviets responded on June 24 with a complete blockade of all land and water traffic between Berlin and the western zones. In addition they disrupted the supply of electricity from the main power plant located in the Soviet zone.[18]

To the Soviet Union, the currency reform represented only part of a bigger problem, the western Allies' efforts to create an independent West German democratic state.[19] Americans indeed saw economic unity as a step toward political unity. On July 1, only days after the beginning of the blockade, they instructed the German Minister Presidents to create a Parliamentary Council (Parlamentarischer Rat). This council would write the West German constitution based on allied, particularly American, guidelines.[20] A separate West German constitution would effectively seal the division of Germany. The Soviets saw Berlin as the only bargaining chip left in their hands to prevent this division. By the same token, representatives from the democratic parties in Berlin realized that their political future depended on the city's continued independence from the Soviet zone. For all parties involved, economic and political questions were inseparable.

While West Berliners' experience of the currency reform was colored from the outset by the political turmoil of the Soviet blockade, West Germans saw it primarily as an economic watershed. Farmers stopped hoarding food while manufacturers, who had been holding back until the advent of a more stable currency, flooded the market with goods. Newspapers documented the magical appearance almost overnight of goods that had been scarce since the end of the war: bicycles, buckets, tableware, furniture, tools, and textiles among others.[21] A witness later recalled that the day after the currency reform "the shop windows were full; everything was available. Where the merchandise came from, I don't know; from one day to another; inexplicable."[22] The currency reform turned Germans from black market operators into capitalist consumers. Western Germany's economic problems did not evaporate overnight but they shifted from a shortage of material to a shortage of cash.[23] In early July a Munich resident wrote to his friend in Berlin: "It is amazing how everything has changed in the past three weeks. Nobody talks about calories anymore because there is enough to eat. The stores are full of goods, there are plenty of papers and magazines to be had. The only thing we don't have is money."[24] The sudden re-emergence of a consumer market set the stage for Germany's "economic miracle" of the 1950s.

Even in West Berlin the economic situation improved somewhat. On the day of the introduction of the new currency in West Berlin, Colonel Howley declared the "inauguration of a better economy which will bring more food, reconstruction, and a higher living standard."[25] Even though Howley made the statement before the beginning of the Soviet blockade, the airlift later helped realize his economic predictions. West Berliners actually felt economically more secure during than before the blockade because a steady stream of essential goods flowed into the city.

While the currency reform brightened West Germany's postwar prospects, economic conditions in the Soviet zone deteriorated. *Newsweek* correspondent John E. Thompson, reported that "while there is no confirmation of reports of food riots in the Soviet zone, there are excellent reports that economic and food conditions are critical and deteriorating rapidly."[26] Thompson had gathered complaints from residents testifying to the inability of the Soviets to feed the people in their zone. West German observers reported similarly bleak conditions. Prices remained at almost the same high level as before the currency reform and the black market continued to flourish. Worse still for Soviet occupation officials, the West German D-Mark became the preferred, if illegal, currency for citizens in the East.[27] The widening economic gulf between East and West Germany provided western powers with further ammunition for the assertion of the western system's political and economic superiority. By the same token the economic success of the currency reform in the western zones gave Berliners an incentive much stronger than any abstract concept of freedom and democracy to resist communism.

As the success of the airlift and the currency reform became apparent to Berliners they increasingly conflated the economic and political aspects of the crisis. American opinion polls detected that by the fall of 1948 the German population's concerns had actually shifted away from economic to political security. Between June and November 1948, the percentage of Berliners valuing freedom and democracy as most important rose from thirty-four to fifty-four percent while the percentage of people regarding economic security as most important, dropped from sixty-one to forty percent.[28] Those figures encouraged Americans in their belief that economic support—in the case of Berlin most literally through the airlift—strengthened democracy. The shift in attitudes acquires a somewhat different meaning, however, when analyzed in the context of the steadily improving economic situation in Berlin during the airlift. With Operation Vittles firmly in place, Berliners fared much better. In fact, Colonel Howley reported that by November the military government was able to increase food rations to nearly 2,000 calories, 220 above the pre-blockade level.[29] The American guarantee of economic security allowed the population to ponder the political implications of the blockade. The conjunction between economics and politics also encouraged Berliners to turn against communism as the source of their economic predicament. The struggle against communism thus became inseparable from the struggle for economic security.

Even before the beginning of the blockade, Berliners often blamed the Soviets for their material and food shortages.[30] Their anti-Soviet sentiments resulted from a combination of postwar experiences and historical prejudice. German disdain for Eastern Europeans dated back centuries and intensified when Hitler exploited those prejudices to galvanize support for his campaigns against Poland and the Soviet Union. Yet a significant portion of the mistrust also came from the Soviets' postwar conduct in their zone. They launched their occupation of Germany with a campaign of rape and pillage that reinforced most of the traditional anti-Russian stereo-types. Another obstacle to German rapprochement with the Soviet Union was the slow release of prisoners from Soviet POW camps. The Soviet Union alienated Germans further by dismantling much of the heavy industry in the zone, crippling economic production in the area for decades to come. As a result even the SED (Socialist Unity Party), the official pro-Soviet party in the eastern zone, found it difficult to justify Soviet actions and galvanize support for its political program.[31]

Yet Germans' contempt for Soviet occupiers did not automati-cally translate into affinity for Americans. Their complaints about Americans, however, centered primarily on unfulfilled expectations rather than negative experiences. West Berliners' views of American occupation policies had reached a low point in the period imme-diately preceding the Soviet blockade. In early 1948 the population in the western sectors became increasingly concerned about the city's future and the possibility of a new war. Rumors circulated that the Americans might leave Berlin in the event of a military confronta-tion, because, as an ICD report noted, "the defensive position of America and Great Britain confirms the population's belief that Rus-sia in the end will be successful."[32] The pessimism about the Ameri-can and British commitment to the city revealed a pervasive sense of powerlessness among Berliners.

At the same time, however, Berliners seemed to see the escalating conflict between the two powers as an opportunity to extract a firm commitment from the western Allies to stay in Berlin. By charging that both Americans and the British had adopted a "defensive posi-tion" toward the Soviets, Berliners in fact challenged both to prove them wrong. The specter of a Soviet takeover served as leverage in their interactions with the western Allies. It also helped Germans cultivate a new image of themselves as victims overshadowing the wartime image of Nazi perpetrators. Americans, in turn, became more willing to accommodate Germans in the face of a Soviet threat. The crisis thus served as a catalyst for the consolidation of their relationship.

The launching of the airlift gave powerful expression to the new American role in Germany. After U.S. Military Governor Clay ordered the transport by air of necessary goods into Berlin as an ad hoc response to the blockade, Truman directed him to put "this improvised airlift . . . on a full-scale organized basis."[33] Americans resolved to honor what they perceived as their responsibility toward the Germans in Berlin through the extension of a role they had already played for some time rather than challenging the Soviets directly through an armed convoy from the western zone or resorting to some other military gesture.

The theme of responsibility pervaded the language of American official statements during the crisis. When Secretary of State Marshall issued the first official note of protest to the Soviet government on 6 July, he not only pointed to the western Allies' right to free access to the city as stipulated in the Potsdam agreement but also emphasized "the responsibility which this Government bears for the physical well-being and the safety of the German population in its sector of Berlin." He insisted that the American responsibility was "outstandingly humanitarian in character." The population of West Berlin, particularly its women and children, Marshall claimed, depended on the continued "use of adequate facilities for moving food, medical supplies, and other items indispensable to the maintenance of human life in the western sectors of Berlin."[34] Americans claimed sole responsibility for the feeding and sustenance of the citizens in their sector.

The U.S. Deputy Representative to the United Nations, Philip C. Jessup, also capitalized on the themes of responsibility and humanitarianism when he brought the case before the Security Council on 6 October 1948. "That an effort should be made," he charged, "to deprive two and one-half million men, women, and children of medicines, food, clothing, and fuel, to subject them to cold and starvation and disease, may seem to some a small matter. But to us, the welfare of the people committed to our charge is a matter of serious concern. We cannot be callous to the suffering of millions of people in any country, much less when we have responsibility for them as an occupying power." Capitalizing on the bleak living conditions in Berlin, Jessup left no doubt about whom he saw as perpetrators and victims. He portrayed the people of Berlin as helpless in the face of Soviet aggression while presenting the United States as guardians of the population's welfare. The airlift, Jessup continued, was not only "a symbol of peace and of methods of a pacific settlement" but also "saved the people of Berlin from much of the suffering which the Soviet Government sought to enforce upon them."[35] By intimating that the Soviet Union attempted to starve the population into submission, Jessup elevated his own country and its allies to the position of protectors and providers and Berliners to the status of victims of Soviet aggression and martyrs for freedom and democracy.

The Berlin blockade lent itself particularly well to the victimization of Germans and demonization of Soviets. The helplessness of the population constituted a core element of the American appeal to the Security Council. Germany's victim status validated America's sense of itself as protector. By the same token Americans began to characterize the Soviets in much the same way as they had portrayed the Germans during World War II. They again saw themselves engaged in a struggle between absolute good and absolute evil. Only this time the Germans were the victims of aggression and the Soviet Union played the part of perpetrator. What had dissolved into shades of gray between 1944 and 1948, with increasingly blurred boundaries between victims and perpetrators, enemies and allies, was now turning into a sharp delineation of black and white again.

Food became the most important instrument with which Americans pledged their commitment toward Berlin. For Soviets and Americans—the former by withdrawing food supplies, the latter by feeding the population—food had become a way to assert political and ideological control over the city. Soon after the Americans began the airlift, Soviets in fact offered to feed the population in the western sectors.[36] Testifying before the UN Security Council, the Soviet representative Andrei Vyshinsky declared that his government had repeatedly stated its readiness to assume responsibility to feed the population of Berlin.[37] The Soviet proposal to assume and the American refusal to relinquish that responsibility revealed the political undercurrents of the food situation in Berlin. Both the Soviet Union and the United States saw food as a means to influence the ideological orientation of the population.

Yet food came to mean more than a way to determine the political future of Berlin. Americans used food and material supplies as a way to demonstrate their benevolence to the citizens of Berlin. Their actions followed the prescriptions of anthropologist Margaret Mead who had written in 1943 that the "giving of food is associated the world over with the cherishing of and responsible activities of parents toward dependent children; thus whenever a people feels that its food supply is in the hands of an authority, it tends to regard that authority as to some degree parental." Americans not only acted as "cherishing and responsible parents," but also believed, as Margaret Mead had five years earlier that "no other operation . . . is so effective in proving to an anxious and disturbed people that the powers that be are good and have their welfare at heart."[38] The airlift thus reaffirmed America's paternal role toward the population of Berlin.

Perhaps the most powerful expression of American paternalist benevolence came through the so-called "Candy Bomber." This was the name given to Lieutenant Gail S. Halvorsen, who, shortly after the beginning of the airlift, began dropping little parachutes with

Fig. 5.3 Air Force Lt. Gail S. Halvorsen preparing candy parachutes. Photo:
Landesbildstelle Berlin.

candy from his plane as he approached the Berlin airport (fig. 5.3).
As the measure gained publicity and popularity, particularly among
the juvenile population, airlift commanders organized the candy
drops on a large scale, collecting candy and handkerchiefs for the
parachutes and even organizing special flights that would drop the
parachutes all over Berlin including the eastern sector.[39] This humanitarian gesture endeared the Lieutenant to thousands of children and became one of the most successful publicity stunts of the
airlift.[40] The candy drops acquired symbolic significance because,
like the earliest encounters between GIs and German children, they

Fig. 5.4 Berlin children waiting for the candy drops. Photo: Landesbildstelle Berlin.

focused attention on the most innocent members of the Berlin population (fig. 5.4). As Berlin's fate became identified with that of its candy-craving children, the contrast between Americans and the Soviets appeared even stronger. The Candy Bomber allowed Americans to magnify the pacific and humanitarian nature of their mission, while Germans could use the youthful exposure as evidence of its own deprivation at the hands of the Soviets. The punitive mission of the early postwar period had been transformed into one focused on welfare.

While the candy drops provided evidence on the light side of the American commitment to Germans' well being, the thirty-one American casualties related to the airlift showed the more serious side of that commitment. When a U.S. cargo plane crashed in West Germany in August 1948, killing the entire crew, not only Americans elevated the soldiers to heroic status (fig. 5.5). *Newsweek* reported that Berliners reacted to the accident in much the same way, mourning the loss as their own (fig.5.6). City officials held a memorial

Fig. 5.5 C-47 crashed into a Berlin apartment building in the Friedenau section of Berlin. 25 July 1948. Photo: Landesbildstelle Berlin.

service for the victims attended by 4,000 Berliners.[41] Just as during World War II, Americans interpreted the casualties as a human sacrifice for the preservation of freedom and democracy. Only this time the fallen soldiers had given their lives not only to protect their own families at home but those of their former enemies as well.

Most of the people of West Berlin and West Germany embraced their dependence on Americans. The doubts about the Anglo-American commitment to the city that many of them had expressed in the spring of 1948 evaporated soon after the beginning of the airlift. Already by the end of July, the population almost unanimously assumed that the western powers would stay in the city. Fifty-eight percent of them were convinced that the Americans could not possibly "deliver us to the Russians—they are our protectors."[42] Berlin's women expressed their faith in Americans even more

Fig. 5.6 Wreath made by the Berlin Women's League, District Schöneberg, in honor of the slain pilot. Photo: Landesbildstelle Berlin.

often than men, sixty-nine compared to forty-one percent among men, revealing a gender gap in the German image of Americans.

Yet Berliners also saw their relationship with Americans in the context of their relations with the Soviets. Especially when confronted with the Soviet counter-offer to feed the population of the western sectors, they were well aware of the political implications of the Soviet offer. Most of them, however, deeply mistrusted the Russian offer and therefore advocated the continuation of the airlift. An opinion survey in late summer revealed that most West Berliners either believed that it was impossible for the Soviets to feed all of Berlin or that they would not keep their word.[43] Seven percent preferred the continuation of the western airlift because the American food was better. Only every tenth person in the western sector mentioned communism as the main reason not to accept Russian food supplies.[44] Berliners chose dependence on Americans over the economic uncertainties of dependence on the Soviets.

Despite the general mood of suspicion toward the Soviets, around 120,000 West Berliners registered in the east for food rations. Colonel Howley had "no sympathy with these spineless German backsliders" as he called them. He regarded their action as a political betrayal of the western cause because they were willing to affiliate themselves with the loathsome east for the false promise of better rations. He even suggested to cut them off from western supplies as they began to return to the western sectors in the spring of 1949.[45] Rather than interpreting the defection as an act of economic desperation, Howley saw it as a lack of ideological commitment to the cause of freedom. Food thus assumed ideological significance in the battle between democracy and communism. In Howley's eyes these "deserters" were undermining the airlift and the resolve of the rest of the population. Others, however, chose to interpret the return of these "backsliders" as an encouraging sign of the growing faith in American resolve.

Berliners' rising expectations of American commitment to the city pressured Americans into even greater commitment. *Newsweek* columnist Joseph B. Philips observed that "the unexpected courage shown by the friendly Germans in Berlin has placed an added responsibility on [the Allied authority]." Because of the desperate pleas of the citizens of the western sectors for the continuation of the airlift, Americans felt compelled not to disappoint their protégés. Philips described the situation as "one more verification of the maxim that the victor belongs to the spoil," meaning that Germans, not Americans were reaping the benefits of the American victory in the war.[46]

Yet Americans, too, benefited from the crisis. The Soviet blockade produced a much starker contrast between the two systems than Americans could ever have established through verbal persuasion. The conflict would force Germans to situate themselves firmly in one camp or the other. They could no longer play the wartime allies off against each other. A *Newsweek* bulletin reported in early September that "developments are proving that the U.S. was correct in a fundamental calculation it made in deciding to stay in Berlin—that the Russian blockade would turn the Germans against the Soviets."[47] Faced with an either-or option, West Germans were more likely to choose liberal democracy over socialism.

The location of Berlin in the center of the Soviet zone made the population's unequivocal support for the western Allies essential.[48] Americans reassured themselves of the Berliners' resolve before dedicating themselves wholeheartedly to their protection. Shortly before he launched the airlift, General Clay sought personal assurance from Ernst Reuter that the city's population in the western sectors supported the effort.[49] The airlift could only symbolize democracy's endurance against Soviet encroachments if Berliners embraced the struggle and did not cave in to Soviet pressures. Reuter, whose own political viability depended on the western Allies' presence, convinced the general of the population's reliability.

West Berliners provided proof of their resolve soon after the beginning of the blockade. At a rally organized by the West Berlin Social Democrats on 26 June, two days after the beginning of the blockade, political leaders emphasized the connection between Berlin's demonstration of support for democracy and the western Allies' physical commitment to the city. Franz Neumann, chairman of the Berlin SPD, declared before 80,000 supporters that the western powers' defense of Berlin would not have occurred without the Berliners' support for freedom and democracy. "No democratic country," he asserted, "would have cared about a city that capitulated in the face of dictatorship." Neumann made it clear to his fellow citizens that even if they regarded economics as the root cause of the conflict, their affiliation with the western Allies carried far-reaching political consequences.

Neumann sounded a powerful theme to his listeners: "The cause of Berlin is the cause of the free world."[50] Berlin's politicians and the public pressured Americans into support by turning their struggle into a symbol for the survival of democracy in the free world. Even Americans became more inclined to see the blockade as an attack on the new American-dominated world order. Truman later wrote that "what was at stake in Berlin was not a contest over legal rights . . . but a struggle over Germany and, in a larger sense, over Europe."[51] The symbolic identification of Berlin with the free world became an essential tool in galvanizing international support against the Soviet blockade. The UN representative Jessup declared before the Security Council that "the Soviet Union may pretend it cannot understand why it can be charged with threat of force against the United States, France, and the United Kingdom when a primary consequence of its action falls directly and intentionally upon the civilian population of Berlin for whose well-being the three Western occupying powers are responsible."[52] The American justification for defending West Berlin thus moved beyond right and responsibility to direct identification of the western Allies with the fate of the population.

Americans looked with approval upon the upsurge in public expressions of anti-communism among Berliners and West Germans in the fall of 1948. In September close to 300,000 Germans converged on the Platz der Republik in front of the Reichstag for a massive anti-communist demonstration. Incited by angry speeches, the crowd moved into the eastern sector, began throwing stones, and tore the red flag from atop the Brandenburg gate. In ensuing violent clashes with East Berlin security forces a sixteen-year-old German boy was killed and twenty-three others injured.[53] For West Berliners the politics of anti-communism served as an outlet for their festering anxieties and frustrations about western integration, economic security, and political rehabilitation. *Newsweek* reported that despite the violence, western occupation powers were quite pleased with the evidence of German anti-communism. By 1948 Americans had adopted the specious tautology that every anti-communist was pro-American and every anti-American was pro-communist, a principle that would guide American foreign policy for the next two decades.

In American popular opinion, West Berlin's resistance to the Soviet blockade was a sign of Germany's democratic conversion. In fact, by the fall of 1948, most Americans simply assumed that not only West Berliners but the majority of Germans shared America's definition of and appreciation for their democratic system.[54] Americans found more concrete evidence for this in the December 1948 municipal elections in Berlin's western sectors. The Berlin magistrate had scheduled these elections in 1946 with the consent of the East German Socialist Unity Party (SED), the political voice of the Soviet Union. On 30 November, only days before the election was to take place, with an SED defeat at the polls looming, political representatives of the eastern sector convened to abolish the magistrate because of its "disregard for the essential interests of the Berlin population and continuous violations of the constitution."[55] This declaration paved the way for SED functionaries to boycott the elections and establish an independent city government under SED control in the Soviet sector. Despite the eastern boycott, West Berliners voted as scheduled with 86.3 percent of eligible voters participating. The Social Democrats under the leadership of Ernst Reuter and Louise Schroeder captured 64.5 percent of the vote, followed by the Christian Democrats with 19.4 percent, and the Liberal Democratic

Party with 16.1 percent.[56] The election results were warped by the boycott of the eastern parties; yet they showed that West Berliners overwhelmingly opted for democratic parties.

To Americans the results signified the Berliners' choice for freedom, democracy, and western integration. Colonel Howley hailed the outcome of the elections as a courageous decision worthy of praise and attention in the entire free world. This decision, he contended, would show Berliners the way toward a future that would be brighter than they could ever have hoped at the end of the war.[57] The elections fueled American optimism about Germany's progress toward democracy, thus allowing them to embrace Germany as a rehabilitated ally.

Yet the German and American postwar definition of democracy encompassed a peculiar mixture of elements that all but obscured more traditional attributes such as freedom and self-determination. Those new elements included economic prosperity, national security, and anti-communism. The Berlin crisis particularly blurred the difference between anti-communism and democracy. The American-sponsored German newspaper *Die Neue Zeitung* reported in early October that West Berlin's perseverance had convinced Americans to treat Germany less as a defeated enemy and more as an ally. It quoted an American news correspondent who had concluded that the previous six months had shown that Germany was committed to defending freedom.[58] However, what Americans defined as freedom in the context of the Berlin crisis, namely the fight against a communist takeover, Germans were more likely to define as security. This American conflation of security and freedom became obvious in a question asked by a survey conducted shortly after the beginning of the blockade. The pollsters asked Berliners why they thought the western powers should stay. One possible answer to the question was: "they give us security—they mean 'freedom'—otherwise democracy is endangered."[59] The authors' reformulation of security as "freedom" points to the close association they saw between the two. Only five percent of Germans chose this option. The percentage among men and among those with nine or more years of education was significantly higher, eleven percent and nine percent respectively. When the pollsters interpreted the results, they curiously omitted the security aspect of the question, stressing instead freedom as the only associative variable with democracy.[60] It is quite likely, however, that Germans would have responded differently to the question had freedom been the only attribute. Further complicating the matter is the third variable thrown into the equation: democracy. The German interviewees were not asked to choose between security and democracy. On the contrary, the option assumed the universality of the connection between democracy and security/freedom. Thus, Americans in fact presupposed a complex triangular relationship among democracy, freedom, and security. In other words, if security guaranteed democracy and democracy guaranteed freedom, then security must mean freedom.

Yet German ideas of democracy after World War II put freedom much lower on the list of attractions than issues like economic prosperity and military security against the Soviet Union. In addition, their exposure to American-style democracy in the early postwar years had little to do with freedom. From the beginning, American re-education officials left German democratic politicians little leeway to develop indigenous popular support. In addition, Germans would not have been inclined in the mid to late 1940s to regard freedom as the greatest facilitator for the re-establishment of law and order in their own country. To the contrary, too much emphasis on freedom could conceivably threaten the security and social stability Germans were looking for in the postwar period. Under American supervision, Germans had no alternative but to accept and support democratic institutions and democratic practices such as a parliamentary system of government. That did not mean that Germans would not have chosen democracy of their own free will—they had done so after World War I—but their motivation for a return to democracy was different than in 1919. After 1945, they chose democracy because it gave them the best chance to achieve economic prosperity, socio-political stability, and security against the Soviet bloc. In the immediate postwar era they adopted democratic structures and institutions but did not develop a democratic culture.[61]

Ironically, Americans after World War II developed a similar understanding of democracy in their own country. In fact, during the early cold war years Americans were increasingly willing to sacrifice essential civil liberties for the sake of national security. In 1947, Truman cited national security as the main justification for the creation of the Federal Employee Loyalty Program that established review boards for all federal employees in an attempt to weed out disloyal civil servants.[62] The fear of internal subversion escalated in the early 1950s into a general witch-hunt led by the junior senator from Wisconsin, Joseph McCarthy.[63] The emergence of a national cold war consensus that gave highest priority to the fight against communism at home and abroad justified the violation of basic freedoms in the interest of national security. Thus rather than two sides of the same coin, freedom and security became opposites: the former had to give way in the interest of the latter.

The increasing prevalence of national security also contributed to the shift in American occupation priorities. Bolstering Germany's anti-communist political contingent and accelerating its economic recovery took precedence over improving the shortcomings of the re-education and denazification programs. The Berlin blockade significantly softened the Allied resolve in prosecuting former Nazis, accelerating a process that was already well underway.[64] American occupation officials had already turned over the denazification process to German tribunals, so-called Spruchkammern. Many of the original members of these tribunals belonged to the political left,

since Social Democrats and Communists had most ardently opposed Nazism during the Third Reich. With the emergence of the
cold war, however, these anti-fascists themselves increasingly came
under attack from Germans as well as American occupation officials. As a result, many Spruchkammern lost their popular mandate
and many former Nazis escaped conviction.[65] The cold war crippled
the strongest anti-fascist faction in postwar Germany and facilitated
a political shift to the right.

In the United States and Germany, the memory of Nazi war
crimes grew dimmer as stories of daring Air Force pilots flying to
Berlin even under most perilous weather conditions abounded in
the news media.[66] Playing airlift became a favorite pastime for Berlin's children with model planes generously furnished by the occupying forces (fig. 5.7). The airlift also provided perfect material for
Hollywood's movie industry. By December 1948, five major studios
were working on motion pictures about the airlift. They bore titles
like *Berlin Air Corridor, Berlin Air Lift, Berlin Blockade* and *Berlin
Powder Keg.*[67]

The most popular of them, *The Big Lift,* used the airlift as back-
drop for the story of a twisted love affair between an American GI
and a German woman. Released in 1950, the film capitalized on the
heroism of American soldiers, while casting an ambivalent light on
the German beneficiaries of the airlift. The movie's protagonist,
Daniel MacCullough, played by Montgomery Clift, is a navigator on
a cargo plane flying supplies to Berlin during the airlift.[68] At the outset, he falls in love with an attractive young Berlin woman, Frederike
Burkhardt. Frederike gives MacCullough a glimpse of the hardships
she and her fellow citizens are suffering under the blockade. He vows
to take care of her, both personally and through the airlift. His
relationship with Frederike mirrors that between the United States
and Germany. The story takes an unexpected turn, however, as Mac-
Cullough, moments before he is to marry Frederike, finds out that

Fig. 5.7 Berlin children playing "Airlift." Photo: Landesbildstelle Berlin.

she has abused his trust. She planned to marry him only to gain entry to the United States where her true lover, another German emigrant, lives. MacCullough's faith in Germany and the purpose of his job is temporarily shattered.

This twist in the love story illustrates the continued undercurrent of suspicion toward Germany that persisted in the United States. Despite a flood of reports of German food shortages and the hardships of the Berlin population under the blockade, many Americans continued to harbor doubts about the sincerity of Germany's progress toward democracy. Reports of German leniency toward former Nazis and a general resurgence of nationalism fueled those doubts.[69] In April 1949, Representative Chet Holifield of California openly criticized U.S. occupation officials in Germany for what he saw as the "coddling of former Nazis." He drew attention to the March–April 1949 issue of a pamphlet titled "Prevent World War

III." He did not specify which organization was behind its publication, but he quoted extensively from an article in it, which stated that "we resent treating the Germans as though they are now our bosom friends. They have a long way to go to prove that they are trustworthy in economics and politics."[70] Such critical expressions indicated that those who still saw evidence of Nazism in Germany had become increasingly frustrated by the fast pace of the German-American rapprochement. The severity of the charges also suggest that those views were becoming increasingly marginal.

Even *The Big Lift* carefully counters the bleak portrayal of one Germany with the promise of another. In a subplot to the film is the story of another German-American relationship, that of MacCullough's friend Sergeant Paul Kowalski, played by Paul Douglas, and his girlfriend Gertie. Kowalski, who spent part of the war in a German POW camp and who deeply mistrusts all Germans, tries to educate Gertie about American democracy and freedom. Yet in his personal conduct toward Gertie he displays all the negative attributes of an authoritarian stormtrooper. As Frederike's devious plot unfolds, Gertie learns to defy Kowalski's bullying, which she describes in one scene as undemocratic. Her moral triumph over Kowalski marks the symbolic triumph of at least part of the German population over political apathy. Her determination to understand democracy reflects an ultimate faith in the potential for Germany's political rehabilitation. At the same time Gertie's criticism of Kowalski served as a reminder to American GIs that they, too, have to act out the democratic ideals in their day-to-day interactions with the former enemy, giving support to the notion of GIs as ambassadors of democracy. By the end of the film, Frederike has faltered and Gertie has become a model democrat. MacCullough and Kowalski, meanwhile, have triumphed in their struggle to crush the Soviet efforts to take the city. The film's conclusion thus offers hope for

Germany's re-education and assurance of America's democratic and humanitarian integrity.

In reality, Germany's democratization appeared to grow apace with the success of the airlift. After Berliners affirmed their commitment to democratic parties in the December municipal elections, the Soviet negotiating position softened for the first time since the beginning of the blockade. The split of the city into two political entities portended the political division of the rest of Germany, leaving Soviet negotiators little bargaining power. Furthermore, the western counter-blockade hurt the East German economy and increased internal pressure on the Soviets to end the blockade. In January 1949, Stalin broke the deadlock by dropping the currency question from the negotiating agenda. The Soviet Union finally agreed to lift the blockade effective 12 May 1949.[71] Four days earlier, on the fourth anniversary of the German capitulation, the West German parliamentary council had accepted the Basic Law, which formed the constitutional basis for the creation of a separate West German state. By the fall the division of Germany was complete and would persist for more than four decades.

*   *   *

The Berlin crisis of 1948–49 represented a watershed both for the division of Germany and the nascent cold war between the Soviet Union and the United States. Yet the American response to the crisis was not so much a radical departure from previous policy than an expression of the changed relationship between Americans and Germans. It brought into sharper view the image among Americans of themselves as protectors and providers initially of Germans, but later, as the cold war progressed, of all those they deemed threatened by a communist takeover. The airlift also helped solidify the American image of Germans as victims, not only of material hardships but of the Soviets as well. Most of the elements of this relationship were in place before, yet the airlift catapulted them to national and international prominence.

Food played a central role in both the airlift and the transformation of German-American relations. In 1944 Americans were prohibited from providing any food and material aid to the German population. To the contrary, the occupation directive stipulated specifically that Germans were not to receive any aid beyond the "supplies necessary to prevent starvation or widespread disease or such civil unrest as would endanger the occupying forces."[72] Yet in 1948, the situation had changed markedly. During the airlift, Americans openly wooed Germans and used the supply of food as an instrument to demonstrate, as Mead had suggested earlier, their good intentions. The Berliners' dependence on the Anglo-American airlift symbolized Germany's dependence on the United States in economic and security matters.

Yet the airlift moved beyond the consolidation of the provider-dependent relationship between Americans and Germans. It also signified the consensus that had been building between the two countries since the end of the war. This consensus encompassed first the mutual understanding of the close connection between economic recovery and political democratization. The currency reform, the immediate cause of the blockade, was thus seen both as a step toward the re-creation of a western-oriented market economy and as a precondition to the establishment of a democratic West German state. The citizens of West Berlin were willing to forfeit the unity of their city in exchange for the inclusion in the consumer paradise of the democratic West. In the collective memory of the German population the day of the currency reform, 20 June 1948, weighed far more heavily than the founding of the Federal Republic in 1949.[73] The currency reform gave Germans a glimpse of the prosperity of the free market economy setting the stage for the *Wirtschaftswunder* of the 1950s. It allowed them to follow the American model of consumer capitalism. In the context of the cold war, consumer capitalism became more than an economic system. It became for Americans a political tool in the fight against communism. Consumption in the United States meant the freedom to choose, and the freedom to choose was in American eyes the essence of democratic liberalism. For Germans consumption became the essence of their postwar democratic experience. In its first election campaign in 1949, Konrad Adenauer's conservative CDU printed a poster featuring a young woman with a grocery basket full of goods. The caption read: "Finally, we can buy again."[74] For Germans, rather than an outcome of democracy consumerism and prosperity became an end in itself. Affiliation with the democratic West and the adoption of a democratic system in Germany became the means toward that end.

A second aspect of the cold war consensus was the primacy of anti-communism, both in domestic and foreign affairs. In the United States fear of communist subversion created in the 1950s a monolithic and conformist culture that glorified consumerism, traditional gender roles, and hyper-patriotism as the cornerstones of American security and democracy.[75] Anti-communism glossed over any racial, social, or political divisions within American society. For Germans anti-communism became a vehicle for their political redemption in the eyes of the western world. By voicing their strong and most militant opposition to the communist regime in East Germany and Eastern Europe, Germans were able to deflect from their own Nazi past and thus situate themselves ideologically firmly in the camp of the western Allies. In America's increasingly bipolar ideological worldview, German expressions of anti-communism were seen as proof of its commitment to democracy. Anti-communism not only created the illusion of a homogenous American culture, it also homogenized American-German postwar relations.

The preoccupation with anti-communism also weakened the American commitment to denazification in Germany. By 1948 anti-communists had become more reliable as political protégés of the Americans than anti-fascists, leading to the political rehabilitation of several former Nazis and the ousting of committed leftists who had resisted Nazism during the Third Reich.[76] In fact the memory of Germany's wartime atrocities faded in inverse relation to the perceived increase of the communist threat. The emergence of the Soviet Union as the new enemy of both the United States and West Germany accelerated the process of collective amnesia about Nazi Germany and the rapprochement between the two countries. Americans substituted communism for fascism as the main threat to American democracy. Instead of teaching Germans democracy and ethnic, racial, and political tolerance, Americans joined Germans in the creation of a new enemy: the Soviet Union. By 1948, the image of the evil "Red Reich" had overshadowed the image of the Third Reich.

The emphasis Germans and Americans placed on anti-communism after 1948, however, was misleading and does not adequately characterize the essence of their relationship since the end of the war. While anti-communism undoubtedly constituted an important element in the future alliance between the two countries, it had not been a major factor in the transformation of their relationship from enemies to allies. That relationship began to change as the first American troops entered German territory in the fall of 1944, and it changed not so much out of geo-strategic expediency but because of the reciprocity that existed between the personal interactions between soldiers and civilians and the political mission of the occupation. The Berlin airlift represented the culmination of this nexus between culture and politics.

Conclusion

"The process of denazification is less than half done," warned James H. Sheldon of the Non-Sectarian Anti-Nazi League in a letter to several congressional representatives in late March 1949. Indeed, Sheldon argued, "our policies are actually promoting the revival of Nazi forces in the German economy."[1] The occasion for Sheldon's appeal was the impending opening of a German industrial exhibition at New York's Rockefeller Center under the auspices of the American Military Government in Germany. While the League's concerns resonated with some legislators, among them Representative Abraham J. Multer of New York, who read the letter into the *Congressional Record,* it did not stop the exhibition from opening as planned. In defense of the fair Military Governor General Lucius D. Clay emphasized Germany's need to attract American customers and increase its exports in order to revitalize its economy.[2] Four years after the end of the Nazi dictatorship American and German political leaders concentrated on economic development as the best path toward integrating postwar Germany into the western democratic community of nations.

Although U.S. business representatives flocked to the exhibition, Jewish protesters gathered outside Rockefeller Center to remind Americans of Germany's recent atrocities. The Committee to

Combat Anti-Semitism picketed the entrance to the exhibition every day. Among the slogans on placards were "Nazis Keep Your Bloody Goods;" "Today the Volkswagen, Tomorrow the Death Wagon;" and "Our Sons Didn't Die to Rebuild Nazi Industries."[3] Despite the protests, the fair attracted record numbers of visitors and manufacturing orders far exceeded expectations.[4]

The exhibition briefly re-ignited the debate in the United States about the treatment of postwar Germany, pitting economics against ethics. Even before the fair opened reports multiplied about the incomplete process of denazification.[5] Yet American government, military, and business leaders were eager not to let Germany's past interfere with future political and economic alliances. Critics of the new American policy toward Germany found themselves increasingly in the minority. In 1945, Henry Morgenthau's proposals to punish postwar Germany had commanded the attention of the nation's most powerful political figures. By 1949, cultural and political reconciliation had reduced the advocates of punitive policies to a few protesters in front of Rockefeller Center. Doubts about Germany's future political reliability had not vanished entirely, but skeptics had lost their dominant position in American politics. Those eager to establish friendly relations with the heirs of the Nazi Reich drowned out the warnings of the few.

The scenes inside and outside Rockefeller Center refocus attention on the question posed at the beginning of this study: Why did the U.S.-German relationship improve with such speed after the end of World War II? The reasons are obviously complex and multi-faceted. Most scholars have attributed those changes to economic or geo-political concerns. Yet cultural and social factors were not separate from Germany's political and economic rehabilitation. On several levels—personal, local, and international—politics and culture were closely interwoven.

Consideration of culture unites and enhances economic or geo-political interpretations of twentieth century U.S. foreign policy. Both advocates of economic and geo-political interpretations have engaged in what the historian Lawrence Stone has called the "habit of crunching historical explanation into a single one-way hierarchy of causation." Stone wrote these words in 1977 as part of a critique of the new social history. Yet much of the scholarship on U.S.-German relations over the past three decades has followed that approach as well with revisionists advocating the primacy of economics and postrevisionists the primacy of geo-politics. By doing so they narrowed their field of vision considerably and explored only a particular set of questions concerning a privileged group of actors. Stone concluded correctly that this kind of systemization chokes off imaginative historical inquiry. It imposes a false sense of order on a much messier and murkier historical process. Borrowing the language of engineers, Stone described historical explanation as "a nonlinear, multiple-loop feedback system, with many semi-independent variables, each responsively reacting to the influence of some, or all, of the others."[6] This approach does not obliterate the question of causation. It simply rejects the idea that there exists a hierarchy of causation. Rather than assigning culture a place in a linear hierarchy of causation, or denying its causality altogether, one needs to understand culture as an integral element of all other factors of causation.

Thus instead of viewing the cultural approach as an alternative that competes with the political and economic ones, one should regard all three as reciprocal and mutually dependent. By the same token, the local history of U.S.- German personal interactions should not be understood as separate from the international political history of U.S.- German relations. Rather, the stories of German-American personal encounters help us understand better policy-makers' shift in assumptions and attitudes. Political and military leaders shared with ordinary Americans most of their cultural assumptions and prejudices, both positive and negative, about Germany. They did not shed their cultural baggage as they were making policy decisions about postwar Germany. The decision to rebuild Germany was not made in a culturally decontextualized geo-political environment. It was not solely the result of a conscious string of rational and strategically inspired decisions at the central command center in Washington, but one that reflected the cultural change emerging from Americans' encounters with Germans.

Cultural feminization became a powerful catalyst in America's postwar rapprochement with Germany. The preponderance of women and children and the pervasiveness of hunger in early postwar Germany fostered in American GIs a shift from one traditionally male gender role—conqueror—to another—protector and provider. In doing so, Americans redirected their attention from those segments of German society responsible for the Nazi war crimes to those whom Americans universally recognized as victims of the war. They increasingly identified the fate of postwar Germany with that of its women and children. Conceiving of Germany in such a way fostered the willingness in the United States to aid in Germany's material reconstruction and deflected attention from the country's Nazi past. Germans encouraged the image of themselves as victims of harsh material circumstances and of women as the embodiment of Germany's postwar experience. The Trümmerfrau became a national heroic icon. Germans embraced their own cultural feminization as long as it served to dispel the negative image of the hyper-masculine aggressive stormtrooper. Cultural feminization thus translated into an acceptance of economic and military dependence on the American occupiers. By withdrawing into the private sphere and concentrating on the immediate physical needs of food and shelter, Germans effectively denied any responsibility for the actions of the state.

The monolithic image of Germany that the American government had created during the war began to break down as soon as GIs entered Germany. Despite U.S. efforts to sustain the impression of a German populace united in the war effort, GIs encountered a diversity of civilians and former soldiers. GIs' interaction primarily with one part of the German population, young women, eventually helped the United States create a new monolithic image of Germany: feminine victim of war and the Soviet menace. Just as the wartime stereotype had facilitated the war effort, the postwar stereotype facilitated support for Germany's rehabilitation and the cold war. Neither image dealt adequately with the cultural and political complexity of Germany.

The assumption of collective guilt became the first casualty of the gendered reconceptualization of postwar Germany. Even though the political advocates of Germany's collective guilt, chief among them Henry Morgenthau Jr., seemed to have lost the car of the president by the end of 1944, the practical directives of the Supreme Headquarters of the Allied Forces in Europe still reflected that idea. General Eisenhower's non-fraternization order issued in September 1944 became the concrete manifestation of collective guilt. Yet American soldiers were unable or unwilling to apply the theoretical concept to their practical day-to-day interactions with German civilians. As the patterns of interaction during the early occupation demonstrate, fraternization, and with it the idea of collective guilt, became gendered. As a result, Americans began to make distinctions between guilty and innocent Germans not solely on the basis of their level of involvement with the Nazi regime but on the basis of their gender and age as well.

Denazification, closely associated with the question of collective guilt, became the second casualty of the gendered view of postwar Germany. When General Eisenhower announced the relaxation of the non-fraternization ban in the summer of 1945, he cited progress in the process of denazification as the major reason. Yet denazification was far from complete then, nor was it complete by 1949. To the contrary, as James S. Sheldon warned, some of the policies of the military government in Germany actually appeared to foster the rehabilitation and re-integration of Nazi figures into German political and economic life.[7] Practical considerations such as the need for Germany's economic recovery alone could not have convinced Americans that former Nazis could be put to good use in the new Germany. Yet as Americans conceived of postwar Germany as a weakened, feminized country in need of economic assistance, rather than the heir of the aggressive masculine Nazi-state, their support for economic reconstruction was more forthcoming. Thus even if individuals within Washington's political and economic policy establishment were willing to brush aside the process of denazification for the more important prospect of a revitalized European economy, they had to convince the American public of the soundness of their ideas. The cultural feminization of Germany thus provided a useful and powerful service in the redirection of the American popular image of postwar Germany from perpetrator to victim.

Anti-communism acquired a new meaning in the context of Germany's cultural feminization as well. As the conflict between the Soviet Union and the United States intensified, Americans increasingly cast Germany in the position of a weak nation in danger of Soviet usurpation. The Berlin airlift magnified Germany's helplessness in the face of the Soviet blockade. Again, whether as a tool to gain acceptance for a radically different policy course or the result of a genuine sense of responsibility toward a war-ravaged country, Americans exaggerated Germany's victim status in order to obtain political, military, and financial support for Germany. When Colonel Frank Howley, the commandant of the U.S. sector of Berlin, confronted the Soviet blockade in 1948, his response was guided not only by political and strategic considerations. After three years of experience in West Berlin, Howley so closely identified with the population in his sector that he considered them *his* people.[8] Anti-communism became the political justification, ex post facto, for the consolidation of the cultural and personal affinity that had been developing since the earliest days of invasion. It helped Germans to redeem themselves politically and disassociate themselves ideologically from the Nazi past. They had successfully passed on the role of global enemy to the Soviet Union and recast themselves as helpless victims. Anti-communism served as a catalyst rather than a major cause for the German-American rapprochement.

The cultural history of American foreign relations thus reinterprets the familiar concepts of collective guilt, denazification, and anti-communism. For the history of German-American postwar relations the approach uncovers layers of interactions and mutual influence hidden from the official documents of the political and diplomatic agencies. More importantly, however, it shows that the process of rehabilitation began before the emergence of the cold war. It thus refutes one of the major assumptions of postwar German-American relations: that American policy toward Germany became conciliatory as a result of the cold war. In fact, as the preceding study shows, German-American rapprochement was as much a cause as a consequence of the cold war.

If the cultural approach focuses attention on the hidden agents of change in international relations, gender helps uncover important behavioral and attitudinal structures in the relationships among individuals, groups, and nations. The immediate aftermath of World War II was a period of extreme gender consciousness in both the United States and Germany. As both countries returned from war to peace narrowly defined gender roles served as tools to re-establish social order and stability. Gender maps out the way in which individuals, whole cultures, and political elites expressed social, cultural, and national differences. The same binary opposites used to express the differences between men and women also served to express and sometimes legitimize the relations among nations. Among them were attributes like strength versus weakness, aggression versus passivity, provider versus dependent, protector versus victim.

Power difference is a central component of all of these binary opposites. Power is also a central component in the relationship among nations. Not all power differences have to be understood through the lens of gender. Yet whether explicit or implicit, gendered language and gendered conceptualizations were often used to express those asymmetrical international relations. For instance when John F. Kennedy in 1963 articulated his frustration with German demands for reassurance of the American commitment to West Germany and NATO, the president likened the German Chancellor Konrad Adenauer to a wife who constantly asks her husband whether he loves her or not.[9] The asymmetry of the American-German relationship was thus conveniently illustrated in the metaphor of the nagging wife who is utterly dependent on her husband's good will and love.

Kennedy's remarks, poignant as they were, ironically came on the eve of a decisive shift in the power balance between the United States and Germany. By the late 1960s, as a result of a combination of developments, among them the Vietnam war and global economic changes beyond U.S. control, America's political, economic, and military predominance began to wane. Concomitantly, Germany's political deference to the United States began to ebb as well. The shift can best be illustrated in the figure of Willy Brandt who became Germany's chancellor in 1969. As mayor of Berlin in 1961, Brandt had to stand by as the East German police built the wall that permanently sealed the German-German border. Profoundly disappointed by American inaction, he was nonetheless powerless to stop the wall from going up or induce the western Allies to respond more strongly to the East German action. Yet as chancellor, Brandt forged ahead to formulate a foreign policy that distanced itself from the United States and sought the dialogue with Germany's eastern European neighbors. He negotiated treaties with several Eastern bloc countries and succeeded in making the German-German border more permeable. Brandt's *Ostpolitik* was a major step toward Germany's emancipation from America's political and military hegemony. Through the recognition of West Germany's eastern border with Poland and the legitimacy of a separate East German state, Ostpolitik also represented the first manifestation at the highest political level of Germany's acceptance of the consequences of World War II. By the early 1970s, the conceptualization of West Germany in feminine terms was no longer applicable.

Germany's cultural feminization in the early postwar period in many ways paralleled the ways in which Americans were conceptualizing their relationship with weaker nations throughout the twentieth century. John Dower showed that Japan's embrace of its own feminization and infantilization after World War II helped its citizens overcome the humiliation of national defeat.[10] In fact Japan's feminization and infantilization ran so deep that General Douglas MacArthur testified before Congress in 1951 that Japan's level of development should be compared to that "of a boy of twelve as compared to our own development of about 45 years."[11] MacArthur's articulation of the Japanese as an immature race appeared to justify close American control and supervision. It seemed as natural as a parent's supervision and education of a child in its formative years. Kristin Hoganson has shown that anxieties about gender at the turn of the century fueled the rhetoric for war against Spain in Cuba and the Philippines.[12] And Andrew Rotter has argued convincingly that U.S. policy toward India during the cold war was shaped by assumptions of India's effeminacy and emotionalism.[13]

In all of these cases race was a crucial component of the

conceptualization of other nations in feminine terms. Race and gender thus became entwined and mutually reinforcing. Both expressed and legitimized, at least in the eyes of the dominant culture, the power differences that existed between two cultures. In Germany, on the other hand, racial difference played no role in the process of cultural feminization. Ethnic affinity rather than racial difference characterized at least part of the informal relations. If anything, the traditional imperialist racial hierarchy became inverted as African-American soldiers, just like their white counterparts, assumed a position of power over Germans and few Germans challenged the legitimacy of their power. By the same token, Germany's system of racial superiority under the Nazis and the annihilation of six million Jews constituted a vital part of the Allied accusations against the Nazi state. Race and racism thus played themselves out very differently, sometimes contradictorily, in the German postwar environment. Feminization was thus not inextricably linked to the idea of racial inferiority. Americans obviously did not think of Germans as racially or ethnically inferior. Most of them did not even consider them culturally inferior. In fact, in his testimony in 1951, MacArthur called the Germans "a mature race" on the same level as Anglo-Saxons.[14] Yet nonetheless the perception of political, economic, and social weakness of postwar Germany helped in creating among Americans the image of a feminized Germany. Ironically, for both Germans and Americans, the temporary feminization ultimately helped Germans deflect attention from the Nazi past and reestablish a political and economic environment conducive to the reassertion of sovereignty and power.

Close attention to language helps us examine presumably value-free terms like power, imperialism, national security, and credibility in a different light. The language in which American policymakers articulated their attitudes and policies toward other nations relied on symbols, metaphors, and concepts that denoted much more than simple practical considerations. Power is associated with masculinity; credibility alludes to the fear of appearing weak; weakness conjures up the image of effeminacy and infantilism; imperialism can be understood as the paternalistic control of weaker peoples; the concept of dependency invokes a gendered as well as an economic component; even the concept of national security acquires gendered meaning, as Elaine Tyler May has shown in *Homeward Bound*.[15] The cultural connotations of these terms served to naturalize, legitimize, and reinforce existing inequalities. Language also unveils the gendered framework of foreign relations in more explicit ways. Individuals, including policymakers, make use of gendered metaphors to express relations between nations. Kennedy's metaphor of the insecure wife, the frequent use of "rape" as a metaphor when policymakers and pundits speak of foreign invasions, and MacArthur's invocation of immaturity concerning the Japanese all conjured up an air of legitimacy and naturalness of the inequities of power.[16]

One cannot dismiss this language as pure rhetoric anymore than one can accept the language of power politics, national security, and economic primacy as the "real thing." Both practical policy considerations and cultural assumptions converged to produce the foreign policy debates and decisions that we investigate. To privilege geopolitical, economic, or cultural motives over others returns us to the problem of an oversimplified hierarchy of causation and the attendant false sense of order.

The industrial fair at Rockefeller Center captured this reciprocity among culture, politics, and economics perhaps better than any other single event in postwar U.S.–German relations. The protesters outside the fair reminded Americans that the postwar reconciliation between Germany and the United States and Germany's economic reconstruction came at the expense of an accounting of Germany's war crimes. While the Nuremberg trials and other American denazification efforts brought some war criminals to justice, denazification occurred in the context of increasingly cordial relations between Americans and Germans. Americans and Germans had traded justice and moral atonement for economics and ideological anti-communism. By 1949, most Americans and Germans had tacitly agreed, at least for the time being, to mute discussion of the wartime past and focus on the postwar future.

Notes

Introduction

1. For more detail see Collier, *Bridge Across the Sky*, 86–89, 105–107. See also Grathwol, Moorhus, *American Forces in Berlin*, 48–49.

2. In 1947, Americans provided economic assistance to western Europe, including Germany, through the Marshall Plan. They created American Information Centers in most major German cities as a vehicle for the introduction of American culture, literature, and art to the German people. In 1955, Germany joined NATO and reestablished a German military force of limited capability. For an overview see Jonas, *The United States and Germany*, 275–98; Gatzke, *Germany and the United States*, 179–89; Ninkovich, *Germany and the United States*.

3. For more detail on the constitutional history of the Federal Republic see Golay, *The Founding of the Federal Republic of Germany*; Wengst, *Staatsaufbau und Regierungspraxis 1948–1953*, esp. 80; Kleßmann, *Die doppelte Staatsgründung*, 193–202.

4. Jonas, *The United States and Germany*, 286.

5. Largely positive accounts of the occupation include Zink, *The United States and Germany*; Gimbel, *The American Occupation of Germany*; Peterson, *The American Occupation of Germany*; Backer, The Decision to Divide Germany; Backer, *Winds of History*; Browder, *Americans in Post-World War II Germany*.

6. Works on denazification include Bower, *The Pledge Betrayed*; Niethammer, *Entnazifizierung in Bayern*. On both denazification and reeducation see Tent, *Mission on the Rhine*. On political reconstruction see Gimbel, *A German Community under American Occupation*; Kleßmann, *Die Doppelte Staatsgründung*. On American economic policies see Price, *The Marshall Plan and Its Meaning*; Gimbel, *The Origins of the Marshall Plan*; Hogan, *The Marshall Plan*.

7. Realist historians include Kennan, *American Diplomacy*; Spanier,

American Foreign Policy Since World War II, esp. 44–46, 63–66, and more recently Smith, *America's Mission.* William Appleman Williams introduced the revisionist interpretation of American foreign relations in *The Tragedy of American Diplomacy,* esp. 258–75. Bruce Kuklick applied that interpretation to American-Soviet relations during the occupation period in *American Policy and the Division of Germany,* 1–2, 8–10, 226–35. See also LaFeber, *America, Russia, and the Cold War,* esp. 41–42, 47–48; Eisenberg, *Drawing the Line.*

8. See Gehring, *Amerikanische Literaturpolitik in Deutschland;* Lange, *Theater in Deutschland.*

9. Willett, *The Americanization of Germany;* Berghahn, *The Americanisation of West German Industry;* Maase, *Bravo Amerika* and *Amerikanisierung der Alltagskultur?;* Poiger, *Jazz, Rock, and Rebels;* Fehrenbach, *Cinema in Democratizing Germany;* Schivelbusch, *Vor dem Vorhang.*

10. Many of these studies focused on the hardships of families as they tried to locate lost relatives, were expelled from the East, coped with food and fuel shortages, made do without a breadwinner, and rebuilt homes and cities destroyed by the bombs. See for instance Heineman, *What Difference Does a Husband Make?;* Niethammer, *"Hinterher merkt man";* Meyer, Schulze, *Wie wir das alles geschafft haben;* Meyer, Schulze, *Von Liebe sprach damals keiner;* Meyer, Schulze, *Auswirkungen des II. Weltkriegs auf Familien;* Freier, Kuhn, *Das Schicksal Deutschlands liegt in der Hand seiner Frauen;* Ruhl, *Unsere verlorenen Jahre;* Ruhl, *Die Besatzer und die Deutschen;* Ruhl, *Deutschland 1945;* Ruhl, *Frauen in der Nachkriegszeit;* Spindler, *Wie wir hamsterten, hungerten und überlebten;* Broszat, Henke, Woller, eds. *Von Stalingrad zur Währungsreform.*

11. Grossman, "A Question of Silence," 43–63. A controversial and somewhat one-sided treatment of rape during the occupation is Helke Sander and Barbara Johr's monograph, based on a film documentary of the same title, *BeFreier und Befreite.* For details on the impact of occupation troops on a particular community in the 1950s see Höhn, "GIs, Veronicas and Lucky Strikes."

12. Naimark, *The Russians in Germany,* 4.

13. See for instance Heineman, *What Difference Does a Husband Make?;* Höhn, "GIs, Veronicas and Lucky Strikes," Poiger, *Jazz, Rock, and Rebels;* Fehrenbach, *Cinema in Democratizing Germany.*

14. For more detail see Eric Foner, *Reconstruction: America's Unfinished Revolution, 1863–1877* (New York: Harper & Row, 1988).

15. Silber, *The Romance of Reunion,* 6, 64.

16. On Japan see Schaller, *The American Occupation of Japan;* Finn, *Winners in Peace;* on the German constitution see Wengst, *Staatsaufbau und Regierungspraxis.*

17. Dower, *Embracing Defeat,* 138. See also Shibusawa, "America's Geisha Ally."

18. Rotter, "Gender Relations, Foreign Relations," 542. See also *Comrades at Odds.*

19. "Zunahme der weiblichen Bevölkerung"; Stand, 29.10. 1948," Länderrat des amerikanischen Besatzungsgebietes: Memorandum über die soziale Lage in der US-Zone, Handakten Preller, 21, 965. Bundesarchiv Koblenz.

20. Since the early 1980s historians of American foreign relations have moved into that direction. See for instance Dower *War Without Mercy; Michael Hunt, The Making of a Special Relationship: The United and China to 1914* (New York: Columbia University Press, 1983), ix–x; and Hunt, *Ideology and U.S. Foreign Policy,* esp. 12–13; Iriye, *Power and Culture.* Rosenberg, *Spreading the American Dream.*

21. Geertz, *The Interpretation of Cultures,* 312.

22. See for instance Costigliola, *France and the United States;* Hoganson, *Fighting for American Manhood;* see also Emily S. Rosenberg's article on the use of gender ideology for the history of American foreign relations, "Gender," 116–24, esp. 119; Scott, "Gender: A Useful Category of Historical Analysis," 1053–75, esp. 1073.

23. See Scott, *Gender and the Politics of History,* 6.

24. Höhn, "GIs, Veronikas, and Lucky Strikes."

25. Several historians have elaborated on this universalization of German women's postwar experiences. See for instance Heineman, "The Hour of the Woman" and *What Difference Does a Husband Make?* See also Moeller, *Protecting Motherhood,* 2.

Chapter 1. "Know Your Enemy?": American and German Wartime Images

1. Giles, The G.I. Journal of Sergeant Giles, 252, 267.

2. For more detail see Nolan, *Visions of Modernity;* Peukert, *The Weimar Republic.*

3. Dorothy Thompson in "Vansittart, Dorothy Thompson Argue the Hard Peace Question" *Newsweek,* 9 October 1944, 104–11. The influential theologian Reinhold Niebuhr believed that western civilization was in part responsible for the excesses of the Nazi regime. Referring to Hitler's policy toward the Jews, he wrote that "we should be overwhelmed by a sense of guilt in contemplating those aspects of the problem which Hitler did not create but only aggravated," in "Jews After the War," *The Nation,* 21 February 1942, 214.

4. Quoted in Blum, *V Was for Victory,* 31.

5. Capra, *The Name Above the Title,* 332.

6. *Prelude to War,* pt. 1 of series *Why We Fight,* directed by Frank Capra, produced by Office of War Information, Bureau of Motion Pictures, 54 min., 1942, videocassette.

7. Ibid.

8. *The Nazis Strike,* pt. 2 of series: *Why We Fight,* 41 min., 1942.

9. "Vansittart, Dorothy Thompson Argue the Hard Peace Question," *Newsweek,* 9 October 1944, 104, 107, 108.

10. Among the American supporters of Vansittart's theory were William Montgomery McGovern, Henry Morgenthau, and Theodore Kaufman. See Burleigh and Wippermann, *The Racial State*, 7–8.

11. Emil Ludwig, "How to Treat Defeated Germany," *Collier's*, 2 October 1943, 18. See also his more extensive treatment of the subject in *How to Treat the Germans*.

12. Ibid.

13. See for instance "Don't Call Them Vandals, It Isn't Fair to the Vandals," *Newsweek*, 25 October 1943, 112. The article traced German vandalism as far back as the year 455. Leopold Schwarzschild, "Six Delusions About Germany," *New York Times Magazine*, 1 October 1944, 5. Schwarzschild, himself a refugee from Germany, asserted that the master-race idea permeated all of German society.

14. F. W. Foerster, "Peace With Germany: What Is the German 'Problem'?" *The Commonweal*, 7 January 1944, 298.

15. Schultz, *Germany Will Try It Again*. M. W. Fodor summarized her arguments in his review of the book in *Saturday Review of Literature*, 5 February 1944, 8.

16. Fodor, Saturday Review of Literature, 8, 9.

17. Nizer, *What to Do With Germany*, 52, 92.

18. Brickner, *Is Germany Incurable?*, 30, 101. For more information on Brickner's approach see Uta Gerhardt, "A Hidden Agenda of Recovery: The Psychiatric Conceptualization of Re-education for Germany in the United States during World War II," *German History* 14, no. 3 (1996): 297–324. See also Hofstadter, *The Paranoid Style in American Politics*, 3–40.

19. "What Shall We Do With Germany? A Panel Discussion of 'Is Germany Incurable?'" *Saturday Review of Literature*, 29 May 1943, 6, 7.

20. Ibid., 4–6

21. Ibid., 7–8, 10.

22. Morgenthau, *Germany Is Our Problem*, 105.

23. Ibid., 44–63.

24. Roosevelt-Churchill memorandum, 15 September 1944, in *Foreign Relations of the United States: The Conference at Quebec, 1944*, 467 (FRUS hereafter).

25. Henry L. Stimson to the President, 15 September 1944, in Henry L. Stimson Diaries, Yale University Library Manuscript Collection, vol. XLVIII, p. 84; diary entry, 14 September 1944, p. 74.

26. Roosevelt to Hull, 29 September 1944, in *FRUS: The Conferences at Malta and Yalta*, 155.

27. Roosevelt to Hull, 20 October 1944, *FRUS*, 159.

28. Roosevelt at a joint press conference with Winston Churchill at Casablanca, 24 January 1943, in *Public Papers*, vol. 12, 39.

29. Roosevelt at a press conference aboard the U.S.S. Quincy, 23 February 1945, in *Public Papers*, vol. 13, 560.

30. *Public Opinion Quarterly* (Winter 1943), 755.

31. "Mimic," in *Washington Post*, 1 July 1942. Reprinted in Dower, *War Without Mercy*, 34.

32. Dower, *War Without Mercy*, 78–79.

33. *Public Opinion Quarterly* (Winter 1943), 755; (Spring 1943), 173; (Summer 1944), 296. For caricatures of Japanese see Dower, *War Without Mercy*, 182–90.

34. Americans often dismissed reports of German atrocities because they had proven to be false during World War I. On America's anti-German propaganda campaign during World War I see Kennedy, *Over Here*, 24, 53–57.

35. Herzstein, *Roosevelt and Hitler*, 154–55, 184–86. Coughlin did not have any direct connections to fascist organizations, but many of his views appealed to those with openly fascist leanings. For more detail see Brinkley, *Voices of Protest*, 274–75.

36. For more detail see Wyman, *The Abandonment of the Jews*, 42–58.

37. Office of Facts and Figures, Bureau of Intelligence, "Negroes in a Democracy at War," cited in Black and Koppes, "Blacks, Loyalty, and Motion Picture Propaganda," 386.

38. James, "Why Negroes Should Oppose the War," 28–29, 37.

39. Von Eschen, *Race Against Empire*, 33.

40. Avery, *Up From Washington*, 170–71. See also Plummer, *Rising Wind*, 76–77.

41. Myrdal, *An American Dilemma*, 1004.

42. Quoted in Myrdal, *An American Dilemma*, 1009.

43. Ulric Bell and William B. Lewis to Archibald MacLeish, 3 February 1942, quoted in Polenberg, *One Nation Divisible*, 47.

44. Polenberg, *One Nation Divisible* 46, 77–78.

45. Heiden, *Der Führer*, 722, 772–74.

46. "The Enemy and His Future: Reviews of Four Books Dealing With Germany and the German People," *Saturday Review of Literature*, 5 February 1944, 5.

47. Black and Koppes, *Hollywood Goes to War*, 279–301.

48. Doherty, *Projections of War*, 124.

49. Shull and Wilt, *Hollywood War Films*, 215.

50. "Vansittart, Dorothy Thompson," *Newsweek*, 9 October 1944, 108, 110.

51. "The Enemy and His Future," *Saturday Review of Literature*, 5 February 1944, 10.

52. James P. Warburg, "Can the Germans Cure Themselves?" *New York Times Magazine*, 20 August 1944, 11. A similar debate about the connection between German culture and the holocaust ensued recently with the publication of Daniel Jonah Goldhagen's book, *Hitler's Willing Executioners*. Goldhagen found evidence suggesting that the willingness to torture and kill Jews was ingrained in German culture even before the Nazis came to power. The book sparked a heated debate among holocaust scholars in the United States,

Germany, and Israel. For a selection of reviews see Schoeps, ed., *Ein Volk von Mördern?*

53. Emmet Lavery, "The Enemy in Perspective," *The Commonweal,* 19 November 1943, 112, 113.

54. M. Hall, "The Kind of Germans We Need," *Christian Century,* 18 April 1945, 488−90.

55. See Dorothy Thompson in "Vansittart, Dorothy Thompson," 110; Alexander S. Lipsett, "Germans Themselves Held Entitled to Punish the Nazis," *New York Times,* 6 February 1945, 6.

56. "Are Germans Incurable?" *Christian Century,* 6 October 1943, 1128.

57. In a study of the magazine, *Berliner Illustrierte,* Josef Roidl found that the volume of U.S.- related articles increased after 1936 by more than two thirds. In 1938 it actually exceeded the level published in 1927. Most of these articles were either neutral or positive in content. Cited in Hans Dieter Schäfer, "Amerikanismus im Dritten Reich," in Prinz and Zitelmann, *Nationalsozialismus und Modernisierung,* 205.

58. Nolan, *Visions of Modernity,* 108−20; Peukert, *The Weimar Republic,* 178−90; Gassert, *Amerika im Dritten Reich,* 17, 103.

59. Nolan, *Visions of Modernity,* 232−35.

60. Schoenbaum, *Hitler's Social Revolution,* 193; Peukert, *Inside Nazi Germany,* 107.

61. See Barron, *"Degenerate Art,"* 9. Catalog of an exhibition in 1991 at the Los Angeles County Museum of Art and other museums in the United States and Europe, documenting the 1937 Nazi exhibition "Entartete Kunst."

62. Schivelbusch, *Vor dem Vorhang,* 25.

63. For more detail see Jost Hermand, "Bewährte Tümlichkeiten. Der völkisch-nazistische Traum einer ewig-deutschen Kunst," in Denkler and Prümm, *Die deutsche Literatur im Dritten Reich,* 102.

64. Bodo Heinemann, "Die Konvergenz der Einzelgänger. Literatur als Integration des Problematischen Individuums in die Volksgemeinschaft: Hermann Stehr—Emil Strauß—Erwin Guido Kolbenheyer," in Denkler, Prümm, *Die deutsche Literatur im Dritten Reich,* 119. On anti-Americanism in Weimar Germany see also Stefan Zweig, "Die Monotisierung der Welt," *Berliner Börsen-Courier,* 1 February 1925; Rudolph Kayser, "Amerikanismus," *Vossische Zeitung,* 27 September 1925; Nolan, *Visions of Modernity,* 154−55. See also Bollenbeck, *Tradition, Avantgarde, Reaktion,* 260−62.

65. For a more detailed discussion of Nazi propaganda see Reuth, *Goebbels.*

66. Gassert, *Amerika im Dritten Reich,* 109−12; Milde, "Lernen von den Eskimos," 146−58.

67. See especially Ross, *Amerikas Schicksalsstunde.* The book was so popular in Germany that the publisher had brought out twelve editions by 1942. See also Ross, *Unser Amerika* and *Die "Westliche Hemisphäre."*

68. Ross was the most prolific and best known of several Nazi authors on

the United States. Others included Adolf Halfeld, *USA greift in die Welt;* Gieselher Wirsing, *Der masslose Kontinent.* For more detail see Gassert, *Amerika im Dritten Reich,* 111–12.

69. "Schwieriges, ja eigentlich unerklärliches Phänomen." Ross, *Die "Westliche Hemisphäre,"* 214.

70. "Selbstschutzmassnahmen des nationalsozialistischen Staates." Ibid., 215.

71. See *Rund um die Freiheitsstatue: Ein Spaziergang durch die USA,* Ministerium für Volksaufklärung und Propaganda, 1941; *Herr Roosevelt Plaudert,* 1943; Filmarchiv, Bundesarchiv Koblenz.

72. Otto Veit, "Franklin Roosevelts Experiment: Amerikas Abkehr von der Wirtschaftsfreiheit," in *Die Neue Rundschau,* December 1934, 719, 724.

73. "Die USA an der Wende zum Nationalen Sozialismus, " in *Die Koralle,* 7 September 1933, 453. See also Hellmuth Schneider-Landmann's "Die Wirtschaftsrevolution in USA und ihr Revolutionär," in *Deutsche Rundschau,* März, 1934, 149–56; Adolf Reichwein, "Amerikanischer Horizont," *Deutsche Rundschau,* February 1938, 106–13.

74. Gassert, *Amerika im Dritten Reich,* 209–30.

75. "Vortrag Curt Ludwig Freiherr von Gienanth anläßlich der Tagung der Leiter der Reichspropagandaämter am 13. und 14. Juli, 1942 im Reichsministerium für Volksaufklärung und Propaganda, Berlin," Bundesarchiv Koblenz, R 55, No. 606, pp. 13, 14.

76. Nolan, *Visions of Modernity,* 115–16; Peukert, *The Weimar Republic,* 178–90.

77. Gatzke, *Germany and the United States,* 97.

78. *Herr Roosevelt Plaudert.*

79. "Vortrag Curt Ludwig Freiherr von Gienanth," 17.

80. Ross referred here to a series of articles published by Ford in the *Dearborn Independent* in 1920. The collection of articles was published in Germany under the title *Der Internationale Jude;* Ross, *Die "Westliche Hemisphäre,"* 217, 225.

81. Hitler, *Hitlers Zweites Buch,* 124–25; see also Jonas, *The United States and Germany,* 212, 240–41, 244–45.

82. *Hitler's Table Talk,* 188.

83. See for instance, "USA Wohin?" *Die Koralle,* 9 February 1936, 171–73.

84. Schäfer, *Das Gespaltene Bewußtsein,* 146–47.

85. May wrote dozens of adventure stories situated in exotic places, the most famous of them taking place in the American West. See for instance May, *Winnetou I, Winnetou II, Winnetou III.*

86. A survey of several popular magazines and literary journals produced many articles on the American West. See for instance D. H. Lawrence, "Indianische Mysterien," *Neue Rundschau,* January 1934, 79–94; "Promotion mit Winnetou," *Deutsche Rundschau,* May 1936, 148; Gregor Heinrich, "Landnahme

des Weißen Mannes in Amerika," *Deutsche Rundschau,* August 1936, 183–86; "Buffalo Bill mit Hornbrille: Wie William Cody der Held unserer Jugendträume wurde," *Die Koralle,* 22 October 1934, 1178–79; A. E. Johann, " 'Learn' Indianer oder Stirb!" *Die Koralle,* 12 November 1934, 1255–57; "Cowboy-Romantik wie es sie wirklich noch gibt." *Die Koralle,* 19 May 1935, 617–19.

87. Schäfer, "Amerikanismus im Dritten Reich," in Prinz, Zitelmann, *Nationalsozialismus und Modernisierung*, 205.

88. Official announcement of the prize in the magazine *Jugendschriften-Warte,* 45 (1940): 1; cited in Renate Jaroslawski, Rüdiger Steinlein, "Die 'politische Jugendschrift.' Zur Theorie und Praxis faschistischer deutscher Jugendliteratur," in Denkler, Prümm, *Die deutsche Literatur,* 320, 321.

89. Kater, "Forbidden Fruit?", 14. For a more extensive treatment of the subject see Kater, *Different Drummers,* especially 33–56.

90. Friedrich Welter, "Um die Deutsche Musik—Ein Bekenntnis," *Die Musik,* 25 (1933), 728; Cited in Kater, "Forbidden Fruit?" 14, 15.

91. Kater, *Different Drummers,* 47.

92. Kater, "Forbidden Fruit?" 20, 24; *Different Drummers,* 48.

93. Schäfer, *Das Gespaltene Bewußtsein,* 176. See also Kater, *Different Drummers,* 71–75, 148–57.

94. Peukert, *Inside Nazi Germany,* 166.

95. Kater, "Forbidden Fruit?", 28.

96. Schäfer, *Das Gespaltene Bewußtsein,* 167.

97. Cited in Gassert, *Amerika im Dritten Reich,* 115. The figures are 340 books between 1924 and 1930; 442 books between 1933 and 1939.

98. Saunders, *Hollywood in Berlin,* 129, 181, see also illustrations 38, 39, 41, 44.

99. Schäfer, "Amerikanismus im Dritten Reich," in Prinz, Zitelmann, *Nationalsozialismus und Modernisierung,* 203–4.

100. Jeffrey Herf has called this phenomenon "reactionary Modernism." In *Reactionary Modernism.* For a critical assessment see Rabinbach, "Nationalsozialismus und Moderne," 110.

101. For a more detailed discussion of American consumer society in the 1920s see Perrett, *America in the Twenties,* especially 348–53; Parrish, *Anxious Decades,* 74–81.

102. "Hier Amerika!" in Schäfer, *Das gespaltene Bewußtsein,* illustration 35.

103. Shäfer, "Amerikanismus im Dritten Reich," in Prinz, Zitelmann, *Nationalsozialismus und Modernisierung,* 203.

104. *Berliner Tageblatt,* 15 February 1936.

Chapter 2. Crossing the Border: The Breakdown of the Fraternization Ban

1. Drew Middleton, "Into Germany With the First Army," *New York Times Magazine,* 8 October 1944, 5.

2. "Policy, Relationship Between Allied Occupying Troops and Inhabitants of Germany," 12 September 1944, Appendix to letter from Eisenhower to Commanding Generals, File 091–4 (Germany), Adjutant General's Records 1944, SHAEF, RG 331, NA.

3. The demand for unconditional surrender of all Axis powers was announced during the Conference at Casablanca between President Roosevelt and Prime Minister Churchill in January 1943. See transcripts of press conference, Casablanca, January 24, 1943 in *FRUS: The Conferences at Washington, 1941–1942, and Casablanca, 1943*, 727. At the Quebec Conference in the fall of 1944, the Allies further discussed Germany's unconditional surrender.

4. Henke, *Die Amerikanische Besetzung Deutschlands*, 96, 205–52.

5. The Joint Chiefs of Staff document JCS 1067 took effect in its final version on 10 May 1945. See U.S. Department of State, *Documents on Germany, 1944–1985*, 15–32.

6. Henke, *Die Amerikanische Besetzung Deutschlands*, 203–204.

7. "Zunahme der weiblichen Bevölkerung; Stand, 29.10.1946," Länderrat des amerikanischen Besatzungsgebietes: Memorandum über die soziale Lage in der US-Zone, Handakten Preller, Z1, 965, Bundesarchiv Koblenz.

8. For a detailed discussion of various reasons for the non-fraternization policy see *Fraternization with the Germans*, 10–13.

9. *Pocket Guide to Germany*.

10. Ibid., 7

11. Ibid., 9.

12. Ibid., 10, 4.

13. *New York Times Magazine*, 8 October 1944, 32.

14. *The Pocket Guide*, 28.

15. Ludwig, Vansittart, and Morgenthau were the leading proponents of a harsh peace with Germany. See Morgenthau Jr., *Germany Is Our Problem;* Ludwig, "How to Treat Defeated Germany," *Collier's*, October 1943, 18; "Vansittart, Dorothy Thompson," *Newsweek*, 9 October 1944, 104, 107–108.

16. *Pocket Guide*, 2, 36–48, 17–18.

17. Message from Eisenhower to General Marshall, 4 October 1944, File 091–4 (Germany), Adjutant General's Records 1944, SHAEF, RG 331, NA.

18. "Policy, Relationship Between Allied Occupying Troops and Inhabitants of Germany," 3, 5–6.

19. "Nazis Organize Guerilla Army for Underground War to Death," *Newsweek*, 30 October 1944, 59.

20. "Germany: Heavings," *Time*, 25 September 1944, 37.

21. Ibid.

22. "German Cassino," *Newsweek*, 2 October 1944, 30.

23. *Fraternization with the Germans*, 18.

24. See Wyman, *The Abandonment of the Jews*, 322–25.

25. Abzug, *Inside the Vicious Heart*, 19.

26. Quoted in Abzug, *Inside the Vicious Heart*, 30.

27. Interview with Fred Bohm, The Fred R. Crawford Witness to the Holocaust Project, Emory University, Atlanta, Georgia, quoted in Abzug, *Inside the Vicious Heart*, 33.

28. See figure 2.1 in this volume.

29. Stefan Heym, "Germans Hear a New Master's Voice," *New York Times Magazine*, 3 December 1944, 54.

30. "Friends or Enemies?" *Newsweek*, 2 October 1944, 54.

31. Clifton Daniel, "If You Should Meet a German—How Would You Handle Him?", *New York Times Magazine*, 10 December 1944, 11.

32. Message from General Eisenhower to 12th Army Group (Personal for Bradley), 17 September 1944, File 91–4 (Germany), Adjutant General's Records, 1944, SHAEF, RG 331, NA.

33. Message from General Marshall to General Eisenhower, 21 September 1944, File 91–4 (Germany), Adjutant General's Records, 1944, SHAEF, RG 331, NA.

34. Message from Eisenhower to Commanding Generals, 26 September 1944, File 91–4 (Germany), Adjutant General's Records, 1944, SHAEF, RG 331, NA.

35. "Occupation: Unofficial Mercy," *Time*, 2 October 1944, 63.

36. Ibid.

37. Arthur Goodfriend, Report to: Chief, Special and Information Services, Subject: "Fraternization between Germans and American Officers and Men," Report to Chief, Special and Information Services, File 250.1–1, G-1 (Personnel), SHAEF, RG 331, NA., p. 1.

38. Dispatch to *Stars and Stripes*, Liege, Paris, from correspondent Leiser en route with the Ninth Army, 14 March 1945, File 250.1–1, G-1 Division (Personnel), SHAEF, RG 331, NA.

39. Goodfriend, "Fraternization," 2–3.

40. Ibid, 8.

41. "Letter from Germany," *American Mercury*, 61 (August 1945), 157–58.

42. Percy Knauth, "Fraternization: The Word Takes on a Brand-New Meaning in Germany," *Life*, 2 July 1945, 26.

43. Wolff-Mönckeberg, *On the Other Side*, 27 May 1945, 125.

44. Ibid., 1 June 1945, 127.

45. "Germany: Chaos and Comforts," *Time*, 16 April 1945, 38; See also *Fraternization with the Germans*, 18.

46. Wolff-Mönckeberg, *On the Other Side*, 20 April 1945, 114.

47. Henke, *Die amerikanische Besetzung Deutschlands*, 89–93.

48. Wolff-Mönckeberg, *On the Other Side*, 1 May 1945, 117; 6 May 1945, 120. See also Udo Haltermann, ed., *So erlebten wir das Ende: Als Deutschland den Zweiten Weltkrieg verlor, Erinnerungen* (Nettetal: Steylerverlag, 1988), 69.

49. "Letter from Germany," *American Mercury*, 61 (August 1945) 157.

50. *Farbige Franzosen am Rhein*. After the publication of the pamphlet the left wing British writer and journalist E. D. Morell published an article titled "The Black Horror on the Rhine" in the *Daily Herald* on 10 April 1920. This term then became the rallying cry for racists in both the United States and Europe. Cited in Pommerin, "The Fate of Mixed Blood Children, 316–17. See also Nelson, "The Black Horror on the Rhine."

51. *American Representation in Occupied Germany*, 102. See also, Pommerin, "The Fate of Mixed Blood Children," 317; Nelson, "The Black Horror on the Rhine," 615.

52. Maria Lorentz, *Die ersten Tage mit den Amerikanern*, (TS, Stuttgart 1977), Projekt "Senioren schreiben Geschichte," J 175, 799, Hauptstaatsarchiv, Stuttgart, p. 4.

53. In some areas, Germans also encountered French Moroccan soldiers. Even though evidence is sketchy and largely anecdotal, there seems to have been again more suspicion toward those African soldiers than African-American soldiers.

54. " Woimmer ein Neger einem deutschen Kind begegnete, verzog sich sein Mund zu einem breiten Grinsen. Dunkle Hände streichelten blonde Haare, griffen in's Gepäck oder in die Brusttasche der Uniform und zauberten Täfelchen brauner Schokolade hervor, für viele der Kleinen die erste Schokolade ihres Lebens." Heinz C. Schade, *Sieger und Besiegte: Amerikaner und Deutsche anno 1945*, (TS, Stuttgart 1977), Projekt "Senioren schreiben Geschichte," J 175, 126 b, Hauptstaatsarchiv Stuttgart, p. 1.

55. "Hauptsächlich verwöhnten sie die Kinder; ihnen wurde Kaugummi und Süssigkeiten gegeben, wasimmer sie wollten. Vor der Bergschule sass ein schwarzer Wachtposten, sein Gewehr in den Himmel gerichtet. Alle paar Minuten feuerte er einen Luftschuss, nur um die Kinder zu belustigen." Ernst Kuch, *Kriegsende in Heidenheim* (TS, Stuttgart 1977), Projekt "Senioren schreiben Geschichte," J 175, 1605, Hauptstaatsarchiv Stuttgart.

56. Niethammer, *"Hinterher merkt man,"* 20–24.

57. "Es waren fast durchweg Neger, vollblütig und grinsend, die aus dem Wagen zum Vorschein kamen, doch alle gutmütig und freundlich." *Über die Kriegsereignisse 1945 und das Ausmaß der Zerstörungen im Zweiten Weltkrieg: 1948–1952*, Hofen, Zipplingen, Kreis Aalen, J 170, Bü. 88, Hauptstaatsarchiv Stuttgart. See also reports from other towns in the same collection, i.e. Zipplingen, Hohenstaufen, Jagstzell.

58. *Berichte von Gemeinden*, Hohenstaufen, Kreis Göppingen.

59. *Berichte von Gemeinden*, Jagtzell, Kertzingen, Kreis Aalen; Ilsfeld, Kreis Heilbronn; Blumweiler, Kreis Mergentheim. Complaints about rape came from Satteldorf, Kreis Crailsheim; and Herbrechtingen, Kreis Heidenheim.

60. *Berichte von Gemeinden*, Unterwilfingen, Kreis Aalen.

61. *Berichte von Gemeinden*, Zipplingen, Kreis Aalen.

62. Information Control Intelligence Summary (ICIS) No. 16, 27 October 1945, Office of the Military Government for Germany, File 2, Box 154, OMGUS, RG 260, National Records Center, Suitland, Maryland (NRC hereafter).

63. Ann Sloan, letter to author, 17 July 1992.

64. Frieda Berger Webb, interview with author, 20 June 1992. Only years later, when they met in the United States did Frieda learn his real identity.

65. Letter from Brigadier General R. B. Lovett, USA, Adjutant General, to Commanding Generals, Subject: Military Personnel Having Relatives in Occupied Germany, 29 March 1945, File 250.1–4, SHAEF, RG. 331, NA.

66. Letter from Colonel James M. White, GSC, Deputy ACofS, G-2, to G-1, Subject: Military Personnel Having Relatives in Occupied Germany, 26 May 1945, File 250.1, SHAEF, RG. 331, NA.

67. Krause, *So I Was a Sergeant*, 41, 196.

68. *Fraternization with the Germans*, 28.

69. Ralf G. Martin, "What Kind of Peace? The Soldier's Viewpoint," *New York Times Magazine*, 11 March 1945, 5.

70. Bach Jr., *America's Germany*, 265.

71. Ibid., 261, 265–67.

72. Arthur Goodfriend, Report to: Chief, Special and Information Services, Subject: "Fraternization between Germans and American Officers and Men," Report to Chief, Special and Information Services, File 250.1–1, G-1 (Personnel), SHAEF, RG 331, NA., p. 3.

73. "Legacy of Hate," *Newsweek*, 3 September 1945, 45.

74. Levin, *In Search*, 229.

75. Ibid., 198.

76. "The Problem of Non-Fraternization," Paper prepared by CCMS (Air) School, from G. L. Worthington, Air Commodore, Assistant Chief of Staff, A-4, to G-1 (Personnel), 29 April 1945, File 250.1–1, G-1, SHAEF, RG 331, NA, p.1.

77. Ibid., 1–2.

78. For a detailed plan of the orientation campaign led by the Publicity and Psychological Warfare Section, Twelfth Army Group, see "Policy, Relationship between Allied Occupying Troops and Inhabitants of Germany," Memorandum from Headquarters, Twelfth Army Group, to Chiefs of Staff Sections, File 91–4 (Germany), Adjutant General's Records, SHAEF, RG 331, NA.

79. *Fraternization with the Germans*, 21.

80. See list of seventy-four American non-fraternization announcements made on AFN Stations, March 1945, File 250.1–5, G-1 (Personnel), SHAEF, RG 331, NA.

81. "Policy, Relationship between Allied Occupying Troops and Inhabitants of Germany," Memorandum from G-5 (Civil Affairs Div., Legal Branch) to G-1 (Personnel), 17 February 1945, File 250.1–2, G-1 (Personnel), SHAEF, RG 331, NA.

82. Memorandum to Colonel Brooks from Lieutenant Colonel E. C.

Woodall, AAG, 26 March 1945, File 250.1–2, G-1 (Personnel), SHAEF, RG 331, NA.

83. Letter from Colonel H. H. Newman, Assistant Adjutant General, by direction of the Supreme Commander to Commanding Generals, Sixth Army Group, Twelfth Army Group, Headquarters 21 Army Group; Subject: Non-Fraternization by Germans, 10 March 1945, File 091–1 (Germany), Adjutant General's Records, 1945, SHAEF, RG 331, NA.

84. Memorandum from Douglas H. Schneider, Assistant Chief Division for Control of German Information Services, Psychological Warfare Division, to McClure, 30 May 1945, File 250.1–11, G-1 (Personnel), SHAEF, RG 331, NA.

85. Letter from Eisenhower to Marshall "Eyes Only," 2 June 1945, File 250.1–6, G-1 (Personnel), SHAEF, RG 331, NA.

86. See letter from ETOUSA, signed Eisenhower, to Commanding Generals; Subject: Non-Fraternization Order, 8 June 1945, File 250.1–6, G-1 (Personnel), SHAEF, RG 331, NA.

87. Press Statement from Eisenhower, 14 July 1945, File 250.1–11, G-1 (Personnel), SHAEF, RG 331, NA.

88. Memorandum from Colonel William S. Paley, Psychological Warfare Division, to Brigadier General Robert A. McClure, Subject: Non-Fraternization Policy, 30 May 1945, File 250.1–11, G-1 (Personnel), SHAEF, RG 331, NA.

89. Press Statement from Eisenhower, 14 July 1945, File 250.1–11, G-1 (Personnel), SHAEF, RG 331, NA.

90. In July 1945 the Nuremberg war crimes trial of the Nazi elite had not even begun yet. For more information on denazification see Kleßmann, *Die Doppelte Staatsgründung,* 78–92; Conot, *Justice at Nuremberg.*

91. On the cancellation of non-fraternization see Message from U.S. Group Control Council to Headquarters USFET for Action; Subject: Non-Fraternization, 28 September 1945; and Message from USFET, Main, signed Eisenhower, to Commanding posts, 29 September 1945, File 261.01, OMGUS, RG 260, NRC.

92. Clifton Daniel, "If You Should Meet a German—How Would You Handle Him?" *New York Times Magazine,* 10 December 1944, 11.

93. "Legacy of Hate," *Newsweek,* 3 September 1945, 44.

94. Saul Padover, "Why Americans Like German Women," *American Mercury,* 63 (September 1946), 357.

95. See "The Quarter's Poll," *Public Opinion Quarterly* (Fall 1945), 385. Disapproval of fraternization decreased somewhat among older women and increased among older men.

96. See Kuklick, *American Policy and the Division of Germany,* 194–95; Thilo Vogelsang, *Das Geteilte Deutschland* (München: DTV, 1966), 28–29; Eisenberg, *Drawing the Line,* 167–76.

97. In both the Soviet and French zones, relations between the civilian population and the occupation troops were tense, in sharp contrast to the cordiality observed in the U.S. zone. For more information see Klaus-

Dietmar Henke, "Politik der Widersprüche: Zur Charakterisierung der französischen Militärregierung in Deutschland nach dem zweiten Weltkrieg," in Scharf, Schröder, *Die Deutschlandpolitik Frankreichs*, 53–56; Naimark, *The Russians in Germany*, 69–140.

Chapter 3. Villians to Vicitms: The Cultural Feminization of Germany

1. James P. O'Donnell, "Do the Fräuleins Change Our Joe?" *Newsweek*, 24 December 1945, 50.

2. Percy Knauth, "Fraternization: The Word Takes on a Brand-New Meaning in Germany," *Life*, 2 July 1945, 26.

3. See "German-American Relations in Germany: Frequency of Group Contacts," 13 November 1946, Surveys Branch, Information Control Division (ICD hereafter), Report No. 27, File 6, Box 158, OMGUS (Rear), RG 260, p. 2; "Contacts between Germans and Americans," 24 February 1948, ICD Opinion Surveys, Report 94, OMGUS Berlin, Germany, File 6, Box 159, OMGUS, RG 260, NRC, p. 4.

4. Saul Padover, "Why Americans Like German Women," *American Mercury*, September 1946, 357.

5. Gray, *The Warriors*, 61. See also Krause, *So I Was a Sergeant*, 141.

6. Gray, *The Warriors*, 65–67.

7. Levin, *In Search*, 275–76, 279.

8. *Fraternization with the Germans*, 81–82.

9. Dispatch from correspondent Leiser to *Stars and Stripes*, Liege, Paris, en route with the Ninth Army 14 March 1945, File 250.1–1, G-1 Division (Personnel), SHAEF, RG 331, NA.

10. *Fraternization with the Germans*, 176.

11. Naimark, *The Russians in Germany*, 69–140, esp. 113–15; also Grossmann, "A Question of Silence," 43–63.

12. Knauth, "Fraternization," 26.

13. "Fraternization Code Honored in Breach," *New York Times*, 13 June 1945, 5.

14. Shukert, Scibetta, *War Brides of World War II*, 134.

15. *Fraternization with the Germans*, 136–39. See also "Deutsche Mädchen," *Frankfurter Rundschau*, 7 December 1946, 3. "Besatzung und Deutsche Frauen," *Süddeutsche Zeitung*, 12 June 1946, 2.

16. *Fraternization with the Germans*, 139.

17. "Fraeuleins Stay in U.S. Compound," *New York Times*, 4 March 1946, 5. See also *Fraternization with the Germans*, 132.

18. Shukert, Scibetta, *War Brides of World War II*, 132.

19. *Fraternization with the Germans*, 41, Table II

20. Kaethe Sears, letter to author, 8 June 1992.

21. Quoted in Shukert, Scibetta, *War Brides of World War II*, 129.
22. *Fraternization with the Germans*, 44–45.
23. Ann Sloan, letter to author, 17 July 1992.
24. Kaethe Sears, letter to author, 8 June 1992.
25. Ann Sloan, letter to author, 17 July 1992.
26. Liese-Lore Mathewson, letter to author, 21 June 1992.
27. Shukert, Scibetta, *War Brides of World War II*, 129.
28. Zink, *The United States in Germany*, 139–40. See also Prinz, ed., *Trümmerzeit in München*, 317–18.
29. "Interview-Auszug über Hamsterfahrten," Kuhn, ed., *Frauen in der Deutschen Nachkriegszeit*, 151–52.
30. Kirst, *Das Schaf im Wolfspelz*, 76.
31. Ann Sloan, letter to author, 17 July 1992.
32. "Junge, alleinstehende Frauen, deren Männer in Gefangenschaft, vermisst, oder gefallen, haben unregelmässigen Männerverkehr, mit Kraftfahrern, Ausländern, jedenfalls solchen, die ihnen Naturalien zubringen." In "Berichte der Familienfürsorgerinnen verschiedener nordrhein-westfälischer Städte über die Wohnverhältnisse, Ernährungsverhältnisse, Bekleidung und allgemeine Notlage der Bevölkerung," June 1947, cited in Kuhn, *Frauen in der Deutschen Nachkriegszeit*, vol. I, 44. Shukert, Scibetta, *War Brides of World War II*, 129–30; see also Ann Sloan's letter to the author, 17 July 1992.
33. The Marshall Plan allocated economic aid to Western European countries including the western zones of Germany. See Michael J. Hogan, *The Marshall Plan: America, Britain, and the Reconstruction of Western Europe, 1947–1952* (New York, 1987), 40, 129. See also *The Marshall Plan and Germany: West German Development within the Framework of the European Recovery Program*, ed. Charles Maier with the assistance of Günter Bischof (New York, 1991). On the Berlin airlift see Uwe Prell and Lothar Wilker, eds., *Berlin Blockade und Luftbrücke 1948/49: Analyse und Dokumentation* (Berlin, 1987); Avi Shlaim, *The United States and the Berlin Blockade, 1948–49: A Study in Decision-Making* (Berkeley, 1983); Daniel F. Harrington, "The Berlin Blockade Revisited," *The International History Review* 6 (February 1984): 88–112; and Hans Herzfeld, *Berlin in der Weltpolitik, 1945–1970* (Berlin, 1973), 230–71.
34. *Fraternization with the Germans*, 40. The drastic variations among the divisions could be explained in part by their role during the war. While the 4th Armored Division was engaged in active combat, the Quartermaster Corps stayed behind the lines to provide primarily food and clothing for the troops. The latter's distance from the fighting might have produced less hatred toward German civilians.
35. USFET *Report of Operations, 8 May–30 September 45*, Annex No. 11; Preventive Medicine Division, *Quarterly Report, 8 May-30 September 45*, Section III, "Venereal Disease Control." Cited in *Fraternization with the Germans*, 76.

There is reason to doubt the accuracy of the latter figure of eigthy-nine percent because racism pervaded the reports on army discipline in the American zone. News articles gave still different figures.

36. "Services: Disabilities and VD," *Newsweek*, 22 July 1946. See also "Medicine: The GI and VD," *Newsweek*, 2 September 1946

37. *Wirtschaft und Statistik*, 1950, 540−41. In 1934, one in 364 were infected with gonorrhea and one in 1,460 were infected with syphilis. See *Wirtschaft und Statistik*, 1949, 273−75. German newspapers reported widely on the problem of VD among Germans. See "Berlins Krankheitskurve seit 1945," *Der Tagesspiegel*, 23 January 1948; "TBC und Geschlechtskrankheiten," *Frankfurter Rundschau*, 16 November 1948.

38. For more information on the introduction of penicillin and its effect on the spread of venereal disease see Allan Brandt, *No Magic Bullet: A Social History of Venereal Disease in the United States since 1880* (New York, 1987), 161−82.

39. Sample of cartoons in *Newsweek*, 16 June 1947, 49.

40. *Wirtschaft und Statistik*, 1967, 391. See also Barbara Willenbacher, "Zerrüttung und Bewährung der Nachkriegs-Familie," [Breakdown and Endurance of the Postwar Family] in Broszat, Henke, Woller, eds. *Von Stalingrad zur Währungsreform*, 600−1;

41. Habe, *Our Love Affair with Germany*, 10; "Occupation: GI Legacy in Germany," *Newsweek*, 16 June 1947, 48.

42. Headquarters, USFET, to Commanding Generals, Subject: Paternity Claims by Non-Nationals, 5 March 1946, File 291.1, OMGUS, RG 260, NRC.

43. Letter, Ruth Haas, Wiesbaden, to Military Government, Subject: Recognition of Paternity, Application for Assistance, December 1948, File 291.1, OMGUS, RG 260, NRC.

44. Letter, Office of Military Government for Hesse, signed Robert W. Bruce, Assistant Executive Officer, to Ruth Haas, 15 December 1948, File 291.1, OMGUS, RG 260, NRC.

45. "Occupation," *Newsweek*, 16 June 1947, 48.

46. Message from USFET Main, signed Eisenhower, to Commanding Posts, 29 September 1945, RG 260, File 261.01, Box 87.

47. Circular 181, "Marriage," Headquarters U.S. Forces, European Theater, 19 December 1946, RG 332, File 291.1, Box 310

48. Public Law No. 271 went into effect on 28 December 1945. It was designed to speed up the process of immigration for spouses and children of citizen members of the armed forces. At this time most applications came from English-speaking countries such as Great Britain and Australia. For debate and Presidential approval of the bill see *Congressional Record*, 79th Cong., 1st sess., 10−12 December 1945, vol. 91, pt. 9:11738, 12341−2, 12547. "Bill to Facilitate the Admission into the United States of the Alien Fiancées or Fiancés of members of the Armed Forces of the United States," *Congressional Record*, 79th Cong., 2d sess., 10−29 June 1946, vol. 92, pt. 6:6919, 7317−18, 7602, 8016.

49. "Fräulein Trouble," *Newsweek*, 24 September 1945, 49.

50. "Three Former U.S. Soldiers Appeal to President Truman," *New York Times*, 23 January 1946, 6.

51. *Newsweek*, 4 February 1946, 58. It is unclear whether or what kind of punishment Horton received for his unilateral action.

52. Letter from H. R. Bull, Major General Chief of Staff, Headquarters USFET, to Chief of Operations, GSC, UNRRA, Arolsen, Germany, Subject: Alleged Marriage of UNRRA Employees to Germans, July 1946, File 291.1, ETO/USFET, RG 332, NRC.

53. Robert R. Rodgers, "2 Ex-GIs Wed German Girls in 'Loop-Hole' Ceremonies," *Stars and Stripes*, 6 July 1946, 1. Article attached to letter from H. R. Bull, Major General Chief of Staff, Headquarters USFET, to Chief of Operations, GSC, UNRRA, Arolsen, Germany, Subject: Alleged Marriage of UNRRA Employees to Germans, July 1946, File 291.1, ETO/USFET, RG 332, NRC.

54. Letter from E. L. Northcutt to General Joseph T. McNarney, 29 June 1946, File 291.1, ETO/USFET, RG 332, NRC.

55. Letter from Joseph Carl Korber to General Joseph T. McNarney, 9 December 1946, File 291.1, ETO/USFET, RG 332, NRC.

56. Letter from Richard Graham to General McNarney, 15 December 1946, File 291.1, ETO/USFET, RG 332, NRC. See also letter from William R. Fuchs in the same collection.

57. Headquarters USFET, Sec. IV, Circular 128, Subject: Marriages, 12 September 1946, File 291.1, ETO/USFET, RG 332, NRC. In June 1946 Congress passed the "Bill to facilitate the admission into the United States of the alien fiancées or fiancés of members of the armed forces of the United States." Known as Public Law 471, it served as the basis for Circular 128. On 19 December, 1946, it was replaced by a new directive, Circular 181. See *Congressional Record*, 79th Cong., 2nd sess., 10–29 June 1946, vol. 92, pt. 6, 6919, 7317–78, 7363, 7602, 8016.

58. Headquarters USFET, Circular 181, Subject: Marriages, 19 December 1946, File 291.1, ETO/USFET, RG 332, NRC.

59. Ibid.

60. *Congressional Record*, 79th Cong., 2nd sess., June 10–29, 1946, vol. 92, 8016.

61. The file on the case of Maylie and Kettler comprised fourteen documents between the dates of 30 January 1947 and 21 July 1947. The two finally gained permission to marry on 24 August 1947. File 291.1, OMGUS, RG 260, NRC.

62. Headquarters, Company "K," 16th Infantry Regiment, APO 742-A, signed Captain Raymond H. Smith, to Commanding Officer, 3rd Battalion, 16th Infantry Regiment, US Army, 14 February 1947; Headquarters 3rd Battalion, 16th Infantry Regiment, from Lieutenant Col. Edwin A. Machen to Commanding Officer, Hq Berlin Command, OMGUS, APO 742-A US Army, not dated, File 291.1, OMGUS, RG 260, NRC.

63. Appendix D to Application for Permission to Marry, from John R. Himes, Chaplain, to Commanding Officer, 3rd Battalion, 16th Infantry Regiment, 15 February 1947, File 291.1, OMGUS, RG 260, NRC.

64. OMGUS, Combined Travel Board, Subject: Statistical Report on German Fiancées, 12 June 1947, File 291.1, OMGUS, RG 260, NRC. See also "3000 Ehen beantragt," *Frankfurter Rundschau,* 27 September 1947, 3; Fast Zweihundert Eheschliessungen," *Frankfurter Rundschau,* 23 October 1947.

65. *Immigration and Naturalization Service: Annual Report 1950,* Table 9A; *Annual Report 1949,* Table 9A.

66. "German-American Relations in Germany: Frequency of Group Contacts," 13 November 1946, Surveys Branch, ICD, Report No. 27, File 6, Box 158, OMGUS (Rear), RG 260.

67. For more information see Verband der Deutsch-Amerikanischen Clubs/Federation of German-American Clubs, e.V., ed. *40 Jahre, 1948–1988,* 4. Later some women's clubs emerged, and most of the men's clubs began to admit women.

68. James P. O'Donnell, "Berlinomania," *Newsweek,* 21 January 1946, 60; see also "Occupation Blues," *Newsweek,* 9 December 1946.

69. Saul Padover, "Why Americans Like German Women," *American Mercury,* September 1946, 354.

70. Jeremy Noakes, Geoffrey Pridham, eds., *Nazism, 1919–1945: A History in Documents and Eyewitness Accounts,* vol. 1 (New York: Schocken Books, 1988), 449.

71. Claudia Koonz, *Mothers in the Fatherland: Women, the Family, and Nazi Politics,* (New York: St. Martin's Press, 1987), 55.

72. For more information on women's role in Nazi Germany see, Koonz, *Mothers in the Fatherland,* 199–200. On assumptions about women's roles in the United States see Beard, *Women as a Force in History,* 37.

73. Rupp, *Mobilizing Women for War,* 151. The American government exerted similar pressure on women. Susan Hartman wrote that "the [American] media emphasized the feminine motivations behind women's willingness to step out of customary roles. Patriotic motives were not ignored; but also highlighted was women's determination to serve their families albeit in novel ways." *The Homefront and Beyond,* 23.

74. "The Problems of German Women," ICD Weekly Intelligence Summary, 2 February 1946 (No.29), File 3, Box 154, OMGUS, RG 260, NRC.

75. Friedel Deisinger, "Die Schuld der Deutschen Frauen," *Frankfurter Rundschau,* 7 December 1945.

76. Rupp, *Mobilizing Women for War,* 151.

77. Kuhn, *Frauen in der Deutschen Nachkriegszeit,* 56.

78. Ibid., 151–55.

79. Ann Sloan, letter to the author, 17 July 1992. See also Thurnwald, *Gegenwartsprobleme Berliner Familien,* 10; also Moeller, *Protecting Motherhood,* 12.

"Zunahme der weiblichen Bevölkerung; Stand: 29.10.1948," Länderrat des amerikanischen Besatzungsgebietes: Memorandum über die soziale Lage in der US-Zone, Handakten Preller, 21, 965, Bundesarchiv Koblenz; Ann Sloan to author, 17 July 1992.

80. Helga Prollius, "Ein Königreich für einen Mann?" *Constanze*, No. 7, 1948, 17.

81. "Da sah man keine ausgehungerten und von Strapazen zerfurchten Gesichter, sondern alle Soldaten machten einen höchst geschonten und wohlbefindlichen Eindruck." Ilse Welli Holzhäuser, No Title, TS, Stuttgart 1977, Projekt "Senioren Schreiben Geschichte," J 175, 490, Hauptstaatsarchiv Stuttgart.

82. Anneliese Uhlig, quoted in Shukert and Scibetta, *War Brides of World War II*, 130. See also her four-part series recounting her marriage to an American soldier and her travel to the United States. "Ich heirate nach Amerika," *Der Regenbogen*, October 1948, 17–18; January 1949, 14–15; February 1949, 8–9 March 1949, 17–18.

83. Shukert and Scibetta, *War Brides of World War II*, 128.

84. Food rations in the American zone fluctuated constantly and varied by region. For more detail see Zink, *The United States in Germany*, 293–300; and Clay, *Decision in Germany*, 263–70. "The Occupation Viewed One Year After," Weekly Intelligence Summary, Information Control Intelligence Summary (ICIS), No. 52, 27 July 1946, ICD, RG 260, file 4, box 154; Weekly Opinion Summary, ICD Opinion Surveys Unit, Marburg Area, 19 November 1946, ICD, RG 260, file 4, box 146.

85. The 1948 Hollywood film *A Foreign Affair* explores the connections between GIs' fraternization with German women and their duties as providers at home. For an interpretation of the film see Emily Rosenberg, " 'Foreign Affairs' after World War II: Connecting Sexual and International Politics," *Diplomatic History* 18 (Winter 1994): 59–70. See also Georg Schmundt-Thomas, "Hollywood's Romance of Foreign Policy," 187–97.

86. May, *Homeward Bound*, 76.

87. For more detail see Rupp, *Mobilizing Women for War*, 86, 172.

88. "Germany Meets the Negro Soldier: GIs Find More Friendship and Equality in Berlin than in Birmingham or on Broadway," *Ebony*, October 1946, 5/6.

89. "Germany Meets the Negro Soldier," 7.

90. See for instance Roi Ottley, "No Color Line for Fräuleins," *Pittsburgh Courier*, 8 December 1945; Ollie Stewart, "What Negro GIs Learned from Women in Europe," *Negro Digest*, September 1947, 24–27; Allan Morrison, "An Aryan Myth Dies," *Stars and Stripes*, 15 July 1945, reprinted in *Negro Digest*, October 1945, 45–47.

91. Several articles on the subject of African-American soldiers in Germany were reprinted in the *Negro Digest*. See Allan Morrison, "An Aryan Myth Dies," *Stars and Stripes*, 15 July 1945, reprinted in *Negro Digest*, October 1945, 45–

47. Roi Ottley, "No Color Line for Frauleins," *Pittsburgh Courier,* 8 December 1945, reprinted in *Negro Digest,* February 1946, 11–12. Ollie Stewart, "What Negro GI's Learned from Women in Europe," *Negro Digest,* September 1947, 24–27.

92. "Racial: Madchen and Negro," *Newsweek,* 16 September 1946, 29.

93. Smith, *Last of the Conquerors,* 44.

94. Ibid., 67.

95. Potter, Miles, and Rosenblum, *Liberators,* 258.

96. Heide Fehrenbach cites 3,000 by 1950 as the most reliable in, "Rehabilitating Father*land,*" *Signs,* 108. A 1949 article in *Survey* estimates the number of babies of mixed parentage at about 2,100. See Stone, "German Baby Crop" *Survey,* 580. See also Barbara Willenbacher, "Zerrüttung und Bewährung der Nachkriegs-Familie," in Broszat, Henke, Woller, eds., *Von Stalingrad zur Währungsreform,* 600–1.

97. Stone, "German Baby Crop," 583. For more information on the problem of illegitimate children of African-American soldiers in Great Britain see "Their Father Was a Negro," *Newsweek,* 11 March 1946, 41.

98. For more detail on the fate of these children see Fehrenbach, "Rehabilitating Father*land,*"

99. Of the 600 women interviewed, a plurality were from a lower class background. Yet 134 were described as upper class and 180 as middle class; 210 of the women had eight years of basic schooling, the minimum required by German law at the time; 218 reported less, and 172 reported more than the required eight years of schooling; 250 of the women listed no occupation, more than 100 were unskilled workers, 90 semiskilled, 60 skilled, and 90 had professional standing; 62 of the women interviewed were married and living with their husbands at the time of the relationship with the black soldiers.

100. See "German Baby Crop," 583. The survey team had polled 500 black soldiers, 280 of whom had filed marriage applications. Of those 110 were pending, 57 had no response, 91 had been rejected and only 22 had been approved. The same was true for Great Britain. See "Their Father Was a Negro," *Newsweek,* 11 March 1946, 41.

101. Frieda Berger Webb, interview with author, 20 June 1992.

102. "SS Remnants Warn German Women: Bavaria Underground Placards Threaten Reprisals for Any Fraternizing with the Yanks," *New York Times,* 30 September 1945, 37.

103. *Fraternization with the Germans,* 73–76

104. ICD Survey in the U.S. Zone, cited in "U.S. Survey Discloses Returning German Soldiers' Views," *New York Times,* 23 August 1945.

105. Glaser, "The Sentiments of American Soldiers," *The American Journal of Sociology,* 435.

106. Brigadier General Edwin L. Sibert, "The German Mind: Our Greatest Problem," *New York Times Magazine,* 17 February 1946, 7.

107. Richard Joseph with Waverly Root, "Why So Many GIs Like the Germans Best," *Reader's Digest*, March 1946, 5–8.

108. "The Blame for Fraternization," *Newsweek*, 1 October 1945, 12.

109. "U.S. Army Wife in Germany Scorns U.S. Army Officers for Associating with German Girls, Letter to *Stars and Stripes*," in *New York Times*, 3 June 1946.

110. "U.S. Army Puts Total Number of Dependents Going to Europe to Join U.S. Servicemen at 77,200," *New York Times*, 13 January 1946. Apart from the wives the figure included 32,000 children, 4,500 fiancées, and 5,000 other dependents. See also "Arrival of First Group of U.S. Families in Berlin," *New York Times*, 1 May 1946.

111. Headquarters, USFET, Information Control Division, APO 757, U.S. Army, memorandum by Billy Wilder, to Davidson Taylor, Subject: Propaganda through Entertainment, 16 August 1945, reprinted in Willett, *The Americanization of Germany*, 40–44.

112. Rosenberg, "Foreign Affairs," *Diplomatic History*, 62.

113. O'Donnell, "Do the Fräuleins Change Our Joe?," *Newsweek*, 50, 52.

114. According to an Army poll, thirty-four percent of American soldiers who spent no time in Germany had a favorable attitude toward them. Among those with up to four weeks of service in Germany, forty-two percent had a favorable attitude. The figure rose to fifty-four percent for those with up to two months of service and to fifty-nine percent for those with more than two months in Germany. Quoted in *Reader's Digest*, March 1946, 6.

115. Truman, *Memoirs*, 341.

116. "Appointment of Byron Price as President's personal representative in Germany," Press release, 30 August, 1945 in *U.S. Department of State Bulletin*, 12 September 1945, 333.

117. Byron Price, "Relations between the Armed Forces and the German People," *U.S. Department of State Bulletin*, 13 December 1945, 885–86.

118. Ruhl, *Neubeginn und Restauration*, 516.

119. "Offen gesagt," [Openly Said], *Heute*, 1 September 1947, 18. "Hilfsaktion Amerikas für Deutschland," [American Relief for Germany] *Süddeutsche Zeitung*, 22 February 1946; see also "Amerikanische Lebensmittelpakete für die amerikanische Zone," [American Food Packages for the American Zone] *Süddeutsche Zeitung*, 12 June 1946. A 1946 German magazine article explained in great detail the journey of CRALOG and CARE packages from American to German households. See "Pakete von Drüben," [Packages from Over There] *Heute*, 15 August 1946, 5. See also "Wie bekommt man ein Care-Paket," [How does one get a Care-Package], *Heute*, 15 July 1947, 19; "Wieviel kommt von drüben?" [How much comes from over there?], *Heute*, 15 June 1947, 14–15.

120. "Tausende suchen den Onkel in Amerika," *Der Tagesspiegel*, 8 April 1948, 6. See also a more cynical treatment of the subject: "Go Ahead, Darling," *Süddeutsche Zeitung*, 14 June 1946.

121. Clay, *Decision in Germany*, 265–66.

122. Quoted in Best, *Herbert Hoover, the Postpresidential Years*, vol. 2, 298.

123. Clay, *Decision in Germany*, 265.

124. Best, *Herbert Hoover, the Postpresidential Years*, vol. 2, 299.

125. Clay, *Decision in Germany*, 270–71.

126. Germans themselves began to appropriate the fate of German women after the war as the archetypal German experience. For more detail see Heineman, "The Hour of the Woman, 354–95 and *What Difference does a Husband Make?* See also Moeller, *Protecting Motherhood*, 11–14; and Grossman, "A Question of Silence," 49.

127. "The Occupation Viewed One Year After," Weekly Intelligence Summary, Information Control Intelligence Summary (ICIS), No.52, 27 July 1946, ICD, File 4, Box 154, OMGUS, RG 260, NRC.

128. Weekly Opinion Summary, ICD Opinion Surveys Unit, Marburg Area, 19 November 1946, ICD, File 4, Box 146, OMGUS, RG 260, NRC.

129. James P. Warburg, "Can the Germans Cure Themselves?," *New York Times Magazine*, 20 August 1944, 11.

130. Lewis F. Gittler, "Everyday Life in Germany Today," *American Mercury*, October 1945, 400. See also Saul Nelson, "Daily Life in Occupied Germany," *Dunn's Review*, April 1947, 58.

131. "Kann man ein hungerndes Volk umerziehen?" *Süddeutsche Zeitung*, 15 March 1947.

132. The United States allocated approximately twelve billion dollars in aid between 1948 and 1951. For more detail on the distribution of Marshall Plan funds see Hogan, *The Marshall Plan*, 161–64, 414–15. "Directive from the Joint Chiefs of Staff to the Commander-in-Chief of the United States Forces of Occupation, July 11, 1947," *Documents on Germany*, 124–35. Even before the announcement of the Marshall Plan, the United States had shipped more than 2.3 million tons of food to Germany. See "Wieviel kommt von Drüben?" [How much comes from over there?], *Heute*, 15 June 1947, 14–15.

133. Heineman, *What Difference Does a Husband Make?*, 75.

Chapter 4. Selling Democracy: GIs and German Youth

1. Military Government of Germany (MGG hereafter), *Monthly Report of the Military Governor, U.S. Zone*, No. 10, 20 May 1946, Education and Religion Branch (Cumulative Review), 16.

2. For creation of GYA see MGG, *Monthly Report*, 20 May 1946, 17.

3. On the concept of infantile citizenship see Berant, *The Queen of America Goes to Washington City*, 27.

4. Alexis de Toqueville, *Democracy in America* transl. George Lawrence, ed. J. P. Meyer (Garden City, N.Y.: Anchor Books, 1969), 692.

5. MGG, *Monthly Report*, 20 May 1946, 16–19; see also reports of juvenile

delinquency and general political apathy in Tania Long, "Spawn of the Nazi Code: German Youth Has Lost Its Roots and Visibly Grows More Demoralized," in *New York Times Magazine*, 25 November 1945, 8, 32.

6. SHAEF published the *Handbook for Military Government in Germany Prior to Defeat or Surrender*, December 1944. The handbook outlined the major objectives in the re-education effort. An earlier version had appeared in the fall of 1944 but critics considered it too lenient toward Germany. The new Handbook reflected elements of the Morgenthau approach by concentrating on punitive measures. File 552, Box 7, G-5 (Civil Affairs), SHAEF, RG 331, NA. See also Tent, *Mission on the Rhine*, 25–28, 42–43.

7. The guidelines for military government in Germany distributed in early 1945 stated that the objective of re-education was to "assume control of German education by indirect means employing personnel of the existing German educational system in so far as possible, as purged or freed from Nazi and militaristic influence." In *Handbook for Military Government*, par. 812; see also "Educating Hitler Youth: Young German Prisoners of War, Age 12 to 17, Are Taught Democracy by Americans," *Life*, 8 October 1945, 75–82. The title was somewhat misleading since the article itself stated that "Allied policy in Central Europe is to let the enemy work out his own re-education as much as possible."

8. "German Youth Granted Political Amnesty by U.S. Military Government: Exceptions Noted," *New York Times*, 3 July 1946; MGG, Education and Religion (Cumulative Review), Monthly Report, No.22, 1 May 1946–30 April 1947, 33.

9. "Address of Winston Churchill," 6 March 1946, reprinted in *Congressional Record*, 79th Congress, Second Session, vol. 92, pt. 9, A1145–7.

10. Kuklick, *American Policy and the Division of Germany*, 194–98.

11. Eisenberg, *Drawing the Line*, 167, 169–71, 233–34. On the question of unification see also Trachtenberg, *A Constructed Peace*, 20–21.

12. For more information on the economic and political developments in the American zone see Boehling, *A Question of Priorities*.

13. MGG, *Monthly Report*, 20 May 1946, 19.

14. One of those critics, Douglas H. Schneider, Assistant Chief of Psychological Warfare, remarked in a 1945 memorandum that "well contented and well behaved American troops are not bad ambassadors for our country and her ideals." In Memorandum from Schneider to McClure, 30 May 1945, File 250.1–11, SHAEF, RG 331, NA. Schneider's memorandum has been discussed in detail in the second chapter. Byron Price also suggested using soldiers as ambassadors in his report to the President in the fall of 1945. See Price "Relations between the Armed Forces and the German People," *U.S. Department of State Bulletin*, vol. 13 (13 December 1945), 885. Price's report has been discussed in more detail in the third chapter.

15. American military observers and news articles warned repeatedly of the growing apathy and criminal activities of the nation's youth primarily in urban

areas. See "Annual Report OMG Bavaria," July 1945–June 1946, vol. 1, 133, Box 52 A, OMGUS, RG 260, NRC; see also "Annex IV to: Summary of Activities OMGB Bavaria," 26 June 1946, Box 52 B, OMGUS, RG 260, NRC. The report stated that "juvenile delinquency is increasing. Prohibited organizations are being formed." Italian director Roberto Rossellini treated the issue of youth's moral decline and general hopelessness in his movie *Germany Zero Hour,* 1946. The film followed the life of a boy in the ruins of Berlin. The boy prostituted himself for food and finally committed suicide by jumping to his death from an empty bombed-out building.

16. "Jugend auf Schiefer Bahn," *Süddeutsche Zeitung,* 1 March 1946, 4.

17. Chaussy, "Jugend," 207.

18. "Jugend auf Schiefer Bahn," *Süddeutsche Zeitung,* 1 March 1946, 4.

19. Havighurst, *Report on Germany,* 84. The problem of juvenile delinquency troubled other zones as well. For a discussion on British policy see Smith, "Juvenile Delinquency," 39–63.

20. "Jugend auf Schiefer Bahn," *Süddeutsche Zeitung,* 1 March 1946, 4.

21. Havighurst, *Report on Germany,* 84.

22. "Jugend bedroht vom Nihilismus," *Frankfurter Rundschau,* 9 April 1946, 4.

23. Long, "Spawn of the Nazi Code," *New York Times Magazine,* 25 November 1945, 8.

24. Ibid.

25. USFET Directive of 7 July 1945, in: "History of Military Government in Land Württemberg-Baden to 30 June 1946", Part V: Education & Religious Affairs, File 13, Box 47, OMGUS, RG 260, NRC.

26. USFET Directive of 25 October 1945, summarized in "History of Military Government."

27. MGG, *Monthly Report,* 20 May 1946, 19.

28. Ibid., 17.

29. Giles, *The GI Journal of Sergeant Giles,* 373.

30. *Fraternization with the Germans,* 140.

31. MGG, *Monthly Report,* 20 May 1946, 17.

32. "Educating Hitler Youth," *Life,* 8 October 1945, 75–82.

33. Excerpt from Minutes of the Wiesbaden Conference: *Statements of Evaluation and Recommendations of Working Committees,* not dated (late 1947), File 1, Box 44, OMGUS, RG 260, NRC.

34. Havighurst, *Report on Germany,* 87.

35. Annual Report OMG Bavaria, July 1945–June 1946, Vol. I Sec. IV: Internal Affairs and Communications, p. 133, Box 52 A, OMGUS, RG 260, NRC.

36. "Hilfe für die Jugend," *Der Tagesspiegel,* 18 April 1946, 2.

37. Semi-Annual Report, Education & Religious Affairs Division, July–December 1946, OMG Württemberg-Baden, Box 39, OMGUS, RG 260, NRC.

38. Ibid.

39. See Lucius D. Clay, *Decision in Germany* (Garden City, N.Y.: Doubleday, 1950), 265.

40. "Kinder betteln um Candy," *Frankfurter Rundschau*, 15 April 1947.

41. "Amerika's Hoffnung auf ein demokratisches Reich drohen am Hunger eines Volkes zusammenzubrechen." "Kinder—Brücke zwischen Völkern," *Die Neue Zeitung*, 30 December 1946, 2.

42. Pollock, *Besatzung und Staatsaufbau*, 111. I thank Wade Jacoby for alerting me to this particular passage.

43. Cited in O'Hanlon, "School Sports as Social Training," 193.

44. Story, "The Country of the Young," 131.

45. "Amerikanischer Sport für die deutsche Jugend," *Die Neue Zeitung*, 23 August 1946, 6. See also "Berliner spielen Baseball," *Die Neue Zeitung*, 22 July 1946, 2.

46. "Besonders geschulte amerikanische Soldaten sind gerade dabei, die deutsche Jugend in die Geheimnisse des neuen Spiels einzuweisen, und die deutsche Jugend geht begeistert mit." "Kleiner Kursus im Baseball-Spiel," *Die Neue Zeitung*, 26 August 1946, 6; 2 September 1946, 8; 9 September 1946, 8; 16 September 1946, 8.

47. "Kleiner Kursus," 26 August 1946, 6.

48. "Softball ohne Wörterbuch," *Heute*, 15 September, 1946 18. "Baseball für die deutsche Jugend," cover story in *Heute*, 9 September 1947.

49. "Reich: Play Ball," *Newsweek*, 23 September 1946, 40.

50. "Youth of Germany Eagerly Joins U.S. Sports Educational Program," *New York Times*, 26 September 1946, 5.

51. Ibid.

52. Ernest O. Hauser, "The Germans Just Don't Believe Us," *Saturday Evening Post*, 3 August 1946.

53. "Unser Lieblingsspiel, Fussball, kennen sie nicht, nur Football, das ist aber ganz was anderes als Fussball." ICD Surveys Unit, "Sonderbericht: Amerikanisches Jugendprogramm in Bamberg," 27 January 1947, File 18, Box 151, OMGUS, RG 260, NRC.

54. ICD , Würzburg Surveys, Subject: "Befragung über das amerikanische Jugendprogramm, Jugendbetätigung," 29 January 1947, p. 3, File 18, Box 151, OMGUS, RG 260, NRC.

55. "Re-Education Seen Forming Half of U.S. Zone Denazification Program," *New York Times*, 16 January 1947.

56. Kahn, *Betrayal*, 184.

57. "Reich: Play Ball," *Newsweek*, 23 September 1946, 40. See also "Militärischer Sport," *Die Neue Zeitung*, 16 September 1946, 7.

58. Kleßmann, *Die Doppelte Staatsgründung*, 149, 286. See also Wolfgang R. Krabbe, "Die FDJ und die Jugendverbände der Bundesrepublik, 1949–1970," *German Studies Review*, 21, no.3 (1998): 525–26.

59. "Kinderfest der 6. Constabulary Squadron," *Die Neue Zeitung*, 12 July 1946, 1.

60. "GIs laden ein," *Heute*, 1 August 1946, 26.

61. "U.S. Armee hilft der deutschen Jugend," *Die Neue Zeitung*, 6 September 1946, 1; for statistical information on youth in the U.S. Zone of Germany see: MGG, *Monthly Report*, Education and Religious Affairs Division, Cumulative Review, No. 22, 1 May 1946–30 April 1947, 40.

62. Office of Military Government for Württemberg-Baden, Stuttgart, Photographs, File 17, Box 43, OMGUS, RG 260, NRC.

63. MGG, *Monthly Report*, Education and Religious Affairs Division, Cumulative Review, No. 10, 20 May 1946, 18.

64. MGG, *Monthly Report*, Education and Religious Affairs Division, Cumulative Review, No. 22, 1 May 1946–30 April 1947, 33, 38.

65. "German Children to Have a Big Yule," *New York Times*, 16 December 1946.

66. Ibid.

67. For more information on the increasing distance, sometimes to the point of open hostility among GIs toward DPs, see Abzug, *Inside the Vicious Heart*, 152–68.

68. MGG, *Monthly Report*, Education and Religious Affairs Division, Cumulative Review, No. 22, 1 May 1946–30 April 1947, 38.

69. "Zuhause ist es ja doch bloss kalt und dunkel." "Spiel und Unterhaltung in vierzehn warmen Zimmern," *Tagesspiegel*, 20 November 1946, 4.

70. U.S. military government sponsored youth centers cropped up all over the zone. See Report on Military Government Operations in the Bremen Enclave, Weekly Detachment Report (Weekly MG Summary No. 76); Youth and Sports Activities, 3 October 1946, p. 4, File 10, Box 142, OMGUS, RG 260, NRC.

71. "Bremen Boys Club: U.S. Sergeant Finances a Lesson in Democracy," *Life*, 9 Decembe, 1946, 36–37. Military government statistics estimated Bremen's male youth at 30,000 in 1946.

72. MGG, *Monthly Report*, Education and Religious Affairs Division, Cumulative Review, No. 22, 1 May 1946–30 April 1947, 40.

73. Letter from Hon. Joseph J. Moriarty, District Judge of the State of Minnesota, to President Harry S. Truman, 26 January 1948. Read into the Congressional Record by Joseph P. O'Hara, Representative from Minnesota, *Congressional Record*, 80th Cong., 2nd sess., 17 February 1948, Vol. 94, pt. 9, A898. Two months later, Rep. O'Hara returned to Moriarty's mission by reading a number of articles about his campaign from Minnesota newspapers, and two citizen's resolutions to support additional aid to Germany, into the Congressional Record. See *Congressional Record*, 80th Cong., 2nd sess., 6 April 1948, Vol. 94, pt. 10, A2156–8.

74. *Congressional Record*, 80th Cong., 2nd sess., 17 February 1948, Vol. 94, pt. 9, A897.

75. "Statistical Information Regarding Youth in the U.S. Zone of Germany—Population and Organization," March 1947, in Military Government, MGG, *Monthly Report,* No. 22, 39.

76. MGG, *Monthly Report,* Education and Religious Affairs Division, Cumulative Review, No. 34, 59.

77. "Sie wollen sich nur verstehen und kennenlernen und miteinander das sein, was sie alle am liebsten sind: junge Mädchen mit dem Herz auf dem rechten Fleck." In "Peggy und Ihre Freundinnen," *Pinguin,* Februar 1949, 32.

78. "Es ist schier unmöglich, unter all' den lustigen Zivilistinnen die Amerikanerinnen und Deutschen voneinander zu scheiden. Fällt erst mal die trennende Uniform, dann wird es erkennbar: junge Mädchen gleichen sich in allen Nationen." In "Peggy und Ihre Freundinnen," *Pinguin,* Februar 1949, 32.

79. "GYA Goes into Fourth Year of Fight to Win Young," *Stars and Stripes,* 16 April 1949.

80. "Statistical Information Regarding Youth in the U.S. Zone of Germany—Population and Organization," March 1947, in Military Government, MGG, *Monthly Report,* No. 22, 40.

81. "Übernahme Amerikanischer Sportgeräte," Gesellschaft zur Erfassung von Rüstungsgut m.b.H., Zweigstelle Württemberg-Baden, 5 May 1947, Z 1, 1000, p. 111, Bundesarchiv Koblenz.

82. "German Children Appraise the Youth Program," Report No. 56, 26 April 1947, ICD Opinion Surveys Hq., OMGUS APO 757, p. 4, File 6, Box 158, OMGUS RG 260, NRC. While military government surveys might not give an altogether objective representation of the thoughts and motivations of Germans during the occupation period, they nonetheless give some indication both about American goals and German expectations. See also Rupieper, *Die Wurzeln der Westdeutschen Nachkriegsdemokratie,* 156–62.

83. The figures ranged from seventeen percent in Heidelberg to nine percent in Munich for boys, and from eleven percent in Frankfurt to six percent in Kassel and Heidelberg for girls; in "German Children Appraise the Youth Program," 4.

84. "German Children Appraise the Youth Program," 6.

85. In Frankfurt thirty-seven percent of the youngsters mentioned food, clothing, and shoes as worthy of improvement, compared to only four percent in Heidelberg. The Kassel and Munich youth also perceived the increased provision of food and clothing far less important than the Frankfurters with twelve and nine percent respectively. More Heidelberg youth, on the other hand, demanded an increase in sports events and equipment. While forty-seven percent in Heidelberg voted for an increase in these activities, in Frankfurt, Kassel, and Munich only twelve, fifteen, and thirteen percent found that to be an issue in need of improvement; in "German Children," 9.

86. Rupieper, *Die Wurzeln der westdeutschen Nachkriegsdemokratie,* 158.

87. "Bericht über Jugendinterviews in Frankfurt und Umgebung," Interviewer No. 216, ICD Opinion Surveys Branch, January/February 1947, File 18,

Box 151, OMGUS, RG 260, NRC; see also "Erfahrungsbericht über Interviews mit schulpflichtigen Kindern bis 18 Jahren in Frankfurt," Interviewer No. 211, ICD Opinion Surveys Branch, January/February 1947.

88. "Gunzenhausen—Fragen an Kinder zum amerikanischen Jugendprogramm," ICD-Opinion Surveys Branch, Januar/Februar 1947, File 18, Box 151, OMGUS, RG 260, NRC.

89. When polls asked the children to estimate how many of them had a better knowledge of democracy, however, the opinions split evenly between "all," "most," "about half," and "only some." Thus, while all children had gained some insight into the meaning of democracy, the extent of the influence remained moderate. "German Children," 12.

90. Most parents understood that the program's purpose was the ideological re-education of Germany's youth. Opinion Surveys Unit, Office of the Director of Information Control, "Army Aid to German Youth Activities Evaluated by German Adults," Report No. 46, 19 February 1947, p. 4, File 6, Box 158, RG 260, NRC.

91. Forty-one percent thought that keeping children off the street was the program's most valuable aspect and another nineteen percent thought that giving the children something to do in their spare time was most important. On the other hand, a significant twenty-six percent chose instruction in the American way of life as most valuable. "Army Aid," Appendix, Table V.

92. "Ich möchte meine Kinder daheim haben, denn er ist noch immer der Feind." "Gunzenhausen—Fragen an Eltern zum amerikanischen Jugendprogramm," ICD-Opinion Surveys Branch, Januar/Februar 1947, File 18, Box 151, OMGUS, RG 260, NRC.

93. Rupieper, *Die Wurzeln der westdeutschen Nachkriegsdemokratie*, 157–58.

94. "Im Gegensatz zur Jugenderziehung der Nazizeit." "Jugendbetätigung," 2nd Interview, ICD Opinion Survey's Branch, WK 111, 30 January 1947, Bayreuth, File 18, Box 151, OMGUS, RG 260, NRC.

95. "Dass die Kinder durch das amerikanische Jugendprogramm nicht wie in der Nazizeit ihren Eltern entfremdet, sondern im Gehorsam ihnen gegenüber erzogen werden." "Jugendbetätigung," 5th Interview, 3.

96. Hausen, Karin, "Family and Role Division: The Polarization of Sexual Stereotypes in the Nineteenth Century—an Aspect of the Dissociation of Work and Family Life," in Evans, Lee, *The German Family*, 61–66. Kocka, "Familie, Unternehmer, und Kapitalismus in Reif, (Hg) *Die Familie in der Geschichte*, 168–69.

97. Wagnleitner, *Coca-Colonization*, 201–203.

98. Wagnleitner, *Coca-Colonization*, 202.

99. Heinrch Küpffer, *Swingtime: Chronik einer Jugend in Deutschland, 1937–1951* (Berlin: Frieding, 1987), 112.

100. Ibid., 113. See also Wagnleitner, *Coca-Colonization*, 212.

101. Willett, *The Americanization of Germany*, 86–89. Wagnleitner, *Coca-Colonization*, 199–200.

102. Wagnleitner, *Coca-Colonization*, 270; see also, Fehrenbach, *Cinema in Democratizing Germany*, 54–55.

103. "Das schlimmste Verbrechen war an uns und das zweitschlimmste war an Ihnen." Cited in Schörken, *Jugend 1945*, 94.

104. May, *Homeward Bound*, 10, 87–91.

Chapter 5. Forging a Consensus: Americans, Germans, and the Berlin Airlift

1. Howley, *Berlin Command*, 3.

2. Ibid., 4 (italics mine).

3. Clay, *Decision in Germany*, 381–82.

4. Trachtenberg, *A Constructed Peace*, 78–86; See also Eisenberg, *Drawing the Line*, 409–77.

5. Boehling, *A Question of Priorities*, 3.

6. In July 1946, the U.S. military governor proposed economic unity among the four zones. The Soviet Union and France opposed the measure, but Great Britain joined the United States on 2 December 1946, in a fusion of their respective zones' economies. See "Statement by the American Military Governor Before the Allied Control Council Respecting Economic Unity Among the Four Zones of Occupation, July 20 1946," and "Memorandum of Agreement Between the United States and the United Kingdom on Economic Fusion of Their Respective Zones of Occupation in Germany," Signed in Washington December 2 1946, U.S. Department of State, Documents on Germany, 1944–1985, 90–91, 110–3. On the Level of Industry Plan see Eisenberg, *Drawing the Line*, 327–34. On the Marshall Plan see Hogan, *The Marshall Plan*, 58–59, 414–15.

7. Prell, Wilker, eds., *Berlin Blockade und Luftbrücke 1948/49*, 19.

8. For more information on the economic disputes between the Soviet Union and the Western Allies see Kleßmann, Die Doppelte Staatsgründung, 109–10; see also Kuklick, *American Policy and the Division of Germany*, 210–25.

9. Backer, *Winds of History*, 226–27. Eisenberg, *Drawing the Line*, 395–97, 410.

10. Shlaim, *The United States and the Berlin Blockade*, 113–14.

11. Kleßmann, *Die Doppelte Staatsgründung*, 191–92; see also Harrington, "The Berlin Blockade Revisited," 96.

12. Reuter won the 1946 municipal elections, but a Soviet veto prevented him from taking office. He remained very much in charge behind the scenes, however, and enjoyed strong support among the population. See Tusa, *The Berlin Airlift*, 86–87; see also Lilge, *Deutschland, 1945–1963*, 46–47.

13. Protocol of the session of the Berlin committee of the economic council of the western zones, 20 May 1948, cited in Paul, *Kampf um Berlin*, 155.

14. Herzfeld, *Berlin in der Weltpolitik*, 239; see also Paul, *Kampf um Berlin*, 156.

15. Schwenger, *Ernst Reuter,* 22–64. Appel, *Die Regierenden von Berlin seit 1945,* 49–118; See also Auer, *Ihr Völker der Welt.*

16. Eisenberg, *Drawing the Line,* 409–10.

17. Sokolovsky to Clay, 22 June 1948, *Documents on Berlin,* 64.

18. Shlaim, *Berlin Blockade,* 159–62.

19. According to Clay, Sokolovsky mentioned to him in a conversation on 3 July that "the technical difficulties would continue until we had abandoned our plans for a West German Government." Clay, *Decision in Germany,* 367. The disruption of traffic to and from Berlin actually began in March 1948, after the three western Allies had met in London to discuss the formation of an independent West German State. See Eisenberg, *Drawing the Line,* 400–07; Trachtenberg, *A Constructed Peace,* 78.

20. Instructions contained in "Frankfurter Dokumente." Reprinted in www.documentarchiv.de/brd/frftdok.html. See also Trachtenberg, *A Constructed Peace,* 78.

21. "Der erste Tag mit der D-Mark," *Wiesbadener Kurier,* 22 June 1948.

22. "Am nächsten Tag da waren die Schaufenster voll, gab's alles. Wo die Waren herkamen, weiss ich auch nicht, von einem Tag zum anderen, unerklärlich." Quoted in Niethammer, *Hinterher merkt man, dass es richtig war dass es schiefgegangen ist,* 81.

23. "Cold War: The Price of Peace—Two Worlds," *Newsweek,* 16 August 1948, 26; "Blick hinter die Ladentische," *Marburger Presse,* 30 June 1948.

24. Andreas-Friedrich, *Battleground Berlin,* 232.

25. "Der morgige Tag wird der Auftakt zu einer besseren Wirtschaft sein, die mehr Nahrung, Wiederaufbau und einen höheren Lebensstandard mit sich bringt." "Berlin wird nicht hungern," *Der Tagesspiegel,* 25 June, 1948.

26. "Cold War: The Price of Peace—Two Worlds," *Newsweek,* 16 August 1948, 26.

27. From *Der Leuchtturm,* 1948, No. 1, reprinted in Kleßmann and Wagner, eds., *Das Gespaltene Land,* 291.

28. "Security Versus Freedom in Blockaded Berlin," Report No. 151, Opinion Surveys Branch, 18 December 1948, Information Services Division (ISD), File 24, Box 150, OMGUS, RG 260, NRC. See also, "Germany and Democracy," *Newsweek,* 3 May 1948, 11.

29. Howley, *Berlin Command,* 230.

30. Berlin Opinion Surveys Unit, "Zusammenfassender Volksmeinungsbericht vom 1.–15. April, 1948," April 1948, ICD, File 21, Box 141, OMGUS, RG 260, NRC.

31. Naimark, *The Russians in Germany,* 78–90, 169, 305, 317, 337.

32. "Die defensive Haltung Amerikas und Englands bestärkt die Bevölkerung in ihrer Ansicht, dass Russland schliesslich doch Erfolg haben wird." Berlin Opinion Surveys Unit, "Zusammenfassender Volksmeinungsbericht

vom 1.- 15. April, 1948," April 1948, ICD, File 21, Box 141, OMGUS, RG 260, NRC.

33. Truman, *Memoirs*, vol. 2, 123.

34. "U.S. Protests Soviet Blockade of Berlin: Note from Secretary of State Marshall to Ambassador Panyushkin," 6 July 1948, Department of State Bulletin, Vol. XIX, No. 472 (18 July 1948).

35. "Statement by Philip C. Jessup, Deputy U.S. Representative in the Security Council," 8 October 1948, Department of State Bulletin, Vol. XIX, No. 485 (17 October 1948), 484.

36. Note from the Government of the Union of Socialist Republics to the Governments of the United States, the United Kingdom, and France in the Berlin Situation, 14 July 1948, *Documents on Berlin*, 72.

37. UN Security Council Meeting, 4 October 1948; discussed in "The United States in the United Nations," Department of State Bulletin, Vol. XIX, No. 484 (10 October 1948), 463.

38. Mead, "Food and Feeding in Occupied Territory," 619.

39. Grathwol, Moorhus, *American Forces in Berlin*, 48.

40. "Schokolade fällt vom Himmel," *Sie*, 17 October 1948, 3.

41. "4,000 Bowed Heads," *Newsweek*, 9 August 1948, 27.

42. "Berlin Reactions to the Airlift and the Western Powers," Report No. 130, Opinion Surveys Branch, 23 July 1948, Information Control Division, File 6, Box 159, OMGUS, RG 260, NRC, p. 2.

43. "A Report on Berlin Morale," Memo from Opinion Surveys to Col. G. E. Textor, Director, ICD Surveys Branch, Berlin, 30 July 1948, File 21, Box 141, OMGUS, RG 260, NRC, p. 3.

44. "Some Aspects of Morale in Berlin," Report No. 132, Opinion Surveys Branch, 10 August 1948, Information Services Division, File 6, Box 159, OMGUS, RG 260, NRC, p. 3.

45. Howley, *Berlin Command*, 259.

46. Joseph B. Philips, "The Germans in Berlin," *Newsweek*, 5 July 1948, 41.

47. "Trends Abroad," *Newsweek*, 6 September 1948, 9.

48. Wetzlaugk, *Die Alliierten in Berlin*, 37.

49. Herzfeld, *Berlin in der Weltpolitik*, 247.

50. "Um eine Stadt, die vor der Diktatur in die Knie gegangen wäre, hätte sich kein demokratisches Land gekümert." "Die Sache Berlins ist die Sache der freien Welt," *Der Tagesspiegel*, 27 June 1948, 6.

51. Truman, *Memoirs*, vol. 2, 123.

52. "Statement by Philip C. Jessup, Deputy U.S. Representative in the Security Council," 8 October 1948, Department of State Bulletin, Vol. XIX, No. 485 (17 October 1948), 484.

53. "Berlin: The Planners and the Risk of War," *Newsweek*, 20 September 1948, 36.

54. "Amerika über Deutschland: 'Herald Tribune' spiegelt Meinungs-wandel," *Die Neue Zeitung*, 19 October 1948, 5.

55. "Missachtung elementarster Lebensinteressen Berlins und seiner Bevöl-kerung und ständiger Verletzung der Verfassung." Quoted in Herzfeld, *Berlin in der Weltpolitik*, 265; see also Prell, Wilker, *Berlin Blockade und Luftbrücke*, 46.

56. Herzfeld, *Berlin in der Weltpolitik*, 266.

57. "Respekt vor dem Mut der Berliner," *Der Tagesspiegel*, 7 December 1948. See also Howley, *Berlin Command*, 227–28.

58. "Amerika über Deutschland: 'Herald Tribune' spiegelt Meinungs-wandel," *Die Neue Zeitung*, 19 October 1948, 5.

59. "Berlin Reactions to the Airlift and the Western Powers," Report No. 130, Opinion Surveys Branch, 23 July 1948, Information Control Division, File 6, Box 159, OMGUS, RG 260, NRC, p. 2.

60. The majority, fifty-eight percent, answered that the western powers "cannot deliver us to the Russians—they are our protectors." "Berlin Reactions to the Airlift."

61. For more detail see Stammen, "Politische Kultur-Tradition im Wandel," 11–52.

62. Kutler, *The American Inquisition*, 36.

63. For more detail on McCarthyism see Schrecker, *The Age of McCarthy-ism*.

64. Bower, *The Pledge Betrayed*, 341.

65. Several former functionaries in the Third Reich ended up holding po-litical office in postwar Germany, among them two chancellors, Kurt Georg Kiesinger and Ludwig Erhard, as well as two minister presidents, Franz-Josef Strauß of Bavaria and Hans Filbinger of Baden-Württemberg. See Bower, *The Pledge Betrayed*, 383–84.

66. See, for instance, John E. Thompson, "Lightning, Clouds, Dangerous Cargo, Red Radio Jamming . . . Make Flying the Berlin Corridor a Cold-War Hot Spot," *Newsweek*, 19 July 1948, 26.

67. "Movie Notes: Films on the Airlift." *Newsweek*, 13 December 1948, 16. "Movie Notes-Titles of Berlin Airlift Movies," *Newsweek*, 27 December 1948, 8.

68. *The Big Lift* (1950), directed by George Seaton.

69. See for instance Max Lerner, "Will There Be a Fourth Reich?" *New York Post*, 23 May 1949; John London, "Denazification Fails, German Editor Says," *Washington Post*, 20 June 1949; "Old Hands Run Germany Again," *U.S. News and World Report*, 29 July 1949; Bigelow Boysen, "War Crimes Lawyer Finds Nazi Thinking Unaltered," *Sunday Star*, 24 April 1949.

70. "Blunders in the Making," In *Prevent World War III*, cited in, Con-gressional Record, 81st Cong. 1st Sess. Vol. 95, 7 April 1949, A2081.

71. Eisenberg, *Drawing the Line*, 476.

72. "Directive to the Commander in Chief of the United States Forces of

Occupation Regarding the Military Government of Germany, 10 May 1945," in *Documents on Germany*, 24.

73. In interviews with workers in the industrial Ruhr area, the historian Lutz Niethammer found that most interviewees regarded the currency reform as the watershed event of the postwar period; in Niethammer, *Hinterher merkt man*, 82–83.

74. "Endlich wieder kaufen können." Poster displayed at the Institut für Publizistik, Westfälische Wilhelms-Universität, Münster, Germany.

75. May, *Homeward Bound*, 14.

76. Bower, *The Pledge Betrayed*, 383–84.

Conclusion

1. Congressional Record, 81st Cong., 1st sess. 1949, 95, pt. 13: A1887. The Non-Sectarian Anti-Nazi League had spearheaded American boycotts of German goods to protest Germany's treatment of Jews in the 1930s. For more information see Moshe Gottlieb, "In the Shadow of War: The American Anti-Nazi Boycott Movement in 1939–1941," *American Jewish Historical Quarterly*, 62, no. 2 (1972): 146–61.

2. "General Clay and W. Logan Laud Fair Aims: Fair Picketed; American Association for Democratic Germany Charges Nazi Penetration," *New York Times*, 9 April 1949. The *New York Times* reported almost daily on the exhibition on April 8–11, 19, and 23, the day it closed. The articles never appeared on the front page, however.

3. "Fair Opens," *New York Times*, 10 April 1949.

4. "Fair to Close, Results Discussed," *New York Times*, 23 April 1949.

5. "Blunders in the Making," in *Prevent World War III*, pamphlet cited in Congressional Record, 81st Cong. 1st Sess. Vol. 95, and April 1949, A2081.

6. Lawrence Stone, "History and the Social Sciences in the Twentieth Century," in *The Future of History: Essays in the Vanderbilt University Centennial Symposium*, ed. by Charles F. Delzell (Nashville, Tenn.: Vanderbilt University Press, 1977), 38.

7. Congressional Record, 81st Cong., 1st sess. 1949, 95, pt. 13: A1887.

8. Howley, *Berlin Command*, 3–4.

9. See Schlesinger, *A Thousand Days*, 375.

10. For more detail see Dower, *Embracing Defeat;* Shibusawa, *America's Geisha Ally*.

11. "Military Situation in the Far East." Hearings before the Committee on Armed Services and the Committee on Foreign Relations, United States Senate, Eighty-second Congress, *Inquiry into the Military Facts Surrounding the Assignments in that Area* (Washington, D.C.: U.S. Government Printing Office, 1951). See also Shibusawa, *America's Geisha Ally*, 170–71.

12. Hoganson, *Fighting for American Manhood.*

13. Rotter, *Comrades at Odds.* See also "Gender Relations, Foreign Relations," 521.

14. "Military Situation in the Far East." Quoted in Shibusawa, *America's Geisha Ally,* 170–71.

15. May, *Homeward Bound,* 10.

16. For the use of rape as a metaphor see political and media statements about Iraq's invasion of Kuwait in 1990. For instance "Kuwait: Rape of a Nation," *Newsweek,* March 11, 1991; Michael Kelly, "The Rape and Rescue of Kuwait," *New Republic,* 25 March 1991.

Select Bibliography

Primary Sources

UNPUBLISHED DOCUMENTS

Washington National Records Center, Suitland, Maryland
Record Group 260: Records of the Office of Military Government United States (OMGUS):
Records of the Executive Office.
  Records of the Control Office.
  Records of the Information Control Division.
  Records of the Civil Affairs Division.
  Records of the Educational and Cultural Relations Division.
Records of the Land and Sector Military Governments.
  Records of the Office of Military Government, Bavaria.
  Records of the Office of Military Government, Berlin Sector.
  Records of the Office of Military Government, Bremen.
  Records of the Office of Military Government, Hesse.
  Records of the Office of Military Government, Württemberg-Baden.
Record Group 332: Records of the European Theater of Operations/ United States Forces European Theater (ETO/USFET):
General Records ETO/USFET.
National Archives of the United States, Washington, D.C.
Record Group 331: Records of the Supreme Headquarters American Expeditionary Forces (SHAEF):
  Records of the Adjutant General's Division.
  Records of the Personnel Division.

Records of the Civil Affairs Division.

Records of the Public Relations Division.

Bundesarchiv Koblenz

Z 1: Länderrat des amerikanischen Besatzungsgebietes.

R 55: Reichsministerium für Volksaufklärung und Propaganda.

Nachlaß Max Hildebert Boehm.

Nachlaß Paul Moldenhauer.

FILMS

Herr Roosevelt Plaudert (1943).

Rund um die Freiheitsstatue (1941).

Die Todesmühlen (1945).

Die Brücke (1948).

Welt im Film (1945–1949).

Hessisches Hauptstaatsarchiv Wiesbaden

Abteilung 502: Akten der Staatskanzlei: Schriftverkehr mit der Landesmilitärregierung.

Bayrisches Hauptstaatsarchiv München

Stk 114909: Vorgänge in Cham bei Kriegsende 1945.

Stk 114941: Gesetze etc. der U.S.- Militärregierung und des Kontrollrats 1945–1949.

Stk 114960–62: Amtlicher Verkehr zwischen Staatsregierung und Militärregierung 1945–1949.

Stk 114973–76: Beschlagnahme von Gebäuden, Wohnungen, und Mobilar durch U.S. Streitkräfte 1945–1949.

Stk 115008–10: Sicherheitsstörungen und Ausschreitungen durch Angehörige der Besatzungsmacht.

Nachlaß Christian Hallig.

Nachlaß Hans Ehard.

Nachlaß Fritz Schäffer.

Nachlaß Anton Pfeiffer.

Baden-Würtembergisches Hauptstaatsarchiv Stuttgart

J 151: Sammlung von Maueranschlägen.

J 152: Flugschriftensammlung.

J 153: Plakatsammlung nach 1945.

J 170: Berichte von Gemeinden über die Kriegsereignisse und das Ausmaß der Zerstörung.

J 171: Berichte aus der Nachkriegszeit.

J 175: Beiträge zum Seniorenwettbewerb "Ältere Menschen schreiben Geschichte."

Lorentz, Maria. *Die ersten Tage mit den Amerikanern*. TS, Stuttgart 1977.

Schade,Heinz C. *Sieger und Besiegte: Amerikaner und Deutsche anno 1945*. TS, Stuttgart 1977.

Kuch, Ernst. *Kriegsende in Heidenheim*. TS, Stuttgart 1977.

Landesarchiv Berlin

Repositur 210: Bezirk Zehlendorf.

Repositur 212: Bezirk Steglitz.

Repositur 213: Bezirk Tempelhof.

Repositur 214: Bezirk Neukölln.

Nachlaß Ernst Reuter.

Nachlaß Hans E. Hirschfeld.

PUBLISHED DOCUMENTS

The Berlin Crisis: A Report on the Moscow Discussion, 1948. Department of State Publication 3298. European and British Commonwealth Series 1. Washington D.C.: Division of Publication, Office of Public Affairs, 1948.

Congressional Record. Washington D.C. 1945–1949.

Documents on Berlin, 1943–1963. Edited by Wolfgang Heidelmeyer and Guenther Hindrichs. Munich: Oldenbourg Verlag, 1963.

Foreign Relations of the United States: The Conferences at Washington, 1941–1942, and Casablanca, 1943. Washington, D.C.: U.S. Government Printing Office, 1968.

Foreign Relations of the United States: The Conference at Quebec, 1944. Washington, D.C.: U.S. Government Printing Office, 1955.

Foreign Relations of the United States: The Conferences at Malta and Yalta, 1945. Washington, D.C.: U.S. Government Printing Office, 1955.

Fraternization with the Germans in World War II, Office of the Chief Historian, European Command, Occupation Forces in Europe Series, 1945–1946. Frankfurt a. M., Germany: Office of the Military Government of the United States, 1947.

Hitler's Table Talk, 1941–1944: His Private Conversations. Translated by Norman Cameron and R. H. Stevens. Introduced and with a new Preface from H. R. Trevor-Roper. London: Weidenfeld and Nicholson, 1973, 1953.

Hitlers Zweites Buch: Ein Dokument aus dem Jahr 1928, Eingeleitet und kommentiert von Gerhard L. Weinberg. Stuttgart: Deutsche Verlags-Anstalt, 1961.

Immigration and Naturalization Service. *Annual Report,* 1949–1950.

Merritt Anna J., Richard L. Merritt. Eds. *Public Opinion in Occupied Germany: The OMGUS Surveys, 1945–1949.* Urbana: University of Illinois Press, 1970.

Noakes, Jeremy, Geoffrey Pridham. Eds. *Documents on Nazism, 1919–1945.* 2 vols. New York: Viking Press, 1974.

Pocket Guide to Germany. Washington D.C.: Government Printing Office, 1944.

The Public Papers and Addresses of Franklin D. Roosevelt. Vol. 12 (1943). *The Tide Turns.* Compiled with special material and explanatory notes by Samuel I. Rosenman. New York: Harper & Brothers, 1950.

The Public Papers and Addresses of Franklin D. Roosevelt. Vol. 13 (1944–45). *Victory and the Threshold of Peace.*

Supreme Headquarters Allied Expeditionary Force. *Handbook for Military Government in Germany prior to Defeat or Surrender.* Washington D.C.: Government Printing Office, December 1944.

U.S. Army Department. Civil Affairs Division. Military Government of Germany. *Monthly Report of the Military Governor.* Education, Religion, and Public Welfare Division. 1945–1949.

U.S. Department of State. *Documents on Germany, 1944–1985.* Washington, D.C.: U.S. Government Printing Office, 1985.

——. *Germany 1947–49: The Story in Documents.* Washington, D.C.: U.S. Government Printing Office, 1950.

——. *Bulletin.* Washington, D.C.: Government Printing Office, 1947–1951.

Wirtschaft und Statistik. 1950.

MEMOIRS, DIARIES, NOVELS, CONTEMPORARY ACCOUNTS

Adenauer, Konrad. *Briefe, 1945–1947.* Bearbeitet von Hans Peter Mensing, Rhöndorfer Ausgabe: Stiftung Bundeskanzler Adenauer Haus. Herausgegeben von Rudolf Morsey und Hans-Peter Schwartz. Bonn: Siedler Verlag, 1983.

——. *Briefe, 1947–1949.* Bearbeitet von Hans Peter Mensing, Rhöndorfer Ausgabe: Stiftung Bundeskanzler Adenauer Haus. Herausgegeben von Rudolf Morsey und Hans-Peter Schwartz. Bonn: Siedler Verlag, 1984.

American Representation in Occupied Germany, 1920–21, compiled by the Assistant Chief of Staff, G2, American Forces in Germany. Washington, D.C.: United States Government Printing Office, 1943.

Andreas-Friedrich, Ruth. *Battleground Berlin: Diaries 1945–1948.* New York: Paragon, 1990.

Bach Julian S. *America's Germany: An Account of the Occupation.* New York: Random House, 1946.

Beard, Mary R. *Women as a Force in History: A Study in Traditions and Realities.* New York: Collier, 1971, 1946.

Belfrage, Cedric. *Seeds of Destruction: The Truth About the U.S. Occupation of Germany.* New York: Cameron & Kahn, 1954.

Berger, Thomas and Karl-Heinz Müller. Eds. *Lebenssituationen 1945–1948: Materialien zum Alltagsleben in den westlichen Besatzungszonen.* Hannover: Niedersächsische Landeszentrale zur politischen Bildung, 1983.

Böll, Heinrich. *Das Brot der frühen Jahre.* Cologne: Kiepenheuer und Witsch, 1955.

——. *Children Are Civilians Too.* Translated from German by Leila Vennewitz. New York: McGraw-Hill, 1970.

——. *Niemands Land: Kindheitserinnerungen an die Jahre 1945 bis 1949.* Munich: Deutscher Taschenbuch Verlag 1985.

——. *Wanderer kommst Du nach Spa . . .* Opladen: Verlag Friedrich Middelhauve, 1950.

——. *Der Zug war Pünktlich.* Opladen: Verlag Friedrich Middelhauve, 1949.

Bourke-White, Margaret. *"Dear Fatherland, Rest Quietly:" A Report on the Collapse of Hitler's Thousand Years.* New York: Simon & Schuster, 1946.

Boyle, Kay. *The Smoking Mountain: Stories of Germany During the Occupation.* New York: Knopf, 1952.

Brickner, Richard M. *Is Germany Incurable?* New York: J. B. Lippincott, 1943.

Byford-Jones, Wilfred. *Berlin Twilight.* New York: Hutchinson, 1947.

Byrnes, James F. *Speaking Frankly.* New York: Harper, 1947.

Capra, Frank. *The Name Above the Title: An Autobiography.* New York: Macmillan, 1971.

Christen, Peter. *From Military Government to State Department: How a German Employee Sees the Work of the United States Military Government and the State Department in a Small Bavarian Town, Its Success and Its Handicaps.* Erding: A. P. Wagner, 1950.

Clay, Lucius D. *Decision in Germany.* Garden City, N.Y.: Doubleday, 1950.

Cohn David L. "First in War, Last in Peace." *Atlantic* 177 (January 1946): 217–20.

Connor, Sidney and Carl J. Friedrich, Eds. "Military Government: Germany." *Annals of the American Academy of Political and Social Science.* 267 (January 1950): 28–105.

Davidson, Basil. *Germany, What Now: Potsdam Partition 1945–1949.* London: Muller, 1950.

Dobie, J. Frank. "What I Saw Across the Rhine." *National Geographic Magazine* 91 (January 1947): 575–86.

Dobran, Edward A. *P.O.W.: The Story of an American Prisoner of War during World War II.* New York: Exposition Press, 1953.

Dorn, Walter L. *Inspektionsreisen in der US-Zone: Notizen, Denkschriften und Erinnerungen aus dem Nachlaß.* Übersetzt und herausgegeben von Lutz Niethammer. Stuttgart: Deutsche Verlagsanstalt, 1973.

Dos Passos, John. *Tour of Duty.* Boston: Houghton Mifflin, 1946.

Dreher, Carl. "Close-Up of Democracy." *Virginia Quarterly Review* 23 (Winter 1947): 89–107.

Farbige Franzosen am Rhein: Ein Notschrei deutscher Frauen, 4th ed. Berlin: Hans Robert Engelmann, 1920, 1923.

Ferrel, Robert H., ed. *Off the Record: The Private Papers of Harry S. Truman.* New York: Harper & Row, 1980.

Ford, Henry and Paul Lehmann. *Der Internationale Jude. Ein Welt-problem: Das erste amerikanische Buch über die Judenfrage.* Leipzig: Hammer Verlag, 1921.

Friedmann, Wolf. *The Allied Military Government of Germany.* London: Stevens, 1947.

Friedrich, Carl J. et al. *American Experiences in Military Government in World War II.* New York: Rinehart, 1948.

Gibbs, Philip. *Thine Enemy.* New York: Medill McBridge, 1950.

Giles, Henry E. *The G.I. Journal of Sergeant Giles.* Compiled and edited by Janice Holt Giles. Boston: Houghton Mifflin, 1965.

Glaser, Daniel. "The Sentiments of American Soldiers Abroad toward Europeans." *American Journal of Sociology* 51, no.5 (March 1946): 433–38.

Goguel, Dietrich. *Es war ein langer Weg: Ein Roman unserer Zeit.* Düsseldorf: Komet-Verlag, 1947.

Gollancz, Victor. *Leaving Them to Their Fate: The Ethics of Starvation.* London: Victor Gollancz ltd., 1946.

———. *In Darkest Germany.* London: Victor Gollancz ltd., 1947.

Greene, Harris. *The Mozart Leaves at Nine.* Garden City, N.Y.: Double-day & Co. Inc., 1961.

Griffith, Eldon W. "Retrospect on Germany." *Yale Review* 30 (Sept. 1949): 96–107.

Güstrow, Dietrich. *In Jenen Jahren: Aufzeichnungen eines befreiten Deut-schen.* Munich: Deutscher Taschenbuch Verlag, 1985.

Habe, Hans. *Aftermath.* New York: Viking Press, 1947.

———. *Our Love Affair with Germany.* New York: Putnam, 1953.

Haltermann, Udo, ed. *So erlebten wir das Ende: Als Deutschland den Zweiten Weltkrieg verlor, Erinnerungen.* Nettetal: Steylerverlag, 1988.

Havighurst, Robert J. *Report on Germany.* New York: Rockefeller Foun-dation, 1947.

Heiden, Konrad. *Der Führer: Hitler's Rise to Power.* Boston: Houghton Mifflin, 1944.

Hill, Russell. *Struggle for Germany.* New York: Harper, 1947.

Holborn, Hajo. *American Military Government: Its Organization and Politics.* Washington D.C.: Infantry Journal Press, 1947.

Howley, Frank. *Berlin Command.* New York: G. P. Putnam's Sons, 1950.

James, C. L. R. "Why Negroes Should Oppose the War." C. L. R. James, George Breitman, Edgar Keemer. *Fighting Racism in World War II.* New York: Monat Press, 1980.

Janowitz, Morris. "German Reactions to Nazi-Atrocities." *American Journal of Sociology* 52, no. 2 (September 1946): 141–46.

Kahn, Arthur D. *Betrayal: Our Occupation of Germany.* Brooklyn, N.Y.: Beacon Service Co., 1950.

Keefe, William F. *Two Years Before the Masthead.* Frankfurt a. Main: F. Rudl, 1952.

Kirkpatrick, Clifford. "Reactions of Educated Germans to Defeat." *American Journal of Sociology* 54, no. 1 (July 1948): 36–47.

Kirst, Hans Helmut. *Das Schaf im Wolfspelz: Ein deutsches Leben-Biographische Versuchungen 1945–1957.* Herford: Busse & Seewald, 1985.

Knappen, Marshall M. *And Call It Peace.* Chicago: University of Chicago Press, 1947.

Knauth, Percy. *Germany in Defeat.* New York: A. A. Knopf, 1946.

Kraus, Charles H. *In the Wake of Battle.* Washington D.C.: n.p., 1950.

Krause, Walter C. *So I Was a Sergeant: Memoirs of an Occupation Soldier.* Hicksville, N.Y.: Exposition Press, 1978.

Kuhn, Annette, ed. *Frauen in der Deutschen Nachkriegszeit.* 2 vols. Düsseldorf: Schwann, 1986.

Küpffer, Heinrich. *Swingtime: Chronik einer Jugend.* Berlin: Frieding, 1987.

Larson Ruth. "Postwar Germany as I Saw It." *Education* 70 (February 1950): 370–75.

Levin, Meyer. *In Search.* New York: Horizon Press, 1950.

Lewis, Sinclair. *It Can't Happen Here.* Garden City, N.Y.: Doubleday, Doran & Co. Inc., 1935.

Liddell, Helen. "Education in Occupied Germany: A Field Study." *International Affairs* 26 (1948): 30–62.

Litchfield, Edward H. et al. *Governing Postwar Germany.* Ithaca, N.Y.: Cornell University Press, 1948.

Ludwig, Emil. *The Moral Conquest of Germany.* Garden City, N.Y.: Doubleday, Doran and Co., Inc., 1945.

Lunau, Heinz. *The Germans on Trial.* New York: Storm, 1948.

Mackinnon, Marianne. *The Naked Years: Growing Up in Nazi Germany.* London: Corgi, 1987.

McGovern, James. *Fräulein.* New York: Crown Publishers, 1956.

Mead, Margaret. "Food and Feeding in Occupied Territory." *Public Opinion Quarterly 7* (1943): 618–28.

Middleton, Drew. *The Struggle for Germany.* Indianapolis, Ind.: Bobbs-Merrill Co., 1949.

Morgenthau, Henry. *Germany Is Our Problem.* New York: Harper, 1945.

Muhlen Norbert. "America and American Occupation in German Eyes." *Annals of the American Academy of Political and Social Science* 295 (Sept. 1954): 52–61.

Murphy, Robert D. *Diplomat Among Warriors.* Garden City, N.Y.: Doubleday, 1964.

Myrdal, Gunnar. *An American Dilemma: The Negro Problem and Modern Democracy.* New York: Harper & Brothers, 1944.

Nizer, Louis. *What To Do With Germany.* New York: Ziff-Davis, 1944.

Norman, Albert. *Our German Policy: Propaganda and Culture.* New York: Vantage Press, 1951.

Padover, Saul K. *Experiment in Germany: The Story of an American Intelligence Officer.* New York: Ducll, Sloan, Pearce, 1946.

Pollock, James. *Besatzung und Staatsaufbau nach 1945: Occupation Diary and Private Correspondence 1945–1948.* Herausgegeben von Ingrid Krüger-Bulcke. Munich: Oldenbourg, 1994.

Pyle, Ernie. *Brave Men.* New York: Henry Holt Co., 1943.

Ross, Colin. *Amerikas Schicksalsstunde: Die Vereinigten Staaten zwischen Demokratie und Diktatur.* Leipzig: F. A. Brockhaus, 1935.

———. *Unser Amerika: Der Deutsche Anteil an den Vereinigten Staaten.* Leipzig: F. A. Brockhaus, 1937.

———. *Die "Westliche Hemisphäre" als Programm und Phantom des amerikanischen Imperialismus.* Leipzig: F. A. Brockhaus, 1942.

Ruhl, Klaus-Jörg, ed. *Neubeginn und Restauration: Dokumente zur Vorgeschichte der Bundesrepublik Deutschland 1945–1949.* Munich: Deutscher Taschenbuch Verlag, 1982.

Salomon, Ernst von. *The Answers of Ernst von Salomon to the 131 Questions in the Allied Military Government "Fragebogen."* London: Putnam, 1954.

Schmidt, Bernd and Hannes Schwenger. eds. *Die Stunde Eins: Erzählungen, Reportagen, Essays aus der Nachkriegszeit*. Munich: Deutscher Taschenbuch Verlag, 1982.

Schultz, Sigrid L. *Germany Will Try It Again*. New York: Reynal & Hitchcock, 1944.

Settel, Arthur. *This Is Germany*. New York: Sloane, 1950.

Shirer, William L. *Berlin Diary*. New York: Alfred A. Knopf, 1941.

——. *End of Berlin Diary*. New York: Alfred A. Knopf, 1947.

Smith, Henry Nash. "The Salzburg Seminar." *American Quarterly* 1 (1949): 35.

Smith, Jean Edward. *The Papers of Lucius D. Clay*. 2 vols. Bloomington: Indiana University Press, 1974.

Smith, William Gardner. *Last of the Conquerors*. New York: Farrar, Strauss and Company, 1948.

Speier, Hans. *From the Ashes of Disgrace: A Journal from Germany, 1945–1955*. Amherst: University of Massachusetts Press, 1981.

Spindler, Sonja. *Wie wir hamsterten, hungerten und überlebten*. Frankfurt a. M.: Voto von Eichhorn, 1983.

Stolper, Gustav. *German Realities*. New York: Reynal & Hitchcock, 1948.

Stone, Vernon E. "German Baby Crop Left by Negro GI's." *Survey*, 85 (November 1949): 579–83.

Thurnwald, Hilde. *Gegenwartsprobleme Berliner Familien: Eine Soziologische Untersuchung an 498 Familien*. Berlin: Weidmann, 1948.

Truman, Harry S. *Memoirs*. 2 vols. Garden City, N.Y.: Doubleday, 1964.

Wann, Marie D. *Dependent Baggage: Destination Germany*. New York: Macmillan, 1955.

Warburg, James P. *Germany, Bridge or Battleground*. New York: Harcourt, Brace, 1947.

——. *Germany, Key to Peace*. Cambridge, Mass.: Harvard University Press, 1953.

Werner, Bruno. *Die Galeere*. Frankfurt a. M.: G.B. Fischer, 1958, 1943.

White, William L. *Report on the Germans*. New York: Harcourt, Brace, 1947.

Wolfers, Arnold. *United States Policy Toward Germany*. New Haven: Yale University, Institute of International Studies, 1947.

Wolff-Mönckeberg, Mathilde. *On the Other Side: To My Children from Germany, 1940–1945.* Translated and edited by Ruth Evans. New York: Mayflower Books, 1979.

Zink, Harold. *American Military Government in Germany.* New York: Macmillan, 1947.

Zoller, Albert. *Hitler Privat: Erlebnisbericht seiner Geheimsekretärin.* Düsseldorf: Droste Verlag, 1949.

CONTEMPORARY PERIODICALS

American Magazine, American Mercury, Christian Century, Commonweal, Harper's, Life, New Republic, Newsweek, New Yorker, New York Times, Saturday Evening Post, Stars and Stripes, Survey, Time.

Deutsche Rundschau, Frankfurter Rundschau, Heute, Die Koralle, Die Neue Rundschau, Die Neue Zeitung, Pinguin, Der Regenbogen, Der Spiegel, Stuttgarter Zeitung, Süddeutsche Zeitung, Der Tagesspiegel.

Secondary Sources

Abzug, Robert H. *Inside the Vicious Heart: Americans and the Liberation of Nazi Concentration Camps.* New York: Oxford University Press, 1985.

Ahrens, Hanns D. *Demontage: Nachkriegspolitik der Alliierten.* Munich: Universitas, 1982.

Albrecht, Gerd, ed. *Der Film im Dritten Reich.* Karlsruhe: Doku Verlag, 1979.

Appel, Reinhard. *Die Regierenden von Berlin seit 1945: Die Nachkriegsgeschichte im Spiegel ihrer Bürgermeister.* Berlin: edition q, 1996.

Auer, Peter. *Ihr Völker der Welt: Ernst Reuter und die Blockade von Berlin.* Berlin: Jaron, 1998.

Avery, Sheldon. *Up From Washington: William Pickens and the Negro Struggle for Equality 1900–1954.* Newark: University of Delaware Press, 1989.

Backer, John H. *The Decision to Divide Germany: American Foreign Policy in Transition.* Durham, N.C.: Duke University Press, 1959.

———. *Winds of History: The German Years of Lucius DuBignon Clay.* New York: Van Nostrand Reinhold, 1983.

Barron, Stephanie. *"Degenerate Art:" The Fate of the Avant Garde in Nazi Germany.* Los Angeles: Los Angeles County Museum of Art, 1991.

Becker, Josef, ed. *Dreißig Jahre Bundesrepublik: Tradition und Wandel.* Munich: Vogel, 1979.

Becker, Josef, Theo Stammen and Peter Waldmann, eds. *Vorgeschichte der Bundesrepublik Deutschland: Zwischen Kapitulation und Grundgesetz.* Munich: Wilhelm Fink Verlag, 1979.

Bell, Daniel. *The End of Ideology: On the Exhaustion of Political Ideas in the Fifties.* Fourth Printing. New York: Free Press, 1960, 1967.

Benz, Wolfgang. *Die Bundesrepublik Deutschland.* Bd. 3, *Gesellschaft.* Frankfurt: Fischer Verlag, 1989.

——. *Von der Besatzungsherrschaft zur Bundesrepublik: Stationen einer Staatsgründung, 1946–1949.* Frankfurt a. Main: Fischer Taschenbuch Verlag, 1984.

——. *Neuanfang in Bayern, 1945–1949: Politik und Gesellschaft in der Nachkriegszeit. Munich: Beck, 1988.*

Berant, Lauren. The Queen of America Goes to Washington City: *Essays on Sex and Citizenship.* Durham, N.C.: Duke University Press, 1997.

Berghahn, Volker. *The Americanisation of West German Industry, 1945–1973.* Cambridge, U.K.: Cambridge University Press, 1986.

Bergstrasser, Arnold. "Zum Problem der sog. Amerikanisierung Deutschlands." *Jahrbuch für Amerikastudien* 8 (1963): 13–23.

Bessel, Richard, ed. *Life in the Third Reich.* New York: Oxford University Press, 1987.

Best, Gary Dean. *Herbert Hoover, The Postpresidential Years.* 2 vols. Stanford: Hoover Institution Press, 1983.

Black, Gregory D. and Clayton R. Koppes. "Blacks, Loyalty, and Motion Picture Propaganda in World War II." *Journal of American History,* 73 (1986): 383–406.

——. *Hollywood Goes to War: How Politics, Profits, and Propaganda Shaped World War II Movies.* New York: Free Press, 1987.

Blum, John Morton. *V Was for Victory: Politics and American Culture During World War II.* New York: Harcourt, Brace, Jovanovich, 1976.

Boehling, Rebecca, *A Question of Priorities: Democratic Reforms and Economic Recovery in Postwar Germany.* Providence: Berghahn Books, 1996.

Bollenbeck, Georg. *Tradition, Avantgarde, Reaktion: Deutsche Kontroversen um die kulturelle Moderne, 1880–1945*. Frankfurt a.M." Fischer, 1999.

Botting, Douglas. *From the Ruins of the Reich: Germany 1945–1949*. New York: Crown, 1985.

Bower, Tom. *The Pledge Betrayed: America and Britain and the Denazification in Post-War Germany*. Garden City, N.Y.: Doubleday, 1982.

Brandt, Allan M. *No Magic Bullet: A Social History of Venereal Disease in the United States since 1880*. New York: Oxford University Press, 1987.

Brinkley, Alan. *Voices of Protest: Huey Long, Father Coughlin, and the Great Depression*. New York: Alfred A. Knopf, 1982.

Broszat, Martin, Klaus-Dietmar Henke, and Hans Woller, eds. *Von Stalingrad zur Währungsreform: Zur Sozialgeschichte des Umbruchs in Deutschland*. Munich: Oldenbourg, 1988.

Broszat, Martin, ed. *Zäsuren nach 1945: Essays zur Periodisierung der deutschen Nachkriegsgeschichte*. Munich: R. Oldenbourg Verlag, 1990.

Browder, Dewey. *Americans in Post World War II Germany: Teachers, Thinkers, Neighbors, and Nuisances*. Lewiston, New York: E. Mellen Press, 1998.

Bungenstab, Karl-Ernst. "Entstehung, Bedeutung und Funktionswandel der Amerikahäuser: Ein Beitrag zur Geschichte der amerikanischen Auslandsinformation nach dem Zweiten Weltkrieg." *Jahrbuch für Amerikastudien* 16 (1971): 189–203.

——. "Die Ausbildung der amerikanischen Offiziere für die Militärregierung nach 1945." *Jahrbuch für Amerikastudien* 18 (1973): 195–212.

——. *Umerziehung zur Demokratie? Re-Education Politik im Bildungswesen der US-Zone 1945–1949*. Düsseldorf: Bertelsmann Universitätsverlag, 1970.

Burleigh, Michael and Wolfgang Wippermann. *The Racial State: Germany 1933–1945*. New York: Cambridge University Press, 1991.

Chamberlin, Brewster S. *Kultur auf Trümmern: Berliner Berichte der Amerikanischen Information Control Section, Juli-Dezember 1945*. Stuttgart: Deutsche Verlags-Anstalt, 1979.

Chaussy, Ulrich. "Jugend." in Benz, Wolfgang. Hg. *Die Bundesrepublik Deutschland, Bd. 3, Gesellschaft*. Frankfurt a. M., Germany: Fischer Verlag, 1989.

Clifford, James and George E. Marcus, eds. *Writing Culture: The Poetics and Politics of Ethnography.* Berkeley: University of California Press, 1986.

———. *The Predicament of Culture: Twentieth Century Ethnography, Literature, and Art.* Cambridge, Mass.: Harvard University Press, 1988.

Collier, Richard. *Bridge Across the Sky: The Berlin Blockade and Airlift, 1948–1949.* New York: McGraw-Hill, 1978.

Conot, Robert E. *Justice at Nuremberg.* New York: Carroll & Graf Publishers, 1983.

Costigliola, Frank. *France and the United States: The Cold Alliance Since World War II.* New York: Twayne, 1992.

Dallek, Robert. *Franklin D. Roosevelt and American Foreign Policy, 1932–1945.* New York: Oxford University Press, 1979.

Dastrup, Boyd L. *Crusade in Nuremberg: Military Occupation, 1945–1949.* Westport, Conn.: Greenwood Press, 1985.

Davis, Franklin M. *Come as A Conqueror: The United States Army's Occupation of Germany 1945–1949.* New York: Alfred A. Knopf, 1961.

Denkler, Horst and Karl Prümm, eds. *Die deutsche Literatur im Dritten Reich: Themen, Traditionen, Wirkungen.* Stuttgart: Reclam, 1976.

Doherty, Thomas. *Projections of War: Hollywood, American Culture, and World War II.* New York: Columbia University Press, 1993.

Dorn, Walter L. "Die Debatte über die amerikanische Besatzungspolitik für Deutschland." *Vierteljahreshefte für Zeitgeschichte* 6. Jg., 1. Heft (Januar 1958): 60–77.

Dower, John W. *Embracing Defeat: Japan in the Wake of World War II.* New York: W. W. Norton, 1999.

———. *War Without Mercy: Race and Power in the Pacific War.* New York: Pantheon, 1986.

Eisenberg, Carolyn Woods. *Drawing the Line: The American Decision to Divide Germany, 1944–1949.* New York: Cambridge University Press, 1996.

Enzensberger, Hans Magnus, ed. *Europa in Ruinen: Augenzeugenberichte aus den Jahren 1944–1948.* Munich: DTV, 1995.

Evans, Richard J., and W. R. Lee. *The German Family: Essays on the Social History of the Family in Nineteenth and Twentieth Century Germany.* Totowa, N.J.: Barnes & Noble Books, 1981.

Fehrenbach, Heide. *Cinema in Democratizing Germany: Reconstructing National Identity after Hitler*. Chapel Hill: University of North Carolina Press, 1995.

———. "Rehabilitating Father*land*: Race and German Remasculinization," *Signs: Journal of Women in Culture and Society* 24, No.1 (April 1998): 107–24.

Finn, Richard B. *Winners in Peace: MacArthur, Yoshida, and Postwar Japan*. Berkeley: University of California Press, 1992.

Fish, Stanley. *Is There a Text in This Class: The Authority of Interpretive Communities*. Cambridge, Mass.: Harvard University Press, 1980.

Frankel, Charles. *The Neglected Aspect of Foreign Affairs: American Educational and Cultural Policy Abroad*. Washington D.C.: Brookings Institution, 1965.

Frederiksen, Oliver. *The American Military Occupation of Germany 1945–1953*. Darmstadt: Historical Division Headquarters U.S. Army, Europe, 1953.

Freier, Elisabeth and Annette Kuhn. *"Das Schicksal Deutschlands liegt in der Hand seiner Frauen": Frauen in der deutschen Nachkriegsgeschichte*. Düsseldorf: Schwann Verlag, 1984.

Frevert, Ute. *Women in German History: From Bourgeois Emancipation to Sexual Liberation*. Translated by Stuart McKinnon-Evans in association with Terry Bond and Barbara Norden. New York: Berg, 1990, 1988.

Gardner, Lloyd C. *Architects of Illusion: Men and Ideas in American Foreign Policy, 1941–1949*. Chicago: Quadrangle Books, 1970.

Garraty, John A. *The Great Depression: An Inquiry into the Causes, Course, and Consequences of the Worldwide Depression of the Nineteen-Thirties as Seen by Contemporaries and in the Light of History*. New York: Harcourt Brace Jovanovich, 1986.

Gatzke, Hans-Wilhelm. *Germany and the United States: A "Special Relationship?"* Cambridge, Mass.: Harvard University Press, 1980.

Geertz, Clifford. *The Interpretation of Cultures: Selected Essays*. New York: Basic Books, 1973.

Gerhardt, Uta. "A Hidden Agenda of Recovery: The Psychiatric Conceptualization of Re-education for Germany in the United States during World War II," *German History* 14, no. 3 (1996): 297–324.

Gehring, Hansjörg. *Amerikanische Literaturpolitik in Deutschland 1945–1953: Ein Aspekt des Re-Education Programms*. Stuttgart: Deutsche Verlags-Anstalt, 1976.

Gienow-Hecht, Jessica E. *Transmission Impossible: American Journalism as Cultural Diplomacy in Postwar Germany 1945–1955*. Baton Rouge: Louisiana State University Press, 1999.

Gimbel, John. *The American Occupation of Germany: Politics and the Military 1945–1949*. Stanford, Calif.: Stanford University Press, 1968.

——. *A German Community Under American Occupation: Marburg, 1945–1952*. Stanford, Calif.: Stanford University Press, 1961.

——. *The Origins of the Marshall Plan*. Stanford, Calif.: Stanford University Press, 1976.

Goedde, Petra. "From Villains to Victims: Fraternization and the Feminization of Germany, 1945–1947." *Diplomatic History* 23, no.1 (1999): 1–20.

Golay, John Ford. *The Founding of the Federal Republic of Germany*. Chicago: University of Chicago Press, 1958.

Goldhagen, Daniel Jonah. *Hitler's Willing Executioners: Ordinary Germans and the Holocaust*. New York: Alfred A. Knopf, 1996.

Gottlieb, Moshe. "In the Shadow of War: The American Anti-Nazi Boycott Movement in 1939–1941." *American Jewish Historical Quarterly*, 62, no. 2 (1972): 146–61.

Graebner, William S. *The Age of Doubt: American Thought and Culture in the 1940s*. Boston: Twayne, 1991.

Gramsci, Antonio. *Selections from the Prison Notebooks of Antonio Gramsci*. Edited and translated by Quentin Hoare and Geoffrey Nowell Smith. New York: International Publishers, 1971.

Grathwol, Robert P. and Donita M. Moorhus. *American Forces in Berlin 1945–1994: Cold War Outpost*. Washington, D.C.: Department of Defense Legacy Resource Management Program, Cold War Project, 1994.

Gray, J. Glenn. *The Warriors: Reflections on Men in Battle* . New York: Harper & Row, 1959.

Grosser, Alfred. *The Colossus Again: Western Germany from Defeat to Rearmament*. New York: Praeger, 1955.

Grossmann, Atina. "A Question of Silence: The Rape of German Women by Occupation Soldiers." *October* 72 (Spring 1995): 43–62.

Hammond Paul. "Directives for the Occupation of Germany: The Washington Controversy." In Harold Stein, ed. *American Civil-Military Decisions: A Book of Case Studies.* Birmingham: University of Alabama Press, 1963.

Hanrider, Wolfram. *Germany, America, Europe: Forty Years of German Foreign Policy.* New Haven, Conn.: Yale University Press, 1989.

Harrington, Daniel F. "The Berlin Blockade Revisited." *The International History Review,* vol. 6, No. 1 (February 1984):88–112.

Hartman, Susan M. *The Homefront and Beyond: American Women in the 1940s.* Boston: Twayne, 1982.

Hauser, Karin. "Family and Role Division: The Polarization of Sexual Stereotypes in the Nineteenth Century—an Aspect of the Dissociation of Work and Family Life," in Evans, Richard and W. R. Lee, eds., *The German Family: Essays on the Social History of the Family in Nineteenth-and Twentieth-Century Germany.* Totowa, N.J.: Barnes & Noble, 1981, pp. 51–83.

Heineman, Elizabeth. "The Hour of the Woman: Memories of Germany's 'Crisis Years' and the West German National Identity." *American Historical Review* 101, no. 2 (1996): 354–95.

———. *What Difference Does a Husband Make? Women and Marital Status in Nazi and Postwar Germany.* Berkeley: University of California Press, 1999.

Henke, Klaus-Dietmar. *Die Amerikanische Besetzung Deutschlands* (Munich: R. Oldenbourg, 1995.

Herbst, Ludolf. *Westdeutschland 1945–1955: Unterwerfung, Kontrolle, Integration.* Munich: R. Oldenbourg, 1986.

Hermand, Jost. *Kultur im Wiederaufbau: Die Bundesrepublik Deutschland 1945–1965.* Munich: Nymphenburger Verlagsanstalt, 1986.

Hermand, Jost, H. Peitsch, and K. R. Scherpe; *Nachkriegsliteratur in Westdeutschland, 1945–1949* Berlin: Argument Verlag, 1982.

Herzfeld, Hans. *Berlin in der Weltpolitik 1945–1970.* Berlin: deGruyter, 1973.

Herzstein, Robert F. *Hitler and Roosevelt: Prelude to War.* New York: Paragon House, 1989.

Hess, Gary R. *The United States at War, 1941–1945.* Arlington Heights: Harlan Davidson, Inc., 1986.

Hillgruber, Andreas. *Deutsche Geschichte 1945–1980: Die Deutsche Frage in der Weltpolitik.* 7th ed. Stuttgart: W. Kohlhammer, 1989, 1983.

Hixson, Walter. *George F. Kennan: Cold War Iconoclast.* New York: Columbia University Press, 1989.

Hofstadter, Richard. *The Paranoid Style in American Politics and Other Essays.* New York: Alfred A. Knopf, 1965.

Höhn, Maria. "GIs, Veronikas, and Lucky Strikes: German Reactions to the American Military Presence in the Rhineland Palatinate in the 1950s." (Ph.D. diss. University of Pennsylvania, 1995).

Hogan, Michael J. *The Marshall Plan: America, Britain, and the Reconstruction of Western Europe, 1947–1952.* New York: Cambridge University Press, 1987.

Hoganson, Kristin L. *Fighting for American Manhood: How Gender Politics Provoked the Spanish-American and Philippine-American Wars.* New Haven, Conn.: Yale University Press, 1998.

Hunt, Michael. *Ideology and U.S. Foreign Policy.* New Haven, Conn.: Yale University Press, 1983.

Hurwitz, Harold. *Die Politische Kultur der Bevölkerung und der Neubeginn konservativer Politik.* Cologne: Verlag Wissenschaft und Politik, 1983.

——. *Die Stunde Null der Deutschen Presse: Die Amerikanische Pressepolitik in Deutschland 1945–1949.* Cologne: Verlag Wissenschaft und Politik, 1972.

Iriye, Akira. "Culture and International History." *Explaining the History of American Foreign Relations.* Edited by Michael J. Hogan and Thomas Paterson. New York: Cambridge University Press, 1991.

——. *Power and Culture: The Japanese-American War, 1941–1945.* Cambridge, Mass.: Harvard University Press, 1981.

Jonas, Manfred. *The United States and Germany: A Diplomatic History.* Ithaca, N.Y.: Cornell University Press, 1984.

Kater, Michael H. *Different Drummers: Jazz in the Culture of Nazi Germany.* New York: Oxford University Press, 1992.

——. "Forbidden Fruit? Jazz in the Third Reich." *American Historical Review* 94 (1989): 11–43.

Kennan, George F. *American Diplomacy, 1900–1950.* Chicago: University of Chicago Press, 1951.

Kennedy, David M. *Over Here: The First World War and American Society*. New York: Oxford University Press, 1980.

Kleßmann, Christoph and Georg Wagner, eds. *Das Gespaltene Land: Leben in Deutschland 1945–1990. Texte und Dokumente zur Sozialgeschichte*. Munich: C. H. Beck, 1993.

Kleßmann, Christoph. *Die doppelte Staatsgründung: Deutsche Geschichte 1945–1955*. 4th enl. ed. Göttingen: Vandenhoeck & Ruprecht, 1989, 1982.

Knapp, Manfred, Werner Link, Hans-Jürgen Schröder and Klaus Schwabe. *Die USA und Deutschland, 1918–1975: Deutsch-Amerikanische Beziehungen zwischen Rivalität und Partnerschaft*. Munich: C. H. Beck, 1978.

Kolb, Eberhard. *The Weimar Republic*. London: Unwin Hyman, 1988.

Kolko, Joyce and Gabriel Kolko. *The Limits of Power: The World and United States Foreign Policy. 1945–1954*. New York: Harper & Row, 1972.

Kocka, Jürgen. "Familie, Unternehmer, und Kapitalismus in Reif, Heinz, ed. *Die Familie in der Geschichte*. Göttingen: Vandenhoeck & Ruprecht, 1982. 163–86.

Koonz, Claudia. *Mothers in the Fatherland: Women, the Family, and Nazi Politics*. New York: St. Martin's Press, 1987.

Krabbe, Wolfgang R. "Die FDJ und die Jugendverbände der Bundesrepublik, 1949–1970." *German Studies Review* 21, no. 3 (October, 1998): 525–61.

Kuklick, Bruce. *American Policy and the Division of Germany: The Clash with Russia on Reparations*. Ithaca, N.Y.: Cornell University Press, 1972.

Kutler, Stanley I. *The American Inquisition: Justice and Injustice in the Cold War*. New York: Hill And Wang, 1982.

LaFeber, Walter. *America, Russia, and the Cold War, 1945–1996*. 8th ed. New York: McGraw Hill, 1997.

Lange, Wigand. *Theater in Deutschland nach 1945: Zur Theaterpolitik der amerikanischen Besatzungsbehörden*. Frankfurt: Lang, 1980.

Latour, Conrad F. and Thilo Vogelsang. *Okkupation und Wiederaufbau: Die Tätigkeit der Militärregierung in der amerikanischen Besatzungszone Deutschlands 1944–1947*. Stuttgart: Deutsche Verlags-Anstalt, 1973.

Lears, Jackson. "The Concept of Cultural Hegemony: Problems and Possibilities." *American Historical Review* 90 (1985): 567–93.

Lilge, Herbert, ed. *Deutschland, 1945–1963*. Hannover: Fackelträger Verlag, 1978.

Maase, Kaspar. *Roll Over Beethoven! The Americanization of West German Youth and the Emergence of a New Cultural Balance*. Hamburg: Hamburger Institut für Sozialforschung, 1992.

——. *Bravo Amerika: Erkundungen Zur Jugendkultur der Bundes—republik in den fünfziger Jahren*. Hamburg: Junius-Verlag, 1992.

——. *Amerikanisierung der Alltagskultur? Zur Rezeption US-Amerikanischer Populärkultur in der Bundesrepublik und den Niederlanden*. Hamburg: Hamburger Institut für Sozialforschung, 1990.

Matz, Elisabeth. *Die Zeitungen der U.S. Armee für die Deutsche Bevölkerung*. Münster: Fahle, 1969.

May, Elaine Tyler. *Homeward Bound: American Families in the Cold War Era*. New York: Basic Books, 1988.

May, Lary, ed. *Recasting America: Culture and Politics in the Age of Cold War*. Chicago: University of Chicago Press, 1989.

Meyer, Sibylle and Eva Schulze. *Wie wir das alles geschafft haben: Alleinstehende Frauen berichten über ihr Leben nach 1945*. Munich: C. H. Beck, 1984.

——. *Von Liebe sprach damals keiner: Familienalltag in der Nachkriegszeit*. Munich: C. H. Beck, 1985.

——. *Auswirkungen des II. Weltkrieges auf Familien: Zum Wandel der Familie in Deutschland*. Berlin: Institut für Soziologie der Technischen Universität Berlin, 1989.

Mitchell, Alan, ed. *The Nazi Revolution: Hitler's Dictatorship and the German Nation*. Lexington, Mass.: D. C. Heath and Co., 1990, 1959.

Moeller, Robert G. *Protecting Motherhood: Women and the Family in the Politics of Postwar West Germany*. Berkeley.: University of California Press, 1993.

Moltmann, Günter. "Die Frühe Amerikanische Deutschlandplanung im 2. Weltkrieg." *Vierteljahreshefte für Zeitgeschichte* 5. Jg., 3. Heft (July 1957): 241–64.

——. "Zur Formulierung der amerikanischen Besatzungspolitik in Deutschland am Ende des 2. Weltkriegs." *Vierteljahreshefte für Zeitgeschichte* 15. Jg., 3. Heft (July 1967): 299–322.

Montgomery, John D. *Forced To Be Free: The Artificial Revolution in Germany and Japan.* Chicago: University of Chicago Press, 1957.

Müller-Marein, Josef. *Deutschland im Jahre Eins: Reportagen aus der Nachkriegszeit.* Munich: Deutscher Taschenbuch Verlag, 1984.

Naimark, Norman M. *The Russians in Germany: A History of the Soviet Zone of Occupation, 1945–1949.* Cambridge, Mass.: Harvard University Press, 1995.

Nelson, Keith L. " 'The Black Horror on the Rhine:' Race as a Factor in Post World War I Diplomacy." *Journal of Modern History.* 42, no. 4 (1970): 615.

Niethammer, Lutz. *Entnazifizierung in Bayern: Säuberung und Rehabilitierung unter amerikanischer Besatzung.* Frankfurt a. Main: S. Fischer Verlag, 1972.

———. *"Die Jahre weiss man nicht wo man die heute hinsetzen soll:" Faschismuserfahrungen im Ruhrgebiet.* Berlin: J. H. W. Dietz Verlag, 1983.

———. *"Hinterher merkt man, dass es richtig war, daß es schiefgegangen ist:" Nachkriegserfahrungen im Ruhrgebiet.* Berlin: J. H. W. Dietz Verlag, 1983.

Niethammer, Lutz and Ulrich Borsdorf. Eds. *Zwischen Befreiung und Besatzung: Analyse des US-Geheimdienstes über Positionen und Strukturen deutscher Politik, 1945.* Translated by Franz Brüggemeier. Weinheim: Beltz Athenäum, 1995, 1976.

Ninkovich, Frank A. "The Currents of Cultural Diplomacy: Art and the States Department, 1938–1947." *Diplomatic History* 1 (1977): 215- 37.

———. *The Diplomacy of Ideas: United States Foreign Policy and Cultural Relations, 1938–1950.* New York: Cambridge University Press, 1981.

———. *Germany and the United States: The Transformation of the German Question since 1945.* New York: Twayne, 1995.

Noelle-Neumann, Elisabeth, et al. *The Germans: Public Opinion Polls 1947–1966.* Allensbach: Verlag für Demoskopie, 1967.

Nolan, Mary. *Visions of Modernity: American Business and the Modernization of Germany.* New York: Oxford University Press, 1994.

O'Hanlon, Timothy. "School Sports as Social Training: The Case of Athletics and the Crisis of World War I." In Wiggins, David K., ed. *Sport in America: From Wicked Amusement to National Obsession.* Champaign, Ill.: Human Kinetics, 1995.

Overesch, Manfred. *Deutschland 1945–1949*. Königstein, Ts.: Athenäum, 1979.

Parrish, Michael E. *Anxious Decades: America in Prosperity and Depression, 1920–1941*. New York: Norton, 1992.

Parrish, Thomas. *Berlin in the Balance 1945–1949: The Blockade, the Airlift, the First Major Battle of the Cold War*. Reading, Mass.: Addison-Wesley, 1998.

Paul, Wolfgang. *Kampf um Berlin*. Munich: Albert Langen, Georg Müller Verlag, 1962.

Perrett, Geoffrey. *America in the Twenties: A History*. New York: Simon & Schuster, 1982.

Peters, H. F. "American Culture and the State Department." *American Scholar* 21, no.3 (Summer 1952): 265–74.

Peterson, Edward N. *The American Occupation of Germany: Retreat to Victory*. Detroit: Wayne State University Press, 1977.

Peukert, Detlef J. K. *Inside Nazi Germany: Conformity, Opposition, and Racism in Everyday Life*. New Haven, Conn.: Yale University Press, 1982.

———. *The Weimar Republic: The Crisis of Classical Modernity*. New York: Hill and Wang, 1993, 1989.

Plummer, Brenda Gayle. *Rising Wind: Black Americans and U.S. Foreign Affairs, 1935–1960*. Chapel Hill: University of North Carolina Press, 1996.

Poiger, Uta G. *Jazz, Rock, and Rebels: Cold War Politics and American Culture in a Divided Germany*. Berkeley: University of California Press, 2000.

Polenberg, Richard. *One Nation Divisible: Class, Race, and Ethnicity in the United States Since 1938*. New York: Viking Press, 1980.

Pomerin, Reiner, "The Fate of Mixed Blood Children in Germany." *German Studies Review* 5, no. 3 (1982):

———, ed. *The American Impact on Postwar Germany*. Providence, R.I.: Berghahn Books, 1997, 1995.

Potter, Lou, William Miles, and Nina Rosenblum. *Liberators: Fighting on Two Fronts in World War II*. New York: Harcourt Brace Jovanovich, 1992.

Prell, Uwe and Lothar Wilker, eds. *Berlin Blockade und Luftbrücke 1948/49: Analyse und Dokumentation*. Berlin: Berlin Verlag, 1987.

Price, Harry B. *The Marshall Plan and Its Meaning*. Ithaca, N.Y.: Cornell University Press, 1955.

Prinz, Friedrich and Maria Kraus. *Trümmerleben: Texte, Dokumente, Bilder aus den Münchner Nachkriegsjahren*. Munich: Deutscher Taschenbuch Verlag, 1985.

Prinz, Friedrich, ed. *Trümmerzeit in München: Kultur und Gesellschaft einer Deutschen Großstadt im Aufbruch, 1945–1949*. Munich: C. H. Beck, 1984.

Prinz, Michael and Rainer Zitelmann. *Nationalsozialismus und Modernisierung*. Darmstadt: Wissenschaftliche Buchgesellschaft, 1991.

Pronay, Nicholas and Keith Wilson, eds. *The Political Re-Education of Germany and Her Allies after World War II*. Totawa, N.J.: Barnes & Noble Books, 1985.

Pross, Harry, ed. *Deutsche Presse seit 1945*. Bern: Scherz, 1965.

Rabinbach, Anson. "Nationalsozialismus und Moderne: Technik-Interpretation im Dritten Reich," in *Der Technikdiskurs in der Hitler-Stalin Ära*, ed. by Wolfgang Emmerich and Carl Wege. Stuttgart: G. B. Metzler, 1995, 94–113.

Reif, Heinz, ed. *Die Familie in der Geschichte*. Göttingen: Vandenhoeck & Ruprecht, 1982.

Reuth, Ralf Georg. *Goebbels*. Translated by Kristina Winston. New York: Harcourt Brace & Company, 1993.

Rosenberg, Emily. " 'Foreign Affairs' after World War II: Connecting Sexual and International Politics." *Diplomatic History* 18 (Winter 1994): 59–70.

———. "Gender." *The Journal of American History* 77 (June 1990): 116–24.

———. *Spreading the American Dream: American Economic and Cultural Expansion 1890–1945*. New York: Hill & Wang, 1982.

Rotter, Andrew. "Gender Relations, Foreign Relations: The United States and Southeast Asia 1947–1964." *Journal of American History*, 81, No.2 (September, 1994): 518–42.

———. *Comrades at Odds: The United States and India, 1947–1964*. Ithaca, N.Y.: Cornell University Press, 2000.

Ruhl, Klaus Jörg. *Alltag zwischen Krieg und Frieden*. Darmstadt: Luchterhand, 1984.

———. *Die Besatzer und die Deutschen: Amerikanische Zone 1945–1948*. Düsseldorf: Droste, 1980.

——. *Frauen in der Nachkriegszeit*. Munich: DTV, 1988.

——. *Unsere verlorenen Jahre*. Darmstadt: Luchterhand, 1985.

Rupieper, Hermann-Josef. *Die Wurzeln der westdeutschen Nachkriegsdemokratie: Der Amerikanische Beitrag 1945–1952*. Opladen: Westdeutscher Verlag, 1993.

Rupp, Leila S. *Mobilizing Women for War: German and American Propaganda, 1939–1945*. Princeton, N.J.: Princeton University Press, 1978.

Sander, Helke and Barbara Johr, eds. *BeFreier und Befreite: Krieg, Vergewaltigungen, Kinder*. Frankfurt: Fischer, 1995.

Sandford, John. *The New German Cinema*. London: Oswald Wolff, 1980.

Santer, Eric L. *Stranded Objects: Mourning, Memory, and Film in Postwar Germany*. Ithaca N.Y.: Cornell University Press, 1990.

Saunders, Thomas J. *Hollywood in Berlin: American Cinema and Weimar Germany*. Berkeley: University of California Press, 1994.

Schäfer, Hans Dieter. *Das Gespaltene Bewußtsein: Über deutsche Kultur und Lebenswirklichkeit 1933–1945*. Frankfurt: Ullstein, 1984, 1981.

Schaller, Michael. *The American Occupation of Japan: The Origins of the Cold War in Asia*. New York: Oxford University Press, 1985.

Schiller, Herbert. *Mass Communications and American Empire*. New York: A. M. Kelley, 1970, 1969.

——. *Communication and Cultural Domination*. New York: Pantheon, 1976.

Schmundt-Thomas, Georg. "Hollywood's Romance of Foreign Policy: American GIs and the Conquest of the German Fräulein." *Journal of Popular Film & Television*. 19 (Winter 1992): 187–97.

Schoenbaum, David. *Hitler's Social Revolution: Class and Status in Nazi Germany, 1933–1939*. New York: Norton, 1980, 1966.

Schoeps, Julius H. *Ein Volk von Mördern? Die Dokumentation zur Goldhagen-Kontroverse um die Rolle der Deutschen im Holocaust*. Hamburg: Hoffmann und Campe, 1996

Schörken, Rolf. *Jugend 1945: Politisches Denken und Lebensgeschichte*. Frankfurt: Fischer Verlag, 1994.

Schrecker, Ellen, *The Age of McCarthyism: A Brief History with Documents*. Boston, Mass.: Bedford Books, 1994.

Schrenck-Notzing, Caspar. *Charakterwäsche: Die Amerikanische Besatzung in Deutschland und ihre Folgen.* Frankfurt: Ullstein, 1993, 1981.

Schwartz, Thomas Alan. *America's Germany: John J. McCloy and the Federal Republic of Germany.* Cambridge, Mass.: Harvard University Press, 1991.

Schwenger, Hannes. *Ernst Reuter: Ein Zivilist im Kalten Krieg.* Munich: Piper, 1987.

Scott, Joan W. "Gender: A Useful Category of Historical Analysis." *American Historical Review* 91 (December 1986): 1053–75.

——. *Gender and the Politics of History.* New York: Columbia University Press, 1988.

Scharf, Claus and Hans-Jürgen Schröder, eds. *Die Deutschlandpolitik Frankreichs und die Französische Zone 1945–1949.* Wiesbaden: Franz Steiner Verlag, 1983.

Sherry, Michael S. *In the Shadow of War: The United States Since the 1930s.* New Haven, Conn.: Yale University Press, 1995.

Shibusawa, Naoko. "America's Geisha Ally: Race, Gender, and Maturity in Refiguring the Japanese Enemy, 1945–1964." Ph.D. diss., Northwestern University, 1998.

Schivelbusch, Wolfgang. *Vor dem Vorhang: Das geistige Berlin, 1945–1948.* Munich: Carl Hanser Verlag, 1995.

Shlaim, Avi. *The United States and the Berlin Blockade, 1948–1949: A Study in Crisis Decision-Making.* Berkeley: University of California Press, 1983.

Shukert, Elfrieda Bethiaume and Barbara Smith Scibetta. *War Brides of World War II.* New York: Penguin, 1988.

Shull, Michael S. and David Edward Wilt. *Hollywood War Films, 1937–1945: An Exhaustive Filmography of American Feature-Length Motion Pictures Relating to World War II.* Jefferson, N.C.: McFarland, 1996.

Silber, Nina. *The Romance of Reunion: Northerners and the South, 1865–1900.* Chapel Hill: University of North Carolina Press, 1993.

Smith, David F. "Juvenile Delinquency in the British Zone of Germany, 1945–51." *German History* 12. No.1 (1994): 39–63.

Smith, Jean Edward. *The Defense of Berlin.* Baltimore, Md.: Johns Hopkins Press, 1963.

Smith, Tony. *America's Mission: The United States and the Worldwide Struggle for Democracy in the Twentieth Century*. Princeton, N.J.: Princeton University Press, 1994.

Spanier, John. *American Foreign Policy Since World War II*. 9th Ed. New York: Holt, Rinehart, and Winston, 1983.

Stammen, Theo. "Politische Kultur-Tradition im Wandel," In *Dreissig Jahre Bundesrepublik: Tradition und Wandel*, edited by Josef Becker and Theo Stammen, 11–52. Munich: Vogel, 1979.

Story, Ronald. "The Country of the Young: The Meaning of Baseball in Early American Culture." In *Sport in America: From Wicked Amusement to National Obsession*, edited by David K. Wiggins. Champaign, Ill.: Human Kinetics, 1995.

Tent, James F. *Mission on the Rhine: Reeducation and Denazification in American-Occupied Germany*. Chicago: University of Chicago Press, 1982.

Tompkins, Jane P. *Reader Response Criticism: From Formalism to Post-Structuralism*. Baltimore, Md.: Johns Hopkins University Press, 1980.

Trachtenberg, Marc. *A Constructed Peace: The Making of the European Settlement, 1945–1963*. Princeton, N.J.: Princeton University Press, 1999.

Tunstall, Jeremy. *The Media Are American: Anglo-American Media in the World*. New York: Columbia University Press, 1977.

Tusa, Ann and John. *The Berlin Airlift*. New York: Atheneum, 1988.

Verband der Deutsch-Amerikanischen Clubs/Federation of German-American Clubs, e.V., ed. *40 Jahre, 1948–1988*. Bamberg: Fränkischer Tag, 1988.

Vogelsang, Thilo. *Das Geteilte Deutschland*. Munich: DTV, 1966.

Von Eschen, Penny. *Race Against Empire: Black Americans and Anticolonialism 1937–1957*. Ithaca, N.Y., 1997.

Wagnleitner, Reinhold. *Coca-Colonization and the Cold War: The Cultural Mission of the United States in Austria after the Second World War*. Chapel Hill: University of North Carolina Press, 1994.

Wengst, Udo. *Staatsaufbau und Regierungspraxis 1948–1953: Zur Geschichte der Verfassungsorgane der Bundesrepublik Deutschland*. Düsseldorf: Droste, 1984.

Wetzlaugk, Udo. *Die Alliierten in Berlin*. Berlin: Verlag Arno Spitz, 1988.

White, Leslie A. *The Concept of Cultural Systems: A Key to Understanding Tribes and Nations* . New York: Columbia University Press, 1975.

Wiggins, David K., ed. *Sport in America: From Wicked Amusement to National Obsession*. Champaign, Ill.: Human Kinetics, 1995.

Willenbacher, Barbara. "Zerrüttung und Bewährung der Nachkriegs-Familie." In Broszat, Martin, Klaus-Dietmar Henke, and Hans Woller, eds. *Von Stalingrad zur Währungsreform: Zur Sozialgeschichte des Umbruchs in Deutschland*. Munich: Oldenbourg, 1988.

Willett, Ralph. *The Americanization of Germany, 1945–1949*. London: Routledge, 1989.

Williams, William Appleman. *The Tragedy of American Diplomacy*. New York: W. W. Norton, 1988, 1959.

Willoughby, John. *Remaking the Conquering Heroes: The Postwar American Occupation of Germany*. New York: Palgrave, 2001.

Wolfe, Robert, ed. *Americans as Proconsuls: United States Military Government in Germany and Japan, 1944–1952*. Carbondale: Southern Illinois University Press, 1984.

Wolff, Michael W. *Die Währungsreform in Berlin 1948/49*. Berlin: Walter de Gruyter, 1991.

Woller, Hans. *Gesellschaft und Politik in der Amerikanischen Besatzungszone: Die Region Ansbach und Fürth*. Munich: Oldenbourg, 1986.

Wyman, David S. *The Abandonment of the Jews: America and the Holocaust, 1941–1945*. New York: Pantheon, 1984.

Ziemke, Earl F. *The U.S. Army in the Occupation of Germany, 1944–1946*. Washington, D.C.: Center for Military History, United States Army, 1975.

Zink, Harold. *The United States and Germany, 1944–1955*. Westport, Conn.: Greenwood Press, 1974, 1957.

Index